CRICKET
WORLD CUP 1999

Bruce Smith
Mark Webb & Salim Parvez

CW01019786

HarperCollins*Publishers*

First published in 1999
by Collins Willow
an imprint of HarperCollins*Publishers*
London

1 3 5 7 9 8 6 4 2

A CIP catalogue record for this book is
available from the British Library

ISBN 0 00 218903 8

The HarperCollins website address is:
www.**fire**and**water**.com

Printed in Great Britain by
The Bath Press

CONTENTS

Introduction

The world's top twelve one-day international cricket teams will be competing for the coveted title of World Champions in the Cricket World Cup 1999. It will be the highlight of the sporting calendar in cricket-playing nations around the world. The tournament will be staged primarily in England during May and June 1999. This will be the seventh World Cup and the fourth to be held in England. England has reached the Final on three occasions and has yet to assume the mantle of World Champion.

Prior to the opening match each of the 12 teams will familiarise itself with local conditions in a series of 36 warm-up matches against County sides. There will be 42 matches in all for the cricket fan to follow, from the opening match on Friday 14th May through to the Final at Lord's on Saturday 20th June 1999.

There will be twelve competing nations including England, Scotland, South Africa, Australia, New Zealand, and World Champions Sri Lanka. Games will be played in Scotland, Ireland and the Netherlands, as well as throughout England.

Who will win? Can England reach yet another final and if they do, will they fall at the final hurdle yet again? Can anyone stop the Australians or will the Aussies have peaked a year too early? Can the likes of Scotland create an upset and bring down one of the top Test sides? Can Sri Lanka recapture the form they showed three years ago and create another thrilling upset?

Whether you are watching on TV or planning to get to some games yourself, you will find a wide variety of useful and plain anorak-style information packed into these 224 pages. Central to it all is the National Team section with up to 12 pages dedicated to each of the 12 participating nations. Stats, facts and player profiles provide perfect talking points in the stand or on the sofa. In your pocket or on the arm of your favourite chair, the *Cricket World Cup 1999 Pocket Annual* is a vital companion for any serious one-day cricket fan.

How It Works

The Cricket World Cup will be staged over a five week period commencing on 14th May and finishing with the Final at Lord's on 20th June 1999. The matches will follow standard One-Day rules and will be played on a 50-over per team basis.

The competition starts with 12 teams trying to battle their way to the Final. The 12 teams are composed of the nine Test playing nations plus three qualifiers (Bangladesh, Scotland and Kenya) from the ICC Championship held in Kuala Lumpur in 1997.

Group Round

The teams have been divided into two groups of six. These teams will play each other in the group stage on a round-robin basis, giving a total of 30 matches overall.

Group A: England, India, Kenya, Sri Lanka, South Africa, Zimbabwe

Group B: Australia, Bangladesh, New Zealand, Pakistan, Scotland, West Indies

At the completion of the round robin tournament the top three teams in each group move through to form a single group of six teams. This stage has become known as the Super Six.

The Super Six

The teams qualifying for this stage bring points with them from the round-robin stage. However, they only bring the points they scored against the other two qualifiers from their group.

The top three teams from Group A will play the top three teams from Group B. Teams add the points from these matches to their pre-existing tally. A total of nine matches will be played and the top four teams in the Super Six table qualify for the semi finals.

The Semi-Finals and Final

The semi-finals are simple knockout games. The team finishing top of the Super Six phase will play the team placed fourth for one place in the final. The team placed second will play the team placed third to determine the other final place. The final will be played at Lord's on 20th June 1999.

The Venues

The matches are spread throughout England. All of the 18 First Class Counties will stage at least one Group Round match. In order to further widen interest in the event in Europe, games will also be held in Holland, Scotland and Ireland.

The Super Six matches, semi-finals and final games are scheduled for the English Test Match grounds, namely, Old Trafford, Headingley, Edgbaston, Trent Bridge, and at The Oval and Lord's. Details on all the venues can be found elsewhere in this book.

Prize Money

There is plenty of cash available to the competing teams, with the record prize fund of $1 million being a three-fold increase on 1996. It will be shared as follows:

Winner:	$300,000
Runner-up:	$150,000
Losing semi-finalists:	$100,000 each

The remaining $350,000 will be split between the other teams.

ICC World Cup Trophy

For the first time in the history of the competition, the trophy will be the permanent prize of the Cricket World Cup. The trophy was designed and manufactured in London by Garrard, the Crown Jewellers, and is valued at more than £27,000.

Crafted in silver and gilt, the 60cm trophy weighs 11kgs and features a golden globe held aloft by three silver columns. The globe itself is presented in the form of a stylised cricket ball, while the columns, styled as stumps and bails, represent the three essential pillars of the game – batting, bowling and fielding.

Author's Notes

The squads for the World Cup were not due to be named until some time after this book went to press. As such we have had to make best guesses at the players who are in-line for inclusion in their team's line-ups for the 1999 World Cup. The cut-off deadline for publication was 20th February 1999 and unless otherwise stated information is provided up to that date.

Comments about this book can be sent to Bruce Smith at:

PO Box 382, St. Albans, Herts, AL2 3JD

alternatively he can be contacted via email at:

Bruce-Smith@msn.com

Disclaimer: In a book of this type it is inevitable that some errors will creep in. While every effort has been made to ensure that the details given in this annual are correct at the time of going to press, neither the authors, editor nor the publishers can accept any responsibility for errors within.

Key to Abbreviations

Abb.	What it means
*	not out
†	Captain
+	Wicket-keeper
o-m-r-w	overs-maidens-runs-wickets
100	Number of 100s scored
4wi	Number of 4-wicket hauls
50	Number of 50s scored
Arm	Type of bowler
Ave	Average score
bp	Batting Position
BP	Best Performance (wickets-runs)
CS	Caught/stumped
F	Final
FM	Fast Medium
Gp	Group
HS	Highest Score
I	Innings
L	Lost
LBG	Leg Break Googly (LS Leg Spin)
LF	Left Arm Fast
LHB	Left Hand Batsman
LM	Left Arm Medium Pace
LOB	Left Arm Off Break
M	Maidens bowled
no	not out
NR	No Result
Overs	Number of overs bowled
P	Played
QF	Quarter Final
R/O	Runs per over given up
RF	Right Arm Fast
RLS	Right Arm Leg Spin
RM	Right Arm Medium pace
ROB	Right Arm Off Break (OS Off Spin)

8

Abb.	What it means
RHB	Right Hand Batsman
RFM	Right Arm Fast Medium
Runs	Runs scored
SF	Semi Final
SLA	Slow Left Arm
SLC	Slow Left Arm Chinaman
SLO	Slow Left Arm Off Break
SR%	Success Rate %
T	Tied (drawn)
W	Won
Wi	Wickets taken
WK	Wicket-Keeper

Match Schedule

May	Gp	Match	Venue
Fri, 14th	A	England vs Sri Lanka	Lord's
Sat, 15th	A	India vs South Africa	Hove
	A	Zimbabwe vs Kenya	Taunton
Sun, 16th	B	Australia vs Scotland	Worcester
	B	West Indies vs Pakistan	Bristol
Mon, 17th	B	New Zealand vs Bangladesh	Chelmsford
Tues, 18th	A	England vs Kenya	Canterbury
Wed, 19th	A	Sri Lanka vs South Africa	Northampton
	A	India vs Zimbabwe	Leicester
Thurs, 20th	B	Australia vs New Zealand	Cardiff
	B	Pakistan vs Scotland	Chester-Le-Street
Fri, 21st	B	West Indies vs Bangladesh	Dublin, Ireland
Sat, 22nd	A	England vs South Africa	The Oval
	A	Zimbabwe vs Sri Lanka	Worcester
Sun, 23rd	A	India vs Kenya	Bristol
	B	Australia vs Pakistan	Headingley
Mon, 24th	B	West Indies vs New Zealand	Southampton
	B	Scotland vs Bangladesh	Edinburgh
Tues, 25th	A	England vs Zimbabwe	Trent Bridge
Wed, 26th	A	Sri Lanka vs India	Taunton
	A	South Africa vs Kenya	Amstelveen
Thurs, 27th	B	West Indies vs Scotland	Leicester
	B	Australia vs Bangladesh	Chester-le-Street
Fri, 28th	B	New Zealand vs Pakistan	Derby
Sat, 29th	A	England vs India	Edgbaston
	A	Zimbabwe vs South Africa	Chelmsford
Sun, 30th	A	Sri Lanka vs Kenya	Southampton
	B	West Indies vs Australia	Old Trafford
Mon, 31st	B	Scotland vs New Zealand	Edinburgh
	B	Pakistan vs Bangladesh	Northampton

June	Gp	Match	Venue
Fri, 4th	SS	Group A2 vs Group B2	The Oval
Sat, 5th	SS	Group A1 vs Group B1	Trent Bridge
Sun, 6th	SS	Group A3 vs Group B3	Headingley

Tues, 8th	SS	Group A2 vs Group B1	Old Trafford
Wed, 9th	SS	Group A3 vs Group B2	Lord's
Thurs, 10th	SS	Group A1 vs Group B3	Edgbaston
Fri, 11th	SS	Group A3 vs Group B1	The Oval
Sat, 12th	SS	Group A2 vs Group B3	Trent Bridge
Sun, 13th	SS	Group A1 vs Group B2	Headingley
Wed, 16th	SF	Team 1 vs Team 4	Old Trafford
Thurs, 17th	SF	Team 2 vs Team 3	Edgbaston
Sun, 20th	F	SF1 vs SF2	Lord's

Warm-up Match Schedule

All the teams taking part in the World Cup will play warm-up games against first class county sides in the first half of May. The majority of the games will be at their host venue. See the Venues section of this book to see where each team is based during the World Cup.

May	*Match*	*Venue*
Fri, 7th	England vs Kent	Canterbury
	India vs Leicestershire	Leicester
	Kenya vs Somerset	Taunton
	South Africa vs Sussex	Hove
	Sri Lanka vs Northamptonshire	Northampton
	Zimbabwe vs Worcestershire	Worcester
Sat, 8th	Australia vs Glamorgan	Cardiff
	Bangladesh vs Essex	Chelmsford
	New Zealand vs Hampshire	Southampton
	Pakistan vs Derbyshire	Derby
Sat, 8th	Scotland vs Durham	Chester-le-Street
	West Indies vs Gloucestershire	Bristol
Sun, 9th	England vs Essex	Chelmsford
	India vs Yorkshire	Headingley
	Kent vs Gloucestershire	Bristol
	South Africa vs Kent	Canterbury
	Sri Lanka vs Nottinghamshire	Trent Bridge
	Zimbabwe vs Derbyshire	Derby
Mon, 10th	England vs Hampshire	Southampton
	India vs Nottinghamshire	Trent Bridge
	Kenya vs Glamorgan	Cardiff
	South Africa vs Middlesex	Lord's
	Sri Lanka vs Leicestershire	Leicester
	Zimbabwe vs Warwickshire	Edgbaston
Tues, 11th	Australia vs Somerset	Taunton
	Bangladesh vs Northamptonshire	Northampton
	New Zealand vs Sussex	Hove
	Pakistan vs Lancashire	Old Trafford
	Scotland vs Yorkshire	Headingley
	West Indies vs Surrey	The Oval

May	*Match*	*Venue*
Wed, 12th	Australia vs Worcestershire	Worcester
	Bangladesh vs Middlesex	Lord's
	New Zealand vs Surrey	The Oval
	Pakistan vs Durham	Chester-le-Street
	Scotland vs Lancashire	Old Trafford
	West Indies vs Warwickshire	Edgbaston

THE VENUES

AMSTELVEEN

Address: VRA Ground, Nieuwe Kalfjeslaan 21B,
                Amstelveen
Telephone: 31 20 641 8525
Games: South Africa vs Kenya (A)

This ground, located a few miles south of Amsterdam, boasts a new turf cricket pitch, on which it will host the all-African South Africa vs Kenya fixture. The Dutch team didn't make it to the finals this time but the locals should provide good support for their South African cousins.

The ground was the second to install a grass wicket in Holland and saw international action prior to the World Cup. The Dutch side played a touring South African side in the summer of 1998.

The pavilion houses the offices of the Royal Dutch Cricket Association.

BRISTOL

Address: County Ground, Nevil Road, Bristol, BS7 9E7
Telephone: 0117 910 8000
Games: India vs Kenya (A),
                West Indies vs Pakistan (B)

The county base of Gloucestershire, the ground is set high above the city of Bristol. The wicket is good and locals will perhaps say that it can favour spinners, which may suit India in their game here against Kenya – which will also be the first international to be staged at the ground.

The ground is full of character, fringed by trees, with a solid Edwardian pavilion. Former Gloucestershire heroes are remembered in the Jessop Tavern, and in the Grace Gates. The ground now acts as a general sports centre, with squash and tennis courts, and in winter the turf serves as the target for a golf driving range.

The history book indicates that difficult batting conditions can prevail, as when Tom Goddard took 17 wickets in a day here in 1939. In another Gloucestershire-Middlesex game in 1938, Jim Smith made the fastest uncontrived first class 50 (11 minutes to hit six sixes and two fours). WG Grace scored a triple century here in 1896 against Sussex, a feat matched by WR Hammond in 1934 vs Glamorgan.

CANTERBURY

Address: St Lawrence Ground, Old Dover Road,
                 Canterbury, Kent, CT1 3NZ
Telephone: 01227 456886
Games: England vs Kenya (A)

Established in 1847 and home of county team Kent. The famous lime tree, which stands within the boundary of the pitch, is apparently now diseased and will eventually have to be pulled down. It will nevertheless feature in the World Cup, typifying the charming eccentricity of some of the English venues. The venue will play host to the England team during the pre World Cup period from 4th to 13th May.

CARDIFF

Address: Sophia Gardens, Cardiff, Glamorgan, Wales
Telephone: 01222 300 500
Games: Australia vs New Zealand (A)

Glamorgan, English County Champions in 1997, have continued the redevelopment of Sophia Gardens and the new Indoor School and practice facilities have opened as part of a 15-year three phase development into an 8,000 seater stadium. New seating has been erected at the river end of the ground, and a new scoreboard facility has been completed. The ground takes its name from the wife of the Marquess of Bute.

The club hosts the Australians and plays a one-day match against the South Africans on 8th May in the pre World Cup competition. The Aussies then face New Zealand in the competition proper in Group A. World-class all-rounder Jacques

Kallis will say farewell to his South African colleagues after the World Cup, as he heads for the resident Glamorgan side as overseas player for 1999 and 2000.

The ground boasts a good batting wicket, with the most notable performance from Glamorgan in July 1993 when Viv Richards and Adrian Dale shared an unbeaten partnership of 425 for the fourth wicket in the match with Middlesex.

CHELMSFORD

Address:	New Writtle Street, Chelmsford, Essex
Telephone:	01245 252420
Games:	New Zealand vs Bangladesh (A),
	Zimbabwe vs South Africa (A)

Home of Essex, one of the most successful domestic one day sides of recent times, this ground will stage games between New Zealand and Bangladesh and between Zimbabwe and South Africa. The legendary Graham Gooch played much of his first-class career here hitting a large portion of his 40,000 plus runs into the fast outfield.

The ground has mostly single-tier seating with just one two-level stand – The Tom Pearce Stand.

CHESTER-LE-STREET

Address:	County Cricket Ground, Riverside,
	Chester-Le-Street, County Durham, DH3 3QR
Telephone:	0191 387 1717
Games:	Pakistan vs Scotland (B),
	Australia vs Bangladesh (B)

The home of Durham County Cricket Club, the Riverside is a picturesque location for cricket and has been team home to great one-day players in their twilight years – Ian Botham, Wayne Larkin and David Boon to name three. Australia may benefit from Boon's advice when playing Bangladesh here. The wicket holds no surprises so Scotland shouldn't be able to ambush Pakistan in their encounter.

The building of a Test standard ground on this site was one of the conditions on which Durham were admitted to the County Championship in 1992. In keeping with the nature of the area, the facility is built using traditional materials and has a low profile. As part of a four phase development the capacity of the ground will ultimately reach 20,000, with one side remaining open so as to afford spectators a magnificent view of the 14th Century Lumley Castle.

DERBY

Address: County Cricket Ground, Nottingham Road,
                 Derby, DE2 6DA
Telephone: 01332 383 211
Games: New Zealand vs Pakistan (B)

The city centre ground has a long history, with a fine grandstand that dates back to 1911. Sometimes cold and exposed, the wicket tends to be slow, which won't suit either New Zealand or Pakistan, who meet here on the 28th May. The team which adapts best to the conditions will win the day.

A touring Aboriginal side played here in 1868 when they were entertained by a South Derby side. Nearer to home Derbyshire recorded their highest first class score here of 645 in 1898.

DUBLIN

Address: Clontarf Club Ground, Dublin
Telephone: 00 353 1833 62 14
Games: West Indies vs Bangladesh (B)

Ireland are not represented in the finals this time around, but the Irish team has come so far in recent years that a rousing Irish welcome is likely for both West Indies and Bangladesh when they appear on the 21st May.

EDGBASTON

Address: County Ground, Edgbaston, Birmingham, B5 7QX
Telephone: 0121 446 4422
Games: England vs India (A),
                         A1 vs B3 (SS), Team 2 vs Team 3 (SF)

Birmingham's Edgbaston will host England's game against India in this World Cup, plus a Super Six game and a semi-final clash. Expect a great atmosphere at all these games, especially if the Asian teams continue through to the final stages, where they will benefit from the huge local support.

Edgbaston has seen some great feats. India's Bishen Bedi bowled 12 overs for an incredible six runs here in 1975 against East Africa, the stingiest figures ever in World Cups.

West Indies have been involved in both the smallest margin and largest margin victories here. They beat Pakistan by one run in 1975 and Zimbabwe by 10 wickets in 1983.

If Australia find themselves in a Super Six here they won't want to check the history. In the first-ever Test at Edgbaston in 1902, Australia was bowled out for 36, their lowest total in all international cricket. Victor Trumper scored half the total. No-one else topped five runs, and there were four ducks and three byes. Wilfred Rhodes took seven for 17 in 11 overs in this match, England's best innings bowling against any country at Edgbaston.

EDINBURGH

Address: Grange Cricket Club, Raeburn Place, Edinburgh
Telephone: 0131 317 7247 (Scottish Cricket Association)
Games: Scotland vs Bangladesh (B),
                         Scotland vs New Zealand (B)

Located amongst the parks of Edinburgh make this probably the most picturesque setting of the World Cup. The Scots made it to the finals but play mainly 'abroad' in England so the two home games at this venue, against Bangladesh and New Zealand, will be appreciated by those who remember that former England captain Mike Denness was really a Scotsman!

HEADINGLEY

Address: Headingley Cricket Ground, Leeds,
          Yorkshire, LS6 3BU
Telephone: 0113 278 7394
Games: Australia vs Pakistan (B),
          Group A3 vs Group B3 (SS),
          Group A1 vs Group B2 (SS)

The home of Yorkshire County Cricket club, the Headingley ground was established in 1888 and has seen international cricket since June 1899.

Given the prevailing weather conditions of mid May and early June, most teams winning the toss put the opposition in, anticipating early swing and seam action. That could be an important call when Australia play Pakistan here on 23rd May – Wasim Akram and Glenn McGrath hoping to get that early bowling opportunity.

With such a long history the friendly and knowledgeable Headingley crowd have witnessed some great feats of cricket history, including two Test triple centuries by Don Bradman in 1930 and 1934. The Surrey left-hander John Edrich also made a Test triple hundred here, against New Zealand in 1965. However, probably the most memorable innings for the Yorkshire crowd was their own Geoff Boycott's hundredth hundred, made against Australia in 1977. In 1981 the combined heroics of Botham with the bat and Willis with the ball beat 500-1 odds to defeat Australia by 18 runs, having followed on 227 runs behind and at 135-7 in their second innings.

West Indian bowler W Davis achieved the best ever World Cup bowling performance here in 1983 when he captured seven wickets for 51 against Australia.

Although the wicket is generally believed to aid seam bowling, it has also been friendly in the past to the long tradition of Yorkshire spin bowlers, including Wilfred Rhodes and Hedley Verity, who here produced the greatest of all bowling analyses, 19.4-16-10-10 against Nottinghamshire in 1932.

Spectators at the Kirkstall Lane (north) end sit in the 'Chad' stand, built to form a white background with only the spectators' heads protruding.

HOVE

Address: The County Ground, Eaton Road, Hove,
                East Sussex, BN3 3AN
Telephone: 01273 732161
Games: India vs South Africa (A)

Hove is famous for its deckchairs where spectators can sit in the sun and watch a day's cricket. Home of Sussex, the ground is being kitted out with permanent lighting but there won't be a day/night game in this World Cup.

The easy batting wicket should suit Tendulkar and the powerful South African top order when India meet them here on the second day of the tournament. Could be too chilly for the deckchairs though!

LEICESTER

Address: The County Ground, Grace Road,
                Leicester, LE2 8AD
Telephone: 0116 2832128
Games: India vs Zimbabwe (A),
                West Indies vs Scotland (B)

Home of Leicestershire, Grace Road was an instant sell-out for the India versus Zimbabwe game. The local Asian community didn't show as much enthusiasm for the West Indies versus Scotland game but, considering the West Indies' recent form, this could be an interesting fixture too.

India's wicketkeeper Kirmani achieved the most World Cup dismissals here in 1983 when he took five catches behind the stumps against Zimbabwe.

LORD'S

Address: Swiss Cottage, London, NW8
Telephone: 0171 432 1066
Games: England vs Sri Lanka (A),
                      Group A3 vs Group B2 (SS), Final

Venue for three previous World Cup finals, Lord's will stage its fourth such event when it hosts the final game of the 1999 World Cup on the 20th June. It will host a Super Six game and in addition to staging the final game of the tournament it will also provide for the first when England (hosts) and Sri Lanka (holders) contest Group A points here on the 14th May.

As a ground, Lord's is a mixture of ancient and modern, from the Grace Gates to the futuristic Media Centre that you could mistake for a landing UFO. Lord's owes its name to Thomas Lord who moved the original turf from Dorset square and found his final field in St. John's Wood. The ground has been owned by the Marylebone Cricket Club (MCC) since 1866.

There is a seven feet (2.1 metre) drop across the ground, with the Grandstand side being higher than the Tavern side. This can be used to good effect by bowlers in the know but it also means that the ball skates away to the boundary. The two ends are referred to as the Pavilion and Nursery ends.

The largest World Cup margin of victory was at Lord's in 1975 when England beat India by 202 runs.

NORTHAMPTON

Address: County Cricket Ground, Wantage Road,
                      Northampton, NN1 4TJ
Telephone: 01604 632917
Games: Sri Lanka vs South Africa (A).
                      Pakistan vs Bangladesh (B)

Like some of the other county grounds, Northampton's city centre site has benefited from the national lottery sports fund. The Spencer Pavilion was extended to provide more seating and last year the Indoor Cricket Centre became reality. At the front of the Centre there is a prime viewing area for 300 spectators. Enjoy a beer in Stumps bar during two excellent fixtures.

Sri Lanka against South Africa sold out quickly as World Champions versus champions in waiting, while the 'local derby' of Pakistan against Bangladesh should see a riotous game.

With a capacity of just 4,000 it is the smallest of the main county grounds but this just adds to the intimate atmosphere.

OLD TRAFFORD

Address:	Cricket Ground, Old Trafford, Manchester, M16 OPX
Telephone:	0161 282 4000
Games:	West Indies vs Australia (B), Group A2 vs Group B1 (SS), Team 1 vs Team 4 (SF)

The Old Trafford wicket has acted as scenery for many a one-day drama, both domestic and international. Lancashire's one day teams of the 70s and 80s pioneered some of the techniques and tactics which have become part of the modern one day game.

One of the Lancashire and West Indies greats, Clive Lloyd, took three catches in the match against Sri Lanka in 1975, a current record held jointly with Border, Ahmed and Reeve. The venue saw the lowest total in a full World Cup match scored when England dismissed Canada for 45 in 40.3 overs in 1979.

The Old Trafford wicket usually produces a good game, favouring neither batsmen nor bowlers. Manchester games can be rain affected so it's important for the team batting first to keep up a decent run rate from the off.

As with other English Test grounds, Old Trafford has quite a history behind it. It was established in 1856 and has played hosts to Tests since 1884.

SOUTHAMPTON

Address:	The County Ground, Northlands Road, Southampton, Hampshire, SO15 2UE
Telephone:	01703 333788
Games:	West Indies vs New Zealand (B), Sri Lanka vs Kenya (A)

A pleasant open ground, the Southampton wicket favours batsmen so it may be the place for West Indies' batsmen to regain some confidence against New Zealand. Sri Lanka's hitters could have a ball later in the month against Kenya.

The earliest surviving record of a cricket match in Hampshire dates from 1749 and for more than 20 years before the founding of MCC in 1787, the south-east Hampshire village of Hambledon was the focal point of English cricket and played an important part in the development of the modern game, including the introduction of the third stump, length bowling, 'straight' batting and the limit to the width of the bat.

TAUNTON

Address:	The County Ground, St. James' Street, Taunton, Somerset, TA1 1JT
Telephone:	01823 272946
Games:	Zimbabwe vs Kenya (A), Sri Lanka vs India (A)

The home of Somerset will host an all-African clash when Zimbabwe come up against Kenya, and an all-Asian coming together in Sri Lanka against India. The wicket suits the batsmen as long as the weather holds and, since all four teams have some potent stroke-players, spectators could be in for a run-fest.

Former West Indies star Viv Richards was a regular at Taunton and he scored home team Somerset's highest individual innings score 322 (one of his 15 centuries for them), on this ground versus Warwickshire in 1985. Sri Lanka beat East Africa by 115 runs in a three day game between these two non-Test playing countries which had just participated in the first World Cup.

THE OVAL

Address: The Oval, Kennington, London
Telephone: 0171 582 6660
Games: England vs South Africa (A),
             Group A2 vs Group B2 (SS),
             Group A3 vs Group B1 (SS)

An impressive expanse of green amongst built-up London, The Oval is the home of the Surrey team. A good batting wicket usually allows batsmen to play their strokes after any early morning dampness has gone. As such the captain winning the toss often prefers to put his opponent at the crease first.

The most expensive bowling session in World Cups was performed here by the unfortunate New Zealander M Snedden who came up against a rampant England in 1983. Snedden's twelve overs cost him 105 runs and incredibly included a single maiden over and a two wicket consolation.

The first-ever Test on English soil was played here in September 1880 and this is the historic venue where the legend of the Ashes was born a couple of years later.

Stands rise up vertically around the ground to retain the atmosphere which builds up during a day's carousing at the various bars on the concourse, which enables the spectators to walk all the way around the ground.

TRENT BRIDGE

Address: Trent Bridge, Nottingham, NG2 6AG
Telephone: 0115 982 1525
Games: England vs Zimbabwe (A),
             Group A1 vs Group B1 (SS),
             Group A2 vs Group B3 (SS)

A brand new stand graces Trent Bridge for the World Cup. The new Radcliffe Road Stand is a three storey building which includes indoor nets, some overnight accommodation for young players and an increase in seating capacity of about 2,000.

For the players the days of 'dodgy' wickets are long gone and the current excellent playing surface, which can almost be called 'neutral', has been rewarded with two Super Six ties.

The ground takes its name from the Trent Bridge Inn which was situated on the south side of the ground. In December 1837, the captain and self-appointed manager of the Nottinghamshire team, William Clarke, married the landlady of the inn and the following spring he laid a cricket ground in the meadow attached to the inn which was to become the modern day Test ground.

The addition of the Radcliffe Road Stand is part of a long redevelopment programme that started in 1979.

WORCESTER

Address:	The County Ground, New Road, Worcester, Worcestershire, WR2 4QQ
Telephone:	01905 748474
Games:	Australia vs Scotland (B),
	Zimbabwe vs Sri Lanka (A)

The County Ground, Worcester is one of the most picturesque grounds on the county circuit. Near the city centre and by the riverside, surrounded by trees, it's also famous for its Ladies Pavilion. Australia play their opener here against Scotland, and Zimbabwe versus Sri Lanka could be closer than anticipated a few months ago.

EMERGING STARS

There are actually 180 stars at the World Cup because the players are the best of the best national sides and each is a star in his own club, county or state team. Amongst these players are a select few who are either new enough to surprise even seasoned watchers of the game or coming to their prime in a way that will truly affect the outcome of this competition. We'll discuss a few of these below.

If you are looking for a real emerging star then why not start with South Africa's youngest ever representative player, at 18 years and 314 days: Victor Mpitsang. He is a basketball playing fan of rap music who can bowl fast so let's hope he gets a chance to take the field. Under the tutelage of Donald and Pollock, Mpitsang is likely to find his feet first at this World Cup and could be a force to be reckoned with in future competitions.

England are once again relying mainly on tried and tested players and a certain type of all-rounder who is deemed to suit one day cricket. You'd be hard-pressed to find many players under thirty in the England camp and neither Mark Alleyne nor Vince Wells are spring chickens but they are new to the England scene and looked the part over the winter tour. Both are able practitioners with bat and ball, making runs with one and restricting the opposition with the other.

Lancashire's Andrew Flintoff has youth on his side and, on the basis of last summer's performances, he'll deserve to get his chance. Fellow Lancastrian Ian Austin is a real favourite with the crowd and is a familiar figure in England but not elsewhere in the globe. His full figure provides for solid strokeplay and deceptive pace off the pitch. Not youthful but definitely emerging, Austin is the archetypal one day player, ideally suited to his environment. England fans will be hoping that these qualities will be more important than international experience and that Ian Austin can become an English cricketing hero.

When Bangladesh beat the touring West Indies 'A' team by two wickets in the first of their three game series, Enamul Hoque was named man of the match. Watch out for this canny bowler who accounted for Hinds, Reifer, Sarwan and Bishop in his 4-25 in ten overs performance.

Hasibul Hussain is less controlled than his colleague and often bowls no balls and sprays around the wides. But he is a dangerous fast bowler with youth on his side so don't rule out Bangladesh as an upset team this time around, if not serious contenders for the Super Sixes.

South Africa have such an established side that it's difficult to imagine too many newcomers getting their say in the World Cup campaign. Even Kirsten has returned to form, which restricts the room for new batsmen. Nevertheless watch out for opening bat Bacher and promising batsman Dale Benkenstein who scored 69 in the fifth one day international against the West Indies in the winter. He knows England from a period playing in the Lancashire League and can hammer bowling in any conditions.

Australia are another established side who nurture players and incorporate them steadily into the side so it's a bit of a surprise that Damien Martyn, who was a young prodigy and Australian Under-19 captain, is suddenly back in the picture. His brand of aggressive and wristy right-handed batting could surprise others and delight Aussie followers. He has the talent.

Zimbabwe's Gavin Rennie has also made a comeback through one day cricket, having struggled to fit cricket around his working life. The World Cup should provide an excellent stage for this hard-hitting left-hander.

Bangladesh too have found a young batting star in Javed Omar, an opening batsman who makes a habit of building solid innings. Unproven against top opposition, the World Cup could forge him into an international class opener.

New Zealand's Paul Fleming has made great strides since the last World Cup. He has scored almost 3,000 runs in one day internationals now and averages in the 30s, with a top score of 116 not out. The off side drive is one of his most accomplished strokes.

Yousuf Youhana is one of Pakistan's rising stars and this World Cup will offer a first chance for many to see his gritty defence and dazzling stroke play. From India, check out left hand opener Sadagoppan Ramesh who produced 323 runs in his first three Test matches. He takes fast bowling in his stride and the idea of Ramesh and Tendulkar in partnership should instil panic in the opposition.

People always mention the batting talent of Kenya's Tikolo but there's also a young man called Ravindu Shah who has built some substantial innings, three over fifty, in his five matches so far. His 213 runs have been gathered at a world class average of over 40.

Raw Speed

Batting talent does often take time to mature but raw bowling speed is more often the product of youth. Thomas Odoyo is Kenya's swiftest and he is proclaimed to be one of their brightest prospects for the future. His bowling is currently wayward by international standards but on green English wickets, watch out for at least one sensational set of figures.

Someone whose bowling style seems made for England in May is New Zealand's Simon Doull. He can swing the ball both ways at a brisk medium pace, just the job for wickets such as Headingley, Trent Bridge and Lord's. His one day record isn't great but batsmen should beware. Another line and length bowler who will find English wickets to his liking may be Zimbabwe's Mpumelelo Mbangwa. He is still learning his trade but played at an English school in his youth and has shown promise in a short career. Mbangwa's team mate Henry Olonga is a quick bowler who grabbed nine wickets in Zimbabwe's recent history-making Test victory over Pakistan. His match-winning burst of 4-42 is top stuff and he's a determined young man so, if he can conjure up some accuracy, you'll see his name in lights.

Scotland's young hope is John Blain who was Scotland's youngest capped cricketer for 106 years. Opening the bowling, he has achieved figures of 4-34 against the England Amateur XI and bowled figures of 10-3-12-2 against Israel. OK, it's not the big time but the promise exists and Blain has now had professional experience with Northamptonshire. Watch out also for James Brinkley who bowled 38.3 overs at an economical 3.5 an over in domestic cricket last year so expect him to pin down some of the more well-known opposition batsmen.

India have their own new bowling talent too. Agarkar is capable of moving the ball both ways and his smooth action has already accounted for 58 international one day wickets. Shoaib Akhtar is the latest bowling sensation to emerge from Pakistan. On his first overseas tour with the senior side in South Africa, he was clocked faster than Waqar Younis and Allan Donald. He possesses old-fashioned aggression and hot-headedness which should make him a crowd pleaser come May in England.

Stuart MacGill is a spin bowler who made an impression on England's batsmen and supporters during the winter but watch out for 20 year old Daniel Vettori, an off break bowler from New Zealand. He is an attacking bowler, quickish through the air and giving the ball a reasonable amount of spin. Probably the best off spinner in modern cricket however is Saqlain Mushtaq. In the last three and a half years he has picked up 176 wickets in 88 limited overs matches.

All Round Talent

While England still await the emergence of an all-rounder to rival Ian Botham, South Africa seem to have a glut of all-round athletes. Following Pollock is Kallis, and following Kallis is Tony Ondik is Kenya's promising all-rounder, a middle order right-hand batsman and right-arm medium pace bowler, and a good fielder. Three wickets and a high score of 63 show promise. Christopher Cairns comes to mind as an all-rounder currently showing good form for New Zealand and he has a team mate in Craig McMillan who has developed into a handy one day player with a decent batting average in the late 20s and the ability to pick up wickets on a regular basis. He came out of a disciplinary cloud recently and is learning all the time.

Shahid Afridi created a sensation by reaching a limited overs 100 against Sri Lanka off a mere 37 balls in his first outing at the crease. Although primarily a batsman, Afridi also bowls fastish leg-breaks and is an excellent all-round fielder. He was voted Man of the Finals in the 1996-97 World Series Cricket.

A young man who is sure to impress in this World Cup and could become its overall star, is Ricky Ponting of Australia. He has already scored over 2,000 runs at an average around the 40 mark and he is only 25. Naturally aggressive in outlook, with nearly every shot in the book, Ponting complements his batting with brisk medium pace/swing and brilliant fielding in the point/cover region. He's had his personal problems and the media's attention will be on him. If he can play his natural game, he is one of the top five talents on the field in this World Cup.

But if it's a young prodigy you want to look out for this summer, perhaps Hasan Raza will make an appearance. He will turn 17 the day before the opening game and has made his mark with the Pakistan Under-15 side, not least by scoring a stylish 80 against India at Lord's in the final of the Lombard Under-15 World Cup. He promises to be another wristy player in the league of Zaheer Abbas. What names we have to conjure with when considering both the past and emerging stars of the cricket World Cup!

WORLD CUP TEAM DIRECTORY

The following pages contain details of the 12 qualifiers for the 1999 World Cup. As far as possible they follow a similar format and this is detailed below. A key to the abbreviations used in this section can be found on pages 8 and 9.

Introduction:
A look at how each country has been playing into the lead-up to the Finals.

World Cup Record:
This is a record of how the team has performed against the other qualifiers for the World Cup.

Campaign Performance:
How the country has performed in any previous World Cup Finals. This includes the stage reached and the captain for the tournament, along with how the cup was won or lost!

One Day Records:
This section includes a variety of detail ranging from complete one day records, record since the last World Cup and both highest and lowest innings totals in the one day game.

Individual Records:
This section contains details of outstanding performances by players in the previous World Cup tournaments including highest partnership totals.

Player Performances:
This lists the batting and bowling details of every player who has played for their country in the World Cup.

Player Profiles:
A description of the players who are likely to be in their team's final squad of 15. These were written prior to the squads being announced so we have taken our best guesses at who will be included. In many cases there are more profiles than the 15 allowed in each squad.

AUSTRALIA

Aussies True to Form

Australia come to the World Cup with most key players in good form. The potential betting scandal surrounding Warne and Mark Waugh may even have served to bind the players more closely. The team management tried out a number of non-regulars to get the one-day balance right and to keep the Test players on their toes and, in the case of Steve Waugh and Healey, to rest their wounds.

Australia won seven of their one-day games and lost three to head the triangular tournament table. In the first of the three final games McGrath wiped out the England middle and late order to recover a seemingly lost game. Even with the retirement of Taylor, Australia have tremendous strength in batting depth. This side will be looking to turn form into results when it counts, something previous Australian sides haven't quite managed to do. The only potential problem will surely be tiredness after tough back to back Test series.

Team strip: Green shooting stars, etched in white, on a bright traditional yellow print. Stars of the Southern Cross on collar and sleeve-ends.

World Cup Record

	First Year	P	W	L	NR	SR%
Canada	1979	1	1	–	–	100.00
England	1975	4	2	2	–	50.00
India	1983	6	4	2	–	66.66
Kenya	1995-96	1	1	–	–	100.00
New Zealand	1987-88	4	3	1	–	75.00
Pakistan	1975	4	2	2	–	50.00
South Africa	1991-92	1	–	1	–	–
Sri Lanka	1975	4	2	2	–	50.00
West Indies	1975	7	2	5	–	28.57
Zimbabwe	1983	6	5	1	–	83.00
Total		*38*	*22*	*16*	*–*	*57.89*

Year	Pos	Captain	Result
1975	F	IM Chappell	Lost to West Indies by 17 runs
1979	Gp	KJ Hughes	Failed to qualify for semi-finals
1983	Gp	KJ Hughes	Failed to qualify for semi-finals
1987-88	F	AR Border	Won – beat England by 7 runs
1991-92	Gp	AR Border	Failed to qualify for semi-finals
1995-96	F	MA Taylor	Lost to Sri Lanka by 7 wickets

One-Day Records

	Period	P	W	L	T	NR	SR%
All-Time:	… … 70-71 to 98-99	418	229	175	3	11	56.26
Since Last WC:	… … … … …	64	33	31	0	0	51.56

Highest Innings Totals:

Runs	Overs	R/O	Opponents	Venue	Year
328-5	60 overs	5.46	Sri Lanka	The Oval	1975
320-9	60 overs	6.40	India	Nottingham	1983
304-7	50 overs	6.08	Kenya	Vishakaptnam	1995-96
289-4	47.5 overs	6.04	New Zealand	Madras	1995-96

Lowest Completed Innings:

Runs	Overs	R/O	Opponents	Venue	Year
129	38.2 overs	3.36	India	Chelmsford	1983

World Cup Individual Records

100 Pluses

Runs	bp	Player	Opponents	Venue	Year
130	2	ME Waugh	Kenya	Vishakaptnam	1995-96
126no	1	GR Marsh	New Zealand	Chandrigarh	1987-88
126	1	ME Waugh	India	Bombay	1995-96
110	2	TM Chappell	India	Nottingham	1983
110	2	GR Marsh	India	Madras	1987-88
110	2	ME Waugh	New Zealand	Madras	1995-96
102	3	RT Ponting	West Indies	Jaipur	1995-96
101	2	A Turner	Sri Lanka	The Oval	1975
100	1	DC Boon	New Zealand	Auckland	1991-92
100	2	DC Boon	West Indies	Melbourne	1991-92

Partnership Record for each Wicket

	Total	Partnership	Opponents	Year
1st	182	RB McCosker (73), A Turner (101)	Sri Lanka	1975
2nd	144	TM Chappell (110), KJ Hughes (34)	India	1983
3rd	207	ME Waugh (130), SR Waugh (82)	Kenya	1995-96
4th	117	GS Chappell (50), KD Walters (59)	Sri Lanka	1975
5th	138	SG Law (72), MG Bevan (69)	West Indies	1995-96
6th	99	R Edwards (58), RW Marsh (*52)	West Indies	1975
7th	*55	KD Walters (*20), GJ Gilmour (*28)	England	1975
8th	*50	RW Marsh (*50), RM Hogg (*19)	Zimbabwe	1983
9th	*23	GR Marsh (*126), AK Zesers (*8)	N Zealand	1987-88
10th	41	JR Thomson (21), DK Lillee (*16)	West Indies	1975

Four Wicket Hauls

Score	Arm	Player	Opponents	Venue	Year
6-14	LFM	GJ Gilmour	England	Leeds	1975
6-39	RFM	KH Macleay	India	Nottingham	1983
5-21	RFM	AG Hurst	Canada	Birmingham	1979
5-34	RF	DK Lillee	Pakistan	Leeds	1975
5-36	RFM	DW Fleming	India	Bombay	1995-96
5-44	RFM	CJ McDermott	Pakistan	Lahore	1987-88
5-48	LFM	GJ Gilmour	West Indies	Lord's	1975
4-34	LFM	MR Whitney	West Indies	Melbourne	1991-92
4-34	LBG	SK Warne	Zimbabwe	Nagpur	1995-96
4-36	LBG	SK Warne	West Indies	Chandrigarh	1995-96
4-39	RFM	SP O'Donnell	Zimbabwe	Madras	1987-88
4-56	RFM	CJ McDermott	India	Madras	1987-88

Man of the Match Awards

21 Awards: DC Boon (4), ME Waugh (3), TM Moody (2), SR Waugh (2), SK Warne (2), DK Lillee (1), A Turner (1), GJ Gilmour (1), AG Hurst (1), TM Chappell (1), GR Marsh (1), CJ McDermott (1), DM Jones (1)

Batting

Player	First Yr	P	I	no	Runs	HS	Ave	100	50	CS
MG Bevan	95-96	7	5	1	125	69	31.25	–	1	2
DC Boon	87-88	16	16	1	815	100	54.33	2	5	2
AR Border	79	25	24	–	452	67	18.83	–	1	10
GS Chappell	75	5	5	–	129	50	25.80	–	1	3
IM Chappell	75	5	5	–	121	62	24.20	–	1	–
TM Chappell	83	4	4	–	139	110	34.75	1	–	1
GJ Cosier	79	3	2	–	6	6	3.00	–	–	1
WM Darling	79	3	3	–	51	25	17.00	–	–	–
GC Dyer	87-88	8	4	–	50	27	12.50	–	–	9/2
G Dymock	79	3	2	1	14	10	14.00	–	–	–
R Edwards	75	5	4	1	166	*80	55.33	–	2	–
DW Fleming	95-96	6	1	–	0	0	–	–	–	2
GJ Gilmour	75	2	2	1	42	*28	42.00	–	–	1
IA Healy	91-92	14	11	2	110	31	12.22	–	–	17/3
AMJ Hilditch	79	3	3	–	143	72	47.66	–	1	1
TG Hogan	83	4	4	2	24	11	12.00	–	–	2
RM Hogg	79	8	5	4	29	*19	29.00	–	–	1
DW Hookes	83	6	6	–	133	56	22.16	–	1	3
KJ Hughes	79	8	8	1	218	69	31.14	–	2	3
MG Hughes	91-92	1	1	1	0	*0	–	–	–	–
AG Hurst	79	3	2	2	6	*3	–	–	–	–
DM Jones	87-88	16	16	2	590	90	42.14	–	5	6
TJ Laughlin	79	1	1	–	8	8	8.00	–	–	–
SG Law	95-96	7	6	2	204	72	51.00	–	1	–
GF Lawson	83	4	4	–	24	16	6.00	–	–	–
S Lee	95-96	2	1	–	9	9	9.00	–	–	1
DK Lillee	75	9	3	1	19	*16	9.50	–	–	–
RB McCosker	75	5	5	–	120	73	24.00	–	1	–
CJ McDermott	87-88	17	11	–	43	14	3.90	–	–	4
GD McGrath	95-96	7	1	1	0	*0	–	–	–	1
KH Macleay	83	4	4	–	19	9	4.75	–	–	1
AA Mallett	75	3	1	–	0	0	–	–	–	1
GR Marsh	87-88	13	13	1	579	*126	48.25	2	2	2
RW Marsh	75	11	11	4	220	*52	31.42	–	2	17/1
TBA May	87-88	6	3	1	16	15	8.00	–	–	1

Player	First Yr	P	I	no	Runs	HS	Ave	100	50	CS
TM Moody	87-88	11	11	1	212	57	21.20	–	2	3
JK Moss	79	1	1	–	7	7	7.00	–	–	2
SP O'Donnell	87-88	7	4	–	15	7	3.75	–	–	4
RT Ponting	95-96	7	7	–	229	102	32.71	1	–	1
GD Porter	79	2	1	–	3	3	3.00	–	–	1
BA Reid	87-88	14	5	2	10	*5	3.33	–	–	4
PR Reiffel	95-96	5	4	3	27	*13	27.00	–	–	3
MA Taylor	91-92	9	9	–	206	74	22.88	–	2	1
PL Taylor	87-88	9	7	3	34	*17	8.50	–	–	1
JR Thomson	75	8	5	2	51	21	17.00	–	–	1
A Turner	75	5	5	–	201	101	40.20	1	–	3
MRJ Veletta	87-88	4	4	1	136	48	45.33	–	–	–
MHN Walker	75	5	3	–	33	18	11.00	–	–	1
KD Walters	75	5	5	1	123	59	30.75	–	1	–
SK Warne	95-96	7	5	2	32	24	10.66	–	–	2
ME Waugh	91-92	12	12	–	629	130	62.90	3	2	5
SR Waugh	87-88	23	22	7	580	82	38.66	–	4	8
KC Wessels	83	3	3	–	92	76	30.66	–	1	1
MR Whitney	91-92	7	3	2	22	*9	22.00	–	–	–
GM Wood	83	5	5	1	144	73	36.00	–	1	1
KJ Wright	79	3	2	–	29	23	14.50	–	–	5
GN Yallop	79	9	9	3	247	*66	41.16	–	2	–
AK Zesers	87-88	2	2	2	10	*8	–	–	–	1

Bowling

Player	Overs	M	Runs	Wi	Ave	BP	4wi	R/O
MG Bevan	32	1	156	3	52.00	2-35	–	4.87
DC Boon	1	0	17	0	–	–	–	17.00
AR Border	73	1	342	9	38.00	2-27	–	4.68
GS Chappell	18	0	88	0	–	–	–	4.88
IM Chappell	7	1	23	2	11.50	2-23	–	3.28
TM Chappell	19.4	0	98	4	24.50	3-47	–	4.98
GJ Cosier	27.2	4	95	5	19.00	3-54	–	3.47
G Dymock	31	7	64	2	32.00	1-17	–	2.06
DW Fleming	45.2	3	221	12	18.41	5-36	1	4.87
GJ Gilmour	24	8	62	11	5.63	6-14	2	2.58
TG Hogan	47	2	172	6	28.66	2-33	–	3.65
RM Hogg	78	9	271	10	27.10	3-40	–	3.47
MG Hughes	9	1	49	1	49.00	1-49	–	5.44

Player	Overs	M	Runs	Wi	Ave	BP	4wi	R/O
AG Hurst	32	6	119	7	17.00	5-21	1	3.71
DM Jones	1	0	5	0	–	–	–	5.00
TJ Laughlin	9.1	0	38	2	19.00	2-38	–	4.14
SG Law	5	0	23	0	–	–	–	4.60
GF Lawson	38	7	127	5	25.40	3-29	–	3.34
S Lee	7	2	31	0	–	–	–	4.42
DK Lillee	98	8	400	12	33.33	5-34	1	4.08
CJ McDermott	149	8	599	27	22.18	5-44	2	4.02
KH Macleay	44.5	6	163	8	20.37	6-39	1	3.63
AA Mallett	35	3	156	3	52.00	1-35	–	4.45
TBA May	44	1	213	4	53.25	2-29	–	4.84
TM Moody	51	2	240	7	34.28	3-56	–	4.70
SP O'Donnell	60.4	6	261	9	29.00	4-39	1	4.30
GD Porter	18	5	33	3	11.00	2-13	–	1.83
BA Reid	122.4	10	512	9	56.88	2-38	–	4.17
PR Reiffel	36	3	163	5	32.60	2-18	–	4.52
PL Taylor	47.4	1	218	6	36.33	2-14	–	4.57
JR Thomson	76.5	10	290	7	41.42	3-51	–	3.77
MHN Walker	57.2	10	210	6	35.00	3-22	–	3.66
KD Walters	17	1	85	1	85.00	1-29	–	5.00
SK Warne	68.3	3	263	12	21.91	4-34	2	3.83
ME Waugh	53	1	269	5	53.80	3-38	–	5.07
SR Waugh	155.1	6	722	24	30.08	3-36	–	4.65
MR Whitney	66	12	215	9	23.88	4-34	1	3.25
GN Yallop	22	0	110	3	36.66	2-28	–	5.00
AK Zesers	15	1	74	1	74.00	1-37	–	4.93

BEVAN, Michael Gwyl   LHB/SLC
Born: 8 May 1970, Belconnen, ACT   *New South Wales*

Also known as 'Bev' and 'Pita', Bevan is one of the world's premier one day middle-order batsmen, often producing key innings under pressure. One of his most memorable moments was driving Roger Harper for four at the Sydney Cricket Ground, clinching a last ball victory for Australia against the West Indies in the 1995-96 season. He one day debuted against Sri Lanka at Sharjah in the Australasia Cup in 1993-94. His average scaled the heights above 60 with over 3000 runs scored and a high score of 108 not out, proving that he is an awesome tower of strength in the Australian middle order. He has had some left arm wrist spin bowling success too, with nearly 30 wickets and an economy rate below five per over. Bevan played for Yorkshire from 1995 to 1996 and moved to Sussex for 1998, one of a number of Australians to gain recent experience in English conditions. He hit a 95 not out in the Benson & Hedges last season and scored 323 runs in ten visits to the crease in the Sunday League.

BLEWETT, Gregory Scott   RHB/RM
Born: 29 October 1971, Adelaide   *South Australia*

Greg Blewett made his one day debut against South Africa at Wellington, New Zealand in the Centenary Tournament of 1994-95. An international average of 21 or so doesn't quite reflect the fluent strokemaker you see at the crease. He likes to pull, hook, cut and cover drive. He has been used primarily in the troublesome number three spot for Australia, bringing to the position an assured presence. He has worked hard to overcome his former weakness against spin bowling. On the other hand in international games his highest score is 57 and in all one day games he has yet to put together a century. This son of former South Australian captain, Bob Blewett, scored centuries in each of his first two Tests (joining Bill Ponsford and Doug Walters as the only Australians ever to do so) and was involved with Steve Waugh in amassing the 14th highest partnership in Test history (in the course of making his best international score of 214 in Johannesburg in 1997). Blewett is a specialist bat-pad catcher and a handy, although not that economical, medium pace bowler.

DALE, Adam Craig   LHB/RFM

Born: 30 December 1968, Ivanhoe, Queensland   *Queensland*

Adam Dale has come from the obscurity of playing for the state Second
XI in Victoria, to taking the new ball for Australia. Dale's medium
pace swing bowling first came to prominence in the domestic one day
competition a few years ago. He had a bumper Shield season in 1996-
97, taking over 40 wickets at 21 apiece, including 6/43 in the final. This
earned him a surprise call-up for the one day games in South Africa.
He made his one day debut against South Africa at East London, in the
first one day international of the 1996-97 series. He has bowled nearly
150 overs since, at just over four per over, although his 17 wickets
haven't come very rapidly. He is always hard to get away, an attribute
that has earned a good economy rate. Dale has a habit of surviving not
out (four out of six innings) and therefore can boast a rather deceptive
average of 24.

FLEMING, Damien William   RHB/RFM

Born: 24 April 1970, Bentley, Western Australia   *Victoria*

Damien Fleming is a right arm seam bowler with an especially cunning
outswinger (leg cutter) and a fast yorker. He made his one day debut
against South Africa at Perth in the World Series of 1993-94 and took a
hat trick in his debut Test in the following year. His international career
has been curtailed by persistent injury to his shoulder and hamstrings.
Nevertheless he has taken over 60 one day international wickets at a
reasonable strike rate and economy. He bowled well at the
Commonwealth Games and again in the Test series against Pakistan.
His batting is a complete no-no at international level!

GILCHRIST, Adam Craig   LHB/WK

Born: 14 November 1971, Bellingen, New South Wales   *W. Australia*

Adam Gilchrist is one of Australia's most exciting young players. He
has deservedly acquired a name for himself as an enterprising player
who can always be relied upon to make a valuable contribution to his
team's fortunes. Behind the stumps, he is reliable, enthusiastic and
athletic, perhaps more comfortable keeping to faster bowlers than to
spinners. As a batsman, his penchant for playing attacking shots, cuts
and drives, and for punishing loose bowling makes him a particularly
enjoyable player to watch. Although his elevation to national honours
was not without controversy (as it was made at the expense of the ever-
popular Ian Healy), such has been the extent of Gilchrist's progress

since moving to Western Australia that he has become a fixture in Australia's one day international side – as both a keeper and dashing opening batsman - over recent seasons. He made three brilliant one day international centuries during 1998 – this included a measured 100 against South Africa in Sydney in January, a blazing 118 off 117 balls against New Zealand at Lancaster Park in February, and a superb 103 which saw him anchor Australia's successful pursuit of a mammoth total of 8/315 set by Pakistan in Lahore in November. In 43 matches he scored over 1,300 runs at an average of 35.29, putting together four hundreds and four fifties.

GILLESPIE, Jason Neil   RHB/RF
Born: 19 April 1975, Darlinghurst, New South Wales   South Australia
After numerous promising seasons Gillespie was selected as a replacement for Craig McDermott for the 1996 World Cup. He debuted in the Titan Cup in India, but couldn't crack a Test spot immediately. He got his chance in the West Indies and went on to tour South Africa. He made his one day debut against Sri Lanka at Colombo in the 1996-97 series. Gillespie's style is direct, bowling at the stumps, especially back, have kept him out of cricket at different times but he had a successful Ashes tour of England last time around, taking a seven wicket haul at Headingley, so English conditions suit him.

HEALY, Ian Andrew   RHB/WK
Born: 30 April 1964, Spring Hill, Brisbane   *Queensland*
The rumour was that Healy played with a hand injury during the winter and that typifies the commitment of the player. He is capable of turning a game, especially in his killer combination with spinner Shane Warne. His one day debut was against Pakistan at Lahore in the 1988-89 season and over 1,300 one day runs at an average of 35+ means that, although not a regular one day player, Healy may find himself guiding the younger players towards the difficult task of taking the World Cup. He has scored nearly 8,000 first class runs and has proved himself a handy batsman over the years, in the mould of Marsh or Knott. He averages in the 30s, a very useful figure for any true keeper. And Healy is one of the best keepers of modern times as more than 600 first class catches and over 50 stumpings testify. Healy has probably eclipsed Rod Marsh as Australia's greatest ever keeper, not just because of his glove work but his ability to hold together the lower order with his

never say die attitude. He combines brilliantly with Warne to intimidate the best batsmen.

JULIAN, Brendon Paul   RHB/LFM
Born: 10 August 1970, Hamilton, New Zealand   Western Australia
Julian made his one day debut against England at Lord's, in the 1993 Texaco Trophy, and was back against England during the winter. He has completed ten matches and taken 15 wickets at the not very economic rate of 5.2 per over, although in domestic cricket he's got a better record just over the four per over mark. A batting average of 12.6 doesn't make him an all-rounder so he'll do well to make the team on a regular basis.

KASPROWICZ, Michael Scott   RHB/RF
Born: 10 February 1972, South Brisbane, Queensland   Queensland
A consistent wicket-taker since the time of his first class debut for Queensland in the 1989-90 season, Michael Kasprowicz is a tall and lanky right arm fast bowler who has overcome regular injury woes in the early part of his career to become one of Australia's most highly regarded pacemen. He made the step up to international one day cricket against the West Indies at Melbourne in the World Series of 1995-96. Kasprowicz displays sufficient variation and bowls with a suitably tight line and length to ensure that he is never an easy bowler to counter, although his economy is under question. Kasprowicz's stock ball is a leg-cutter delivered just short of a length and he can produce a deceptively quick faster ball – a ball which he used with particularly stunning effect during his sensational seven wicket haul in the second innings of the Sixth Test against England at The Oval in 1997 – which troubles batsmen. Complementing his talents with the ball are his qualities as a handy late-order batsman and a safe (albeit unspectacular) fielder.

LANGER, Justin Lee   LHB/RM/WK
Born: 21 November 1970, Perth, Western Australia   Western Australia
This slightly built but gritty batsman is a prolific scorer at first-class level and he already has over 20 centuries to his name. Langer weathered a pace bowling assault from Curtly Ambrose and Courtney Walsh in each innings of his debut Test to compile 20 and 54. He made his one day debut against Sri Lanka at Sharjah in the Australasia Cup of 1993-94. In more recent times, he has remained a fringe member of the national side, but his maiden Test century – albeit amid the

astonishing run feast in Peshawar in the second match of the 1998 series against Pakistan – indicates that he may well be ready to take the next step. In 1998 Langer had a prolific season in England. In one day cricket tournaments he averaged 38.81 in the Sunday League, 27.2 in the Benson & Hedges and a mighty 109 in the NatWest. His 114 not out in the NatWest shows how important he may be to Australia in England in 1999.

LEHMANN, Darren Scott   LHB/SLO
Born: 5 February 1970, Gawler, South Australia   Victoria
A top score of 103 in international one dayers and an average in the mid 30s goes some way to demonstrating that Darren Lehmann is a free scoring left-handed batsman who combines a natural penchant for playing swashbuckling attacking shots – particularly through the covers and mid-wicket - with an ability to apply the most deft and inventive touches to his strokes behind the wicket. To complete the picture Lehmann is an occasional left arm orthodox spin bowler and competent slip and short leg fielder. From the time that he burst on to the first class scene in Australia as a 17 year old in the 1987/88 season, Lehmann has built an imposing CV, including a first class average over 50 and the record for the most number of runs scored in a single domestic one-day season in Australia, but has arguably been overlooked as an Australian international. He played his first international one day game against in-form Sri Lanka at Colombo in the 1996/97 series. His 28 innings have resulted in 782 runs at an average of 34 and he's proved a handy, if uneconomic, bowler. Lehmann was another Aussie to bring his talents to the UK in 1998 and his 41.36 average in the Sunday League and 380 runs in Benson & Hedges (average 119, two not outs) should set alarm bells ringing in Australia's opponents' dressing rooms.

MARTYN, Damien Richard   RHB/ROB
Born: 21 October 1971, Darwin, N.Territory   Western Australia
A former member of the Australian Cricket Academy and a previous Australian under 19 captain, Damien Martyn is an aggressive and wristy right-handed middle order batsman. His career stalled in the years following his meteoric promotion to the senior Australian team at the age of 21. Although he has continued to work hard at his game both physically and mentally, such was his decline that he has only chalked up the relatively modest total of 20 or so one day internationals over

the last six years, following a one day debut against West Indies at Sydney in the 1992/93 World Series. Nevertheless, he was recalled to the national side for one day tours of India, Sharjah, Pakistan, Bangladesh and the winter series against England. His batting average of under 17 doesn't come close to his domestic performance so perhaps 1999 is the year for Martyn to make his comeback and fulfil that early promise.

MACGILL, Stuart Charles Glyndwr   RHB/LBG
Born: 25 February 1971, Mount Lawley, Perth   *New South Wales*
MacGill has recently overcome doubts about his temperament to perform admirably in Pakistan and at home against England. He turns the ball as far as Warne without quite the same control. He makes a reasonably short, straight approach to the wicket and his repertoire encompasses excellent variation. His trademark delivery is a relatively flat and short leg break which pitches on about the line of the right handed batsman's off stump and turns to finish outside it, but he also bowls a nicely aimed top spinner and a flipper which, whilst it does not spin appreciably, is cleverly disguised. MacGill has the advantage of being new to many batsmen in the World Cup competition, although there won't be many spinning wickets like the Sydney one where he took seven for 50 against England in the Test. He spins the ball hard and, if he can maintain accuracy, could be a match winner. Tail end batsmen can't pick his bowling variations so he can also tidy up an innings inexpensively. Scored some runs in the winter but proved vulnerable against fast accurate pace.

MCGRATH, Glenn Donald   RHB/RF
Born: 9 February 1970, Dubbo, New South Wales   *New South Wales*
Glenn McGrath has taken over from Craig McDermott as Australia's fast bowling spearhead and is one of the world's premier pace bowlers. Known as 'Millard' or 'Pigeon' he can generate genuine pace and bounce to complement his accuracy and ability to move both the new and old ball. He made a fine contribution in Pakistan and against England in 1998-99 after being sidelined for the Commonwealth Games and before because of injury. He has a classic run up and action, bowling a nagging line at top pace. A fierce competitor, he can be sharp with his tongue as well as with the ball, enjoying the intimidation of tail enders. He can't bat to save himself and usually gives the impression he wants to get out to get on with his real job. He made his one day debut against South Africa at Melbourne in the

World Series of 1993-94 and came to international prominence on the 1995 tour to the Caribbean, producing consistently hostile spells of fast bowling to intimidate the West Indians and capture 17 wickets during the four Tests, including a then-career best of 6-47. He seems to need to rant and rave as he gets fired up but is top class and should harvest a good crop of wickets in an English summer. During the winter triangular tournament McGrath joined a select group of Australians to take 100 or more wickets in one day internationals.

MILLER, Colin Reid   RHB/ROB, FM
Born: 6 February 1964, Footscray, Victoria   *Tasmania*
Colin Miller is an all-rounder who can get involved in a game in any capacity. He bowls off-spin but can convert back to medium pace when required. He may find himself bowling the latter style to be effective in English conditions. He is a capable bat and enthusiast in the field – a good team player, but with little one day experience. Nicknamed 'Funky' on account of his outgoing nature, Miller has played for three Australian States, Holland's national team, and a number of European and Asian clubs. Miller's career was primarily built on his reputation as a strongly built right-arm paceman who could move the ball both ways (mostly off the wicket) and who had the capacity to vary his pace cleverly. Miller's decision in a club game in Hobart to revert from bowling pace to off-spin (on account of a niggling ankle injury) was the catalyst for him to begin mixing both styles of bowling. He grabbed 12 for 119 against South Australia at Bellerive in January 1998 (an all-time record for a Tasmanian bowler in a Sheffield Shield match). In the 1997-98 season he rewrote 'Chuck' Fleetwood-Smith's 63 year old record for the highest number of wickets taken in a Shield season. He then emerged, at the age of 34, as a valued member of Australia's history-making team which toured Pakistan in 1998.

PONTING, Ricky Thomas   RHB/RM/WK
Born: 19 December 1974, Launceston, Tasmania   *Tasmania*
Ponting is a highly successful one day player but can he put a late night drinking incident and three match ban and fine behind him? A precocious talent, Ponting debuted for his state at the age of 17, and his first-class career has described a steady upward curve since that point, with a one day debut against South Africa at Wellington in the New Zealand Centenary Tournament of 1994-95. He has scored over 2,000 runs at an average around the 40 mark. Naturally aggressive in outlook, with nearly every shot in the book, Ponting complements his batting

with brisk medium pace/swing and brilliant fielding in the point/cover region. He could also double as reserve wicketkeeper.

SLATER, Michael Jonathon   RHB/LB

Born: 21 February 1970, Wagga Wagga, NSW   New South Wales

Michael Slater is a dashing, nimble-footed opening bat who has destroyed new ball attacks world-wide. Known as 'Slats' or 'Sybil', he was rewarded for scoring over 1,000 runs in his first full season with NSW in 1992-93 with a trip to England for the Ashes in 1993. He scored a century in his second Test at Lord's. The NSW partnership of Slater and Taylor has formed a very effective opening partnership for Australia. Slater made his one day debut against South Africa at Melbourne in the 1993-94 World Series and he has striven to improve his limited overs game as he seeks to become a complete international cricketer. He is one of the fittest Australian first-class cricketers and another Australian who played some cricket in England in 1998 and in general found the conditions difficult; he still managed to clobber 410 runs in ten completed innings in the Sunday League. His international one day record isn't quite as impressive but he's on an improving curve. If he can reproduce the stunning stroke play of the fifth Test against England then he can take Australia all the way. He plays strokes with great freedom and shot selection could be his problem.

WARNE, Shane Keith   RHB/LBG

Born: 13 September 1969, Ferntree Gully, Melbourne   Victoria

The fact that Shane Warne took a wicket in his first over back in international cricket this winter was less significant in the long run perhaps than his taking over the one day captaincy when Steve Waugh had to rest through injury. Warne, captain of Victoria, proved an inspirational and tactically astute leader and victory in the series must have given him renewed confidence. He completed his one hundredth one day match during the triangular tournament, at which point he had bowled 939.3 overs and taken 153 wickets including a best performance of 5-33 and restricting batsmen to 4.14 runs per over. The stats don't do justice to the pleasure which Warne's enthusiastic and entertaining play has brought to millions of cricket fans worldwide while revitalising the art of leg spin. In 1995, Warne reached 200 Test wickets in only his 42nd Test, building a solid foundation to what may be a long and impressive career. Warne combines a complete armoury of leg spinner, top spinner, googly and flipper, with enormous spin and considerable accuracy. He bowls from a few paces and varies his pace and flight well. His bleached blond hair and outgoing personality on the field have earned him the nickname of 'Hollywood'. Last year proved a difficult one for him with surgery required on his bowling shoulder, and then revelations that he and Mark Waugh had been fined by the ACB for accepting money from a bookie.

WAUGH, Mark Edward   RHB/ROB, RM
Born: 2 June 1965, Canterbury, Sydney   *New South Wales*

Mark 'Junior' Waugh is one of the most elegant stroke players in world cricket and has a reputation for being one of the most delightful batsmen to watch when in flight, effortlessly dispatching the world's best bowlers to all parts of the ground. He had a superb 1996 World Cup, scoring three centuries as an opening bat. Waugh didn't flinch when the media unearthed the bookmaker scandal during England's winter tour, but responded with excellent and consistent batting form. Once settled, he can bring even the most talented attack to its knees with an awesome array of shot-making. Waugh is a brilliant and versatile fielder. He made his one day debut against Pakistan at Adelaide in the 1988-89 World Series. He has since scored over five and a half thousand runs at an average in the late thirties and a top score of 130, a formidable record. He has also bowled over 500 overs with a best game of 5-24 so watch out for Mark Waugh's new conversion to flighty off breaks.

WAUGH, Stephen Rodger   RHB/RM
Born: 2 June 1965, Canterbury, Sydney   *New South Wales*

Stephen 'Tugga' Waugh is currently rated the world's best batsman. Along with his batting, Waugh is an steady medium pacer and versatile fieldsman. One season after debuting for NSW, Waugh was plunged into the tough international circuit at a time when Australia was at the cricketing cross-roads. Recent times have seen him reign supreme as the most consistent, prolific and mentally tough batsman in the world. One of his many career highlights was a double century against the West Indies at Kingston in 1995, a key factor in the reclaiming of the Sir Frank Worrell Trophy. He was named man of the series for his 429 runs (average 107.25), five vital wickets and six catches. He began his one day career against New Zealand at Melbourne in the 1985-86 World Series Cup. He boasts immense powers of concentration and scores freely to all parts of the field. England worked out a leg side field to stifle Waugh's style but he has the all-round game to combat such tactics. Newly appointed captain of the Test side as well as the one day team, he is one of the deepest thinkers in the game. Waugh will hit the 250 match mark in the West Indies or at the World Cup and he may reach 6,000 runs this year. His top score is 102 not out and he averages over 30 per innings, even though he is often batting for team, not self. His bowling is a useful addition to the armoury and he has bowled a lot of one day overs at four and half an over with a best performance of 4-33.

BANGLADESH

Inaugural Win Possible

First-timers Bangladesh are truly the new tigers on the block – but just
how good or bad they perform is one of the questions being asked by
most in the lead-up to the World Cup. Making their first appearance in
the Finals, they secured their place in the premier event by winning the
Carlsberg ICC Trophy – the official qualifying competition for the
World Cup. That was two years ago in 1997 though and since then the
team has been playing one day games against non-Test playing nations.
Their true worth has therefore yet to be proven against the major
nations and in this respect they could become the Group B whipping
boys. If they are to make their mark on the competition then it could
come against the other ICC qualifiers Scotland when the two clash in
Edinburgh on 24th May. The two teams met in the semi-final of the
tournament with Bangladesh winning by 72 runs.

Team strip: A set-in sleeve and a shirt with a central band featuring a
tiger print, which is bordered with black piping.

Player Profiles

ABEDIN, Minhajul Nannu   RHB/RM, ROB
Born: 25 September 1965, Chittagong
Minhajul Abedin made his debut as long ago as the 1985-86, Asia Cup,
against Pakistan at Colombo (PSS). His 22 innings up to last May had
amassed 313 runs at an average of 14.2 with a high score of 45. In 71
overs at international level, his economy rate was over five and a half
per over. Abedin will be there for his experience and the help he can
give the younger members.

ALAM, Jahangir Talukdar   RHB/LM
Born: 19 April 1968, Dhaka
Jahangir Alam, or Alam Talukdar as he is sometimes known, made his
debut against Australia at Sharjah in the 1989-90 Australasia Cup and
he played in the Presidents Cup at the end of 1997. Neither his batting
nor bowling have been particularly outstanding and he won't be a first
choice but rather a squad player.

AHMED, Shafiuddin Babu   RHB/RFM
Born: 1 June 1973, Dhaka
Shafiuddin Ahmed is a useful pace bowler who usually opens the
attack. He made his debut against Zimbabwe at Nairobi (Gymk) in the
1997-98 President's Cup. His batting is nothing to write home about
but he is capable of protecting his wicket and eeking out a few runs at
the end of an innings. His bowling economy is not the best but a 3-42
performance shows that he can put together a decent spell.

HOSSAIN, Mehrab Opee   RHB/RM
Born: 22 August 1978, Dhaka
Mehrab Hossain is a squad player who debuted against India at Mohali
in the 1997-98 Coca-Cola Triangular Series, 1997-98 and only got one
game in that tournament, scoring six runs and not bowling.

HOSSAIN, Mohammad Shahriar Bidyut   RHB
Born: 1 June 1976
A recent addition to the international team, Hossain made his debut
against ICC Trophy and World Cup rivals Kenya at Nairobi (Gymk), in
the 1997-98 President's Cup and he played against India in the Silver
Jubilee Independence Cup. His first five innings brought just 41 runs at
an average of just over eight and a high score of 16. As a specialist
opening batsman, he plainly has much to prove but the selectors have
stuck with him as a promising option and an innings of 43 against
Maldives and of 37 against West Indies 'A' showed promise towards
the end of last year.

HUSSAIN, Mohammad Hasibul Shanto   RHB/RFM
Born: 3 June 1977, Dhaka
Hasibul Hussain opens the bowling for Bangladesh and, despite a
penchant for bowling no balls and wides, he can be a dangerous
handful. He proved himself against lesser opposition when taking four
for 35 off 5.3 overs in the autumn. He grabbed man of the match in that
game by also scoring 21. His batting average doesn't indicate that he is
an emerging all-rounder but he does have another 21 not out to his
name. His bowling economy is woeful but opening batsmen will have
to watch out. He made his debut against Sri Lanka at Sharjah in the
1994-95 Asia Cup.

ISLAM, Mohammad Aminul Bulbul   RHB/ROB
Born: 2 February 1968, Dhaka

Islam made his debut against India at Chittagong in the 1988-89 Asia Cup and he now leads his side into their first World Cup proper, having won the ICC Trophy in 1997. He has only played 21 internationals in the ten year period although he has played with Bangladesh at the top level, against 'A' sides and so on, much more than that. He has scored 497 runs at an average of 31 and held together the innings from batting at his favourite number four position, with five not out innings. Islam has also bowled at international level and with mixed success. His economy rate of nearly six per over is too high but a best performance of 3-57 indicates that he might bring himself on with his off breaks as a partnership breaker in the right conditions.

KHAN, Mohammad Akram Hussain   RHB/RM
Born: 1 February 1967, Chittagong

Akram Khan is an experienced team member with a consistent batting record since his debut against Pakistan at Chittagong in the 1988-89 Asia Cup. His average is in the 20s and he has amassed over 500 runs, with a high score of 59. He has bowled at this level but without success so don't expect to see him coming on unless a game is unwinnable.

MASHUD, Mohammad Khaled Pilot   RHB/WK
Born: 8 February 1976, Rajshahi

Mashud made his one day international debut against India at Sharjah, in the 1994-95 Asia Cup and he has been the regular wicketkeeper until the latest warm-up games. Apart from his excellent standard of keeping, the most interesting item on his statistical *CV* is a 27 not out knock from his position in the lower order, a great help when Bangladesh need every player's input to count. On the other hand, his batting form in the last few games has not been good, with a few ducks dotted around. Watch out for his stumping skills when Hoque is bowling.

OMAR, Mohammad Javed Belim Golla   RHB
Born: 25 November 1976, Dhaka

Javed Omar is an established opening batsman who started his career slowly but has since shown the promise of building reasonably sized innings in one day cricket. He made his one day international debut against India at Sharjah in the 1994-95 Asia Cup. A high score of 18 after four games must have given cause for concern but in recent games against West Indies 'A' he showed fair form with a solid 32, following a man of the match winning 81 against Malaysia earlier in the autumn.

RAFIQUE, Mohammad   LHB/SLO
Born: 15 May 1970, Dhaka

Mohammad Rafique made his debut against India at Sharjah in the 1994-95 Asia Cup. His first 12 innings produced 194 runs (average 16.16) with a promising high score of 77. He is certainly a good option for fifth bowler with an economy rate under five, a regular haul of wickets and a best performance of 3-55.

RAHMAN, Mafizur Munna   RHB/RM
Born: 10 November 1978

Mafizur Rahman made his debut as recently as in the 1997-98 Asia Cup, against Sri Lanka at Colombo (SSC). He hasn't been given enough opportunities to prove anything yet with a high score of 16 in his first four innings, but he is seen as a prospect for the future. He has done some bowling but without success.

RAHMAN, Naimur Durjoy   RHB/ROB
Born: 19 September 1974, Dhaka

Naimur Rahman is a handy all-rounder with a respectable batting average nearing 20 and a high score of 47 as well as being an option as fifth bowler. His bowling economy isn't top notch and it may be that English conditions don't suit his style. He made his debut against Pakistan at Sharjah in the 1994-95 Asia Cup.

ENGLAND

All-Rounders Hold the Key

England's preparation for the World Cup included a tough winter in Australia and the Sharjah tournament in April. Experience against South Africa last summer could also prove useful if they make the latter stages. For the first time the 15 World Cup players will be contracted until the end of the World Cup competition to the ECB and any appearance they make for their counties will be subject to approval from the England team management, leaving them free to concentrate their minds on the task in hand. England are clearly determined to give their players every chance of winning on home turf.

The triangular tournament Down Under was a good test of form and England blew hot and cold. Alan Mullally took four for 18, his best figures in one-day internationals, to win the first encounter with the Aussies, only for England to get trounced in the follow-up. The next two were shared, with Hick especially showing good form with centuries in Sydney and Adelaide. Veteran left-hander Fairbrother showed his value in one-day cricket by holding England's innings together as they won with three balls to spare in the first against Sri Lanka. Gough, Grimes and Hollioake showed some decent bowling form.

Poor form amongst the bowlers, especially Cork, leaves the job to a selection of all-rounders. The top order looks good but the middle order weak without Thorpe or Ramprakash on form. The all-rounders may not be good enough at top level. Newcomers to the squad who may make it onto the pitch include Scottish-born Yorkshire paceman Gavin Hamilton, Leicestershire batsmen Ben Smith and Darren Maddy and Lancashire's Andrew Flintoff, who played in last summer's test series against South Africa.

Team strip: Blue with red and white of the St George Cross on the sleeve panel and collar.

World Cup Record

	First Year	P	W	L	NR	SR%
Australia … … … … …	1975	4	2	2	–	50.00
Canada … … … … …	1979	1	1	–	–	100.00
East Africa … … … …	1975	1	1	–	–	100.00
Holland … … … …	1995-96	1	1	–	–	100.00
India … … … … …	1975	4	3	1	–	75.00
New Zealand … … … …	1975	6	3	3	–	50.00
Pakistan … … … …	1979	8	3	4	1	42.85
South Africa … … …	1991-92	3	2	1	–	66.66
Sri Lanka … … … … …	1983	6	5	1	–	83.33
UAE … … … … …	1995-96	1	1	–	–	100.00
West Indies … … … …	1979	4	3	1	–	75.00
Zimbabwe … … …	1991-92	1	–	1	–	–
Total … … … … … … … …		*40*	*25*	*14*	*1*	*64.10*

Campaign Performances

Year	Pos	Captain	Result
1975	SF	MH Denness	Lost to Australia by 4 wickets
1979	F	JM Brearley	Lost to West Indies by 92 runs
1983	SF	RGD Willis	Lost to India by 6 wickets
1987-88	F	MW Gatting	Lost to Australia by 7 runs
1991-92	F	GA Gooch	Lost to Pakistan by 22 runs
1995-96	QF	MA Atherton	Lost to Sri Lanka by 5 wickets

One-Day Records

	Period	P	W	L	T	NR	SR%
All-Time: … …	70-71 to 98-99	292	147	135	2	8	51.76
Since Last WC: … … … … …		45	21	22	1	1	47.72

Highest Innings Totals:

Runs	Overs	R/O	Opponents	Venue	Year
334-4	(60 overs)	5.56	India	Lord's	1975
333-9	(60 overs)	5.55	Sri Lanka	Taunton	1983
322-6	(60 overs)	5.36	New Zealand	The Oval	1983
296-4	(50 overs)	5.92	Sri Lanka	Peshawar	1987-88
290-5	(60 overs)	4.83	East Africa	Birmingham	1975

290-4	(49.4 overs)	5.83	West Indies	Jamshedpur	1987-88
280-6	(50 overs)	5.60	Sri Lanka	Ballarat	1991-92

Lowest Completed Innings:

Runs	Overs	R/O	Opponents	Venue	Year
93	36.2	2.55	Australia	Leeds	1975
125	49.1	2.54	Zimbabwe	Albury	1991-92

World Cup Individual Records

100 Pluses

Runs	bp	Player	Opponents	Venue	Year
137	2	DL Amiss	India	Lord's	1975
131	3	KWR Fletcher	New Zealand	Nottingham	1975
130	3	DI Gower	Sri Lanka	Taunton	1983
115	1	GA Gooch	India	Bombay	1987-88
104no	3	GA Hick	Holland	Peshawar	1995-96
102	4	AJ Lamb	New Zealand	The Oval	1983

Partnership Record for each Wicket

	Total	Partnership	Opponents	Year
1st	158	B Wood (77), DL Amiss (88)	East Africa	1975
2nd	176	DL Amiss (137), KWR Fletcher (68)	India	1975
3rd	143	GA Hick (*104), GP Thorpe (89)	Holland	1995-96
4th	115	AJ Lamb (102), MW Gatting (43)	New Zealand	1983
5th	*89	MH Denness (*51), CM Old (*37)	India	1975
6th	98	DI Gower (130), IJ Gould (35)	Sri Lanka	1983
7th	*44	IJ Gould (*14), GR Dilley (*31)	New Zealand	1983
8th	62	DA Reeve (35), D Gough (*26)	Sri Lanka	1995-96
9th	43	RW Taylor (*20), RGD Willis (24)	Pakistan	1979
10th	20	GG Arnold (*18), P Lever (5)	Australia	1975

Four Wicket Hauls

Score	Arm	Player	Opponents	Venue	Year
5-39	OB	VJ Marks	Sri Lanka	Taunton	1983
4-8	RFM	CM Old	Canada	Manchester	1979
4-11	RF	JA Snow	East Africa	Birmingham	1975
4-11	RF	RGD Willis	Canada	Manchester	1979
4-15	RFM	M Hendrick	Pakistan	Leeds	1979
4-30	RFM	CC Lewis	Sri Lanka	Ballarat	1991-92

4-31	RFM	IT Botham	Australia	Sydney	1991-92
4-42	RF	RGD Willis	N.Zealand	Birmingham	1983
4-45	RM/OB	AW Greig	N.Zealand	Nottingham	1975
4-45	RF	GR Dilley	Sri Lanka	Taunton	1983
4-52	OB	EE Hemmings	India	Bombay	1987-88

Man of the Match Awards

24 Awards: GA Gooch (5), AJ Lamb (3); IT Botham (2), CC Lewis (2), GA Hick (2), DL Amiss (1), KWR Fletcher (1), JA Snow (1), CM Old (1), M Hendrick (1), DI Gower (1), G Fowler (1), RGD Willis (1), AJ Stewart (1), NMK Smith (1).

World Cup Player Performances

Batting

Player	First Yr	P	I	no	Runs	HS	Ave	100	50	CS
PJW Allott	1983	7	3	1	8	8	4.00	–	–	1
DL Amiss	1975	4	4	–	243	137	60.75	1	1	1
GG Arnold	1975	3	1	1	18	*18	–	–	–	1
MA Atherton	1995-96	6	6	–	119	66	19.83	–	1	–
CWJ Athey	1987-88	6	6	2	211	86	52.75	–	2	4
IT Botham	1979	22	18	2	297	53	18.56	–	1	10
G Boycott	1979	5	5	1	92	57	23.00	–	1	–
JM Brearley	1979	5	5	–	161	64	32.20	–	2	4
BC Broad	1987-88	3	3	–	67	36	22.33	–	–	1
NG Cowans	1983	1	–	–	–	–	–	–	–	1
DG Cork	1995-96	5	3	–	36	19	12.00	–	–	2
PAJ DeFreitas	1987-88	22	13	3	184	67	18.40	–	1	5
MH Denness	1975	4	4	2	113	*37	56.50	–	–	–
GR Dilley	1983	6	4	2	90	*31	45.00	–	–	1
PR Downton	1987-88	8	5	1	19	9	4.75	–	–	8/1
PH Edmonds	1979	3	2	1	7	*5	7.00	–	–	–
JE Emburey	1987-88	8	7	2	96	*30	19.20	–	–	3
NH Fairbrother	1991-92	14	12	3	373	*75	41.44	–	3	8
KWR Fletcher	1975	4	3	–	207	131	69.00	1	1	1
NA Foster	1987-88	7	4	3	42	*20	42.00	–	–	1
G Fowler	1983	7	7	2	360	*81	72.00	–	4	–
MW Gatting	1983	15	13	2	437	60	39.72	–	3	3
GA Gooch	1979	21	21	1	897	115	44.85	1	8	3

Player	First Yr	P	I	no	Runs	HS	Ave	100	50	CS
D Gough	1995-96	6	4	2	66	*26	33.00	–	–	1
IJ Gould	1983	7	4	1	66	35	22.00	–	–	11/1
DI Gower	1979	12	11	3	434	130	54.25	1	1	2
AW Greig	1975	4	4	–	29	9	7.25	–	–	–
FC Hayes	1975	3	3	–	90	52	30.00	–	1	–
EE Hemmings	1987-88	6	1	1	4	*4		–	–	2
M Hendrick	1979	5	2	1	1	*1	1.00	–	–	3
GA Hick	1991-92	15	14	2	476	*104	39.66	1	4	6
RK Illingworth	1991-92	10	5	3	31	14	15.50	–	–	3
JA Jameson	1975	2	2	–	32	21	16.00	–	–	–
APE Knott	1975	4	2	1	18	*18	18.00	–	–	1
AJ Lamb	1983	19	17	4	656	102	50.46	1	3	9
W Larkins	1979	2	2	–	7	7	3.50	–	–	–
P Lever	1975	4	1	–	5	5	5.00	–	–	1
CC Lewis	1991-92	9	6	2	81	33	20.25	–	–	4
VJ Marks	1983	7	3	–	18	8	6.00	–	–	2
PJ Martin	1995-96	5	4	2	6	3	3.00	–	–	–
G Miller	1979	1	–	–	–	–	–	–	–	–
C M Old	1975	9	7	2	91	*51	18.20	–	1	2
DR Pringle	1987-88	11	7	2	50	*18	10.00	–	–	2
DW Randall	1979	5	5	1	64	*42	16.00	–	–	1
DA Reeve	1991-92	11	7	3	117	35	29.25	–	–	5
RT Robinson	1987-88	7	7	–	142	55	20.28	–	1	1
RC Russell	1995-96	6	4	–	27	12	6.75	–	–	7
GC Small	1987-88	13	4	1	8	5	2.66	–	–	–
NK M Smith	1995-96	3	3	1	69	31	34.50	–	–	1
RA Smith	1991-92	10	10	2	293	91	36.62	–	2	3
JA Snow	1975	3	1	–	2	2	2.00	–	–	–
AJ Stewart	1991-92	15	13	1	345	77	28.75	–	2	8/1
CJ Tavare	1983	7	7	–	212	58	30.28	–	1	2
RW Taylor	1979	5	3	1	32	*20	16.00	–	–	4
GP Thorpe	1995-96	6	6	2	254	89	63.50	–	2	5
PCR Tufnell	1991-92	4	2	2	3	*3		–	–	–
DL Underwood	1975	2	–	–	–	–	–	–	–	2
C White	1995-96	2	1	–	13	13	13.00	–	–	–
RGD Willis	1979	11	4	1	25	24	8.33	–	–	4
B Wood	1975	3	2	–	83	77	41.50	–	1	–

Bowling

Player	Overs	M	Runs	Wi	SR	BP	4wi	R/O
PJW Allott	80.3	10	335	8	41.87	3-41	–	4.16
GG Arnold	29.4	7	70	3	23.33	1-15	–	2.35
CWJ Athey	1	0	10	0	–	–	–	10.00
IT Botham	222	33	762	30	25.40	4-31	1	3.43
G Boycott	27	1	94	5	18.80	2-14	–	3.48
BC Broad	1	0	6	0	–	–	–	6.00
DG Cork	48	2	216	8	27.00	2-33	–	4.50
NG Cowans	12	3	31	2	15.50	2-31	–	2.58
PAJ DeFreitas	187.5	30	742	29	25.58	3-28	–	3.95
GR Dilley	66	4	243	7	34.71	4-45	1	3.68
PH Edmonds	26	3	73	3	24.33	2-40	–	2.80
JE Emburey	79	4	295	6	49.16	2-26	–	3.73
NA Foster	70	1	313	9	34.77	3-47	–	4.47
MW Gatting	12	3	48	1	48.00	1-35	–	4.00
GA Gooch	23	2	115	1	115.00	1-42	–	5.00
D Gough	51	4	238	4	59.50	2-48	–	4.66
AW Greig	31	2	89	6	14.83	4-45	1	2.87
EE Hemmings	59.3	4	274	13	21.07	4-52	1	4.60
M Hendrick	56	14	149	10	14.90	4-15	1	2.66
GA Hick	34	0	189	3	63.00	2-44	–	5.55
RK Illingworth	98.1	6	424	12	35.33	3-33	–	4.31
JA Jameson	2	1	3	0	–	–	–	1.50
AJ Lamb	1	0	3	0	–	–	–	3.00
W Larkins	2	0	21	0	–	–	–	10.50
P Lever	36	3	92	5	18.40	3-32	–	2.55
CC Lewis	50.4	5	214	7	30.57	4-30	1	4.22
VJ Marks	78	9	246	13	18.92	5-39	1	3.15
PJ Martin	44	2	198	6	33.00	3-33	–	4.50
G Miller	2	1	1	0	–	–	–	0.50
CM Old	90.3	18	243	16	15.18	4-8	1	2.68
DR Pringle	90.4	15	366	8	45.75	3-8	–	4.03
DA Reeve	45.2	5	177	9	19.66	3-38	–	3.90
GC Small	103	5	458	11	41.63	2-29	–	4.44
NKM Smith	25.3	2	96	4	24.00	3-29	–	3.76
JA Snow	36	8	65	6	10.83	4-11	1	1.80
GP Thorpe	6	0	28	0	–	–	–	4.66
PCR Tufnell	28	2	133	3	44.33	2-36	–	4.75
DL Underwood	22	7	41	2	20.50	2-30	–	1.86

Player	Overs	M	Runs	Wi	Ave	BP	4wi	R/O
C White	6.3	1	23	0	–	–	–	3.53
RGD Willis	118.1	27	315	18	17.50	4-11	2	2.66
B Wood	12	5	14	0	–	–	–	1.16

Player Profiles

ALLEYNE, Mark Wayne   RHB/RM
Born: 23 May 1968, Tottenham, London   *Gloucestershire*
His one day debut was against Australia at Brisbane in the triangular
tournament earlier this year where he put together some economical
bowling spells and registered a few runs on the board. Another of
England's many all-rounders suitable to the one day format. In first
class cricket he averages in the late 30s and in one dayers in 1998 he
put together an innings of 88 in the Benson and Hedges and kept
batsmen down to around four per over.

AUSTIN, Ian David   LHB/RM
Born: 30 May 1966, Haslingden, Lancashire   *Lancashire*
Austin made his one day debut against Sri Lanka at Lord's in the
Emirates Triangular Tournament in 1998. A journeyman 'Mr Reliable'
Sunday after Sunday in England, he does have that extra aggression
and one day nouse to make him an England one day all-rounder. In the
Sunday League in 1998 he kept batsmen down to 3.3 runs per over and
he bowled 56 overs in the NatWest Trophy for just 111 runs (1.98). His
batting for England has looked ordinary and he's one of a type of
England player who is perhaps good enough but not outstanding.

BROWN, Alistair Duncan   RHB/RLB
Born: 11 February 1970, Beckenham   *Surrey*
Alistair Brown is a very hard hitting but essentially correct middle
order batsman. He is not lacking in confidence, as was revealed when
he slogged Ian Botham for four in the course of a century against
Durham during his first full season. Played as an opener in three one
day internationals against India in 1996, scoring an unusually
circumspect 100 in the third of them, before seeming to lose all form
for the remainder of that season. Returned to form in 1997 for Surrey
and after forcing a return to the first team scored 203 off only 119 balls
against Hampshire in a Sunday league game. Was brought back against

South Africa in the summer of 1998 and averages in the mid-20s. He is a good fielder with a safe pair of hands.

CROFT, Robert Damien Bale   RHB/ROB
Born: 25 May 1970, Morriston, West Glamorgan   Glamorgan
Another bowler from the debut class of 1990, Croft is a practical cricketer who has a decent batting average to go with his consistent off-spin. He broke into the England team in 1996 and made his one day debut for England against Pakistan at Manchester in that year. He has looked a better bet in the one day team because of his all round abilities, including enthusiasm in the field and the odd 20 run knock. His spin lacks penetration at the top level, but Croft can be relied upon to bowl a consistent line and generally gives little away. He's not in the best form of his life but will give his all when called upon.

EALHAM, Mark Alan   RHB/RFM
Born: 27 August 1969, Willesborough   Kent
Son of the Kent stalwart Alan Ealham, Mark Ealham is one of many all-rounders tried by the England selectors to fill the huge gap left by the retirement of Ian Botham. Ealham debuted against India at The Oval in 1996 and he was called up for the winter tournament down under. He bowls a brisk medium pace off a short angled run up, and can move the ball away from the bat late, although he's not the most economical. He excels in the one day game and, like his father, is an exceptional fielder. He can keep the scoreboard moving without resorting to slogging and holds the record for the fastest Sunday League century (44 balls), although for England he has yet to prove himself as a match winner.

FAIRBROTHER, Neil Harvey   LHB/LM
Born: 9 September 1963, Warrington, Lancashire   Lancashire
Neil Fairbrother specialises in winning games of this format. He is vulnerable early in his innings but, once established, keeps the scoreboard ticking over, being an excellent runner between the wickets. He averages over 40 in international one day games and is capable of planning a knock to reach a winning total. A notable century against the West Indies in 1991 firmly established his reputation as a one day player, and he averaged nearly 60 in the 1991-92 World Cup. He is the master of the quick 30 or 40 when rapid runs are required and, although he failed in the final game of the winter tour to Australia, he came out top of the averages this winter with 64.6.

FLINTOFF, Andrew   RHB/RM

Born: 6 December 1976, Preston, Lancashire   *Lancashire*

A promising player who made his Test debut against South Africa at Nottingham in 1998 but who has yet to prove anything at international level. His one day form last summer was consistently good with the bat and he put in some effective bowling on a part-time basis. Certainly a good prospect and capable of building a substantial innings in a one day game. May get a chance if England are getting desperate.

FRASER, Angus Robert Charles   RHB/RF

Born: 8 August 1965, Billinge, Lancashire   *Middlesex*

The Mr Dependable of the England attack, Fraser is a seam bowler in the classic mould, with immaculate length and line, and late movement. His height also allows him to generate pace and bounce. He made a spectacular return to the Test side for last winter's tour to West Indies after a two-year absence and got an MBE for his efforts. He was England's most successful bowler there, as he was against South Africa, with three successive five-wicket hauls. He is the top English player in the world bowling rankings and deserves a chance in the World Cup on his home territory if he is fit – he has suffered with hip problems. Since his one day debut against Sri Lanka at Delhi in the 1989-90 season, Gus has bowled some 348.5 overs and kept the best batsmen in the world to 3.57 runs per over. His batting average, at 13, is also better than some of the so-called all-rounders on the scene.

GOUGH, Darren   RHB/RF

Born: 18 September 1970, Barnsley   *Yorkshire*

A Yorkshire hero, he ran in fast and bowled aggressively during the winter tour to Australia. He is England's key strike bowler and could cause havoc amongst the batting orders of some lesser opposition and keep the better batters in jail at the beginning and end of innings. His main weapon in Australia was the fast yorker, cleaning up tail enders and getting him a hat-trick. In English conditions he will also employ swing and seam. Could be the bowler of the competition. On the downside, as Gough's bowling has improved, his batting has failed to match expectations with an international average of just over 11. He is capable of putting together a dynamic knock late in an innings but too often fails to get started. Gough entered first class cricket in 1990 and has over 500 wickets, 89 of them in one day internationals with a best of 5-44, having made his one day debut against New Zealand at

Birmingham in 1994. Arguably England's premier fast bowler, he made a massive impact on his first tour of Australia by taking 6-49 and making a battling 51 in the drawn Sydney Test. Missed the following winter tour to West Indies through injury. He was back with 6-42 against South Africa, in Leeds in 1998.

HEADLEY, Dean Warren   RHB/RMF
Born: 27 January 1970, Norton   *Middlesex*
After a slow start in the winter this medium pacer came back strongly and showed the kind of athletic commitment to inspire other team members. His stamina and aggression are less useful in the one day game than his line and length. He takes wickets in bursts, is effective against left-handers, but can be inconsistent game to game. He is the grandson of Caribbean cricket legend George Headley, and son of former Worcestershire and West Indies batsman Ron, completing three generations of Test players in the family. He first played in 1990 for Middlesex and made his England one day debut against Pakistan at Manchester in 1996. His batting is never more than adequate for a tailender. In the 1998 domestic season he was much more economical than his current international average of giving away over five per over.

HEGG, Warren Kevin   RHB/WK
Born: 23 December 1968, Whitefield, Lancashire   *Lancashire*
Hegg's keeping is technically sound, and he holds a notable record of 11 catches in a first-class match, set in 1989. He has taken more than 500 catches and more than 50 stumpings in his career. Players like Australia's Healey prove that a specialist keeper can pay off in one day cricket as well as in Tests so perhaps England will change tactics. Hegg's sometimes hard-hitting, batting, like his keeping, is consistent, and has steadily improved, so much so that he averaged over 40 for Lancashire in 1998. If the selectors see sense then Hegg may get his chance in the one day games as he did in the Australian Tests.

HICK, Graeme Ashley   LHB/LOB
Born: 23 May 1966, Salisbury   *Worcestershire*
Always a disappointment to those who have seen him at his best in English first class cricket, Hick continues to both fail and dazzle at the international level. Best these days in attacking mode as per the one-day game. Hick appears to have established himself at number three, from where he can build a match-winning innings if the middle order

can hold down the other end. He can turn his arm over to break a partnership if the conditions suit but is more effective in the slips if the confidence holds up. Hick made his debut against West Indies at Birmingham in 1991 and has scored nearly 3,000 runs at an average of 38.83. His stroke play can be breathtaking so England will hope that this is going to be the moment that he makes the world stage his own.

HOLLIOAKE, Adam John   RHB/RMF
Born: 5 September 1971, Melbourne, Australia   *Surrey*

Adam Hollioake, though born in Australia, first played cricket in Hong Kong and developed his game at school in England. He was introduced to the England side for the one day internationals against Pakistan in 1996 where he enjoyed considerable success with the ball. In the games against Australia in 1997 he hit the winning runs in each game and contributed usefully with both bat and ball. A forceful middle order batsman with a decent average in late 20s, and medium pace bowler with well disguised changes of pace, he regularly takes wickets in one day cricket (best 4-27). After captaining the England A side, he was appointed as England's one day captain with some success until Stewart brought the leadership under one cap again.

HUSSAIN, Nasser   RHB/RLS
Born: 28 March 1968, Madras, India   *Essex*

Hussain was England's highest run scorer in the winter Tests and he should be able to bring his driving, cutting and sound defence to bear in home conditions to shore up England's middle order. Looks comfortable in the pressurised cauldron of international cricket but is not considered totally at home in the one day game, as an average of 23 attests. Considered an England captain in waiting only a year or so ago, Hussain has done well to focus on improving his batting in the England middle order and has adapted his style to the one-day game fairly successfully. He began his Essex career in 1987, where he averages over 40. His international debut was in 1989-90 in the West Indies and he put together a top scoring 207 against Australia, in 1997.

KNIGHT, Nicholas Verity   LHB
Born: 28 November 1969, Watford   *Warwickshire*

Nick Verity Knight (named after the great Yorkshire bowler) started his career at Essex. He was thrust into the Test arena and managed a maiden 50 against the West Indies. A year later against Pakistan, it was obvious he had developed as a player, and the left-handed opener's new approach took him to his first Test century and his one day debut. He fared well on the winter tour of Zimbabwe and New Zealand until breaking a finger in one of the final one day matches. He only managed to get a place as captain for the 1997-98 'A' tour but his attacking style has made him the opening batsman of choice alongside Stewart for one day games and he averages over 40 in internationals. The tactics didn't quite pay off this winter as Knight got out after good starts, averaging 26 through the triangular tournament. An excellent fielder, particularly at slip.

MULLALLY, Alan David   RHB/FM
Born: 12 July 1969, Southend-on-Sea, Essex   *Leicestershire*
The tall left-arm seamer learned his cricket in Western Australia (first class debut 1987). He is a good exponent of swing, and has added extra pace recently. He is steady medium to fast, accurate but sometimes lacking bite and penetration. Having a left-armer in the side disrupts the batsmen and, in the right conditions, Mullally could be deadly with his seam up. He had a fine season for Leicestershire in 1998, achieving a best 7-55 against Nottinghamshire and in one day games bowling very economically, giving away less than three per over in two out of three of the competitions. Generally reckoned to be a better bowler than when he was first picked for England in 1996 (he debuted with Croft and Headley against Pakistan), the Englishman posted best ever figures against Australia recently with a spell of four for 12 in the space of 27 deliveries. Three of Mullally's wickets coincided with a dramatic Australian collapse of four wickets for the addition of just two runs. His previous best was three for 29 against Zimbabwe in Harare.

RAMPRAKASH, Mark Ravin   RHB/ROB
Born: 5 September 1969, Bushey, Hertfordshire   *Middlesex*
Considered by many as the next captain of England, Ramprakash's natural talent has always been apparent and appears now to be harnessed for the good of the team. He had a good tour of Australia, except for the last Test. Once in, his stroke play can set the crowd on fire and propel an innings where it needs to go. He didn't play in the Australian triangular tournament but should come back into the one day team for the World Cup. His exposure to one day cricket has not been high but he is an athletic fielder and useful off-spinner too, able to keep the runs down when required. The Middlesex captain, who

averages in the high 40s in first class cricket, had to wait until his 38th England innings for a maiden century (vs West Indies, Barbados). He followed up with a 154 in Bridgetown and his temperament is now beginning to match his good technique.

STEWART, Alec James   RHB/WK
Born: 8 April 1963, Merton, Surrey   *Surrey*

A top class player with vast experience since his debut in 1981 for his life-time team Surrey, following in father Mickey Stewart's footsteps. Averages in the 40s, is England's top player in the current form tables, and was Test cricket's highest scorer in 1998. He made his one day debut against Sri Lanka at Delhi in the 1989-90 season and has scored over 3,200 runs at an average of 31.17 with a highest score of 116. During the Australian tour he made batting his priority. For one-day duty he does it all: captain, wicket-keeper and opening batsman. As a batsman he has failed to build a one day innings recently (no 50s in the triangular tournament). But when the gaffer takes charge he can counter attack with a full range of strokes. Alec Stewart only once called his leadership qualities into question when he lost his cool during a one-day game vs Sri Lanka. His team appeared to react badly, emphasising how important is the Surrey man's contribution as main motivator and leader.

THORPE, Graham   LHB/RM
Born: 1 August 1969, Farnham, Surrey   *Surrey*

One of the first names on England's team-sheet when fit, but a back injury forced him to miss the end of the summer against South Africa and most of the Australian tour. His presence in the middle-order has been badly missed and Graham Thorpe's fitness could decide England's chances either way. Another Surrey stalwart, Thorpe first played in 1988 and has scored over 30 centuries while averaging over 40 in Test cricket. Thorpe's technique isn't suited to the one day game but his class is sorely needed in an England line-up which collapsed cheaply all too often during the winter.

WELLS, Vincent John   RHB/RM/WK
Born: 6 August 1965, Dartford, Kent   *Leicestershire*

Another England new boy with both batting and bowling talents. He made his debut against Australia at Brisbane this winter. He took eight wickets at just over 19.12 apiece, let go under five runs per over and then contributed 131 runs at an average of 26.2. His initial selection was justified by some consistently economical bowling in summer 1998, although he didn't build an innings bigger than 51 not out in one day cricket last year.

INDIA

A Need to Tread Carefully

After an indifferent start in New Zealand in the winter, India came back to draw their one day series with Tendulkar, the all-time top scorer in World Cup finals, particularly back to form. Kumble, fresh from his Jim Laker equalling ten wickets in an innings, and Srinath, are world top 20 bowlers. There will be plenty of support for this team on its travels. India has proved once before that it can win the World Cup in England and their current players know how to harness English conditions. In preparation for that India has played more one day games since the last World Cup than any of the other qualifiers – 109 in fact with a 45% success rate. They start out in Group A of the competition and their ability to progress to the Super Six stage might well hinge on how they conduct themselves in their group encounter with Sri Lanka. Neutral on-lookers will be hoping that the bad blood from the 1996 competition will have been swept away. They will also be mindful of a recent one day defeat by Zimbabwe who are also in their group.

Team strip: A pastel sky blue with the golden trim from the nation's cricket logo printed across the front and extending into a single sleeve.

World Cup Record

	First Year	P	W	L	NR	SR%
Australia … … … … …	1983	6	2	4	–	33.33
East Africa … … … …	1975	1	1	–	–	100.00
England … … … …	1975	4	1	3	–	25.00
Kenya … … … … …	1995-96	1	1	–	–	100.00
New Zealand … … … …	1975	5	2	3	–	40.00
Pakistan … … … …	1991-92	2	2	–	–	100.00
South Africa … … …	1991-92	1	–	1	–	–
Sri Lanka … … … … …	1979	4	–	3	1	–
West Indies … … … …	1979	6	3	3	–	50.00
Zimbabwe … … … …	1983	6	6	–	–	100.00
Total… … … … … … … …		*36*	*18*	*17*	*1*	*51.42*

Campaign Performances

Year	Pos	Captain	Result
1975	Gp	S Venkataraghavan	Failed to qualify for semi-finals
1979	Gp	S Venkataraghavan	Failed to qualify for semi-finals
1983	F	N Kapil Dev	Won beat West Indies by 43 runs
1987-88	SF	N Kapil Dev	Lost to England by 35 runs
1991-92	Gp	M Azhar-ud-din	Failed to qualify for semi-finals
1995-96	SF	M Azhar-ud-din	Lost to Sri Lanka by default

One-Day Records

	Period	P	W	L	T	NR	SR%
All-Time: … … …	74 to 98-99	390	175	195	3	17	46.91
Since Last WC: … … … … …		109	45	54	1	9	45.00

Highest Innings Totals:

Runs	Overs	R/O	Opponents	Venue	Year
289-6	50 overs	5.78	Australia	Delhi	1987-88
287-8	50 overs	5.74	Pakistan	Bangalore	1995-96

Lowest Completed Innings:

Runs	Overs	R/O	Opponents	Venue	Year
132-3	60 overs	2.20	England	Lord's	1975
158	37.5 overs	4.17	Australia	Nottingham	1983

World Cup Individual Records

100 Pluses

Runs	bp	Player	Opponents	Venue	Year
175no	6	N Kapil Dev	Zimbabwe	Tunbridge Wells	1983
137	2	SR Tendulkar	Sri Lanka	Delhi	1995-96
127no	2	SR Tendulkar	Kenya	Cuttack	1995-96
106	5	VG Kambli	Zimbabwe	Kanpur	1995-96
103no	2	SM Gavaskar	New Zealand	Nagpur	1987-88

Partnership Record for each Wicket

	Total	Partnership	Opponents	Year
1st	163	AD Jadeja (53), SR Tendulkar (*127) Kenya	1995-96	
2nd	127	M Azhar-ud-din (55), SR Tendulkar (84)	N.Zealand	1991-92
3rd	175	SR Tendulkar (137), M Azhar-ud-din (*72)	Sri Lanka	1995-96
4th	142	NS Sidhu (80), VG Kambli (106)	Zimbabwe	1995-96
5th	66	M Azhar-ud-din (93), SV Manjrekar (47)	Australia	1991-92
6th	73	Yashpal Sharma (89), RMH Binny (27)	West Indies	1983
7th	58	N Kapil Dev (40), Madan Lal (27)	Australia	1983
8th	*82	N Kapil Dev (*72), KS More (*42)	N.Zealand	1987-88
9th	*126	N Kapil Dev (*175), SMH Kirmani (*24)	Zimbabwe	1983
10th	27	S Venkataraghavan (*13), BS Bedi (13)	West Indies	1979

Four Wicket Hauls

Score	Arm	Player	Opponents	Venue	Year
5-43	RFM	N Kapil Dev	Australia	Nottingham	1983
4-19	RFM	M Prabhakar	Zimbabwe	Bombay	1987-88
4-20	RFM	Madan Lal	Australia	Chelmsford	1983
4-29	RFM	RMH Binny	Australia	Chelmsford	1983

Man of the Match Awards

18 Awards: SR Tendulkar (4), N Kapil Dev (3), M Amarnath (2), FM Engineer (1), Yashpal Sharma (1), Madan Lal (1), RMH Binny (1), M Prabhakar (1), M Azhar-ud-din (1), SM Gavaskar (1), AD Jadeja (1), NS Sidhu (1).

Batting

Player	First Yr	P	I	no	Runs	HS	Ave	100	50	CS
S Abid Ali	75	3	1	–	70	70	70.00	–	1	–
M Amarnath	75	14	12	–	254	80	21.16	–	1	2
PK Amre	91-92	4	3	1	27	22	13.50	–	–	–
SA Ankola	95-96	1	–	–	–	–	–	–	–	–
K Azad	83	3	2	–	15	15	7.50	–	–	–
M Azhar-ud-din	87-88	22	18	3	665	93	44.33	–	7	6
ST Banerjee	91-92	2	2	1	36	*25	36.00	–	–	2
BS Bedi	75	5	4	1	25	13	8.33	–	–	2
RMH Binny	83	9	7	–	73	27	10.42	–	–	2
FM Engineer	75	3	2	1	78	*54	78.00	–	1	2
AD Gaekwad	75	6	5	–	113	37	22.60	–	–	2
SM Gavaskar	75	19	19	3	561	*103	35.06	1	4	4
KD Ghavri	75	4	3	–	35	20	11.66	–	–	–
AD Jadeja	91-92	13	11	2	237	53	26.33	–	1	4
VG Kambli	91-92	12	11	3	205	106	25.62	1	–	1
N Kapil Dev	79	26	24	6	669	*175	37.16	1	1	12
AR Kapoor	95-96	2	1	–	0	0	–	–	–	–
SC Khanna	79	3	3	–	17	10	5.66	–	–	1
SMH Kirmani	83	8	6	1	61	*24	12.20	–	–	12/2
A Kumble	95-96	7	2	–	27	17	13.50	–	–	8
S Madan Lal	75	11	7	3	122	27	30.50	–	–	1
Maninder Singh	87-88	7	2	1	4	4	4.00	–	–	1
SV Manjrekar	91-92	11	11	–	295	62	26.81	–	1	5
NR Mongia	95-96	7	6	3	69	25	23.00	–	–	4/3
KS More	87-88	14	10	5	100	*42	20.00	–	–	12/6
CS Pandit	87-88	2	1	–	24	24	24.00	–	–	1
BP Patel	75	6	5	1	88	38	22.00	–	–	–
SM Patil	83	8	8	1	216	*51	30.85	–	2	2
M Prabhakar	87-88	19	11	2	45	*11	5.00	–	–	4
VKB Prasad	95-96	7	2	1	0	*0	–	–	–	1
SLV Raju	91-92	11	3	1	4	*3	2.00	–	–	2
BS Sandhu	83	8	4	2	28	*11	14.00	–	–	2
C Sharma	87-88	4	1	–	0	0	–	–	–	–
RJ Shastri	83	14	11	1	185	57	18.50	–	1	6
NS Sidhu	87-88	12	10	–	454	93	45.40	–	6	2

Player	First Yr	P	I	no	Runs	HS	Ave	100	50	CS
L Sivaramakrishnan	87-88	2	–	–	–	–	–	–	–	1
ED Solkar	75	3	2	–	21	13	10.50	–	–	1
K Srikkanth	83	23	23	1	521	75	23.68	–	2	9
J Srinath	91-92	15	9	6	59	*12	19.66	–	–	3
SR Tendulkar	91-92	15	14	2	806	137	67.16	2	8	4
DB Vengsarkar	79	11	10	3	252	63	36.00	–	1	3
S Venkataraghavan	75	6	4	3	49	*26	49.00	–	–	1
GR Viswanath	75	6	5	–	145	75	29.00	–	1	–
Yashpal Sharma	83	8	8	1	240	89	34.28	–	2	2

Bowling

Player	Overs	M	Runs	Wi	Ave	BP	4wi	R/O
S Abid Ali	36	7	115	6	19.16	2-22	–	3.19
M Amarnath	110.3	9	431	16	26.93	3-12	–	3.90
SA Ankola	5	0	28	0	–	–	–	5.60
K Azad	17	1	42	1	42.00	1-28	–	2.47
M Azhar-ud-din	23.5	0	109	5	21.80	3-19	–	4.57
ST Banerjee	13	1	85	1	85.00	1-45	–	6.53
BS Bedi	60	17	148	2	74.00	1-6	–	2.46
RMH Binny	95	9	382	19	20.10	4-29	1	4.02
KD Ghavri	43	4	195	0	–	–	–	4.53
AD Jadeja	24.2	0	120	2	60.00	2-31	–	4.93
N Kapil Dev	237	27	892	28	31.85	5-43	1	3.76
AR Kapoor	20	2	81	1	81.00	1-41	–	4.05
A Kumble	69.4	3	280	15	18.66	3-28	–	4.01
S Madan Lal	116.2	12	426	22	19.36	4-20	1	3.66
Maninder Singh	70	1	280	14	20.00	3-21	–	4.00
SM Patil	9	0	61	0	–	–	–	6.77
M Prabhakar	145.1	10	640	24	26.66	4-19	1	4.40
VKB Prasad	65	1	312	8	39.00	3-45	–	4.80
SLV Raju	88.1	7	366	13	28.15	2-38	–	4.15
BS Sandhu	83	10	297	8	37.12	2-26	–	3.57
C Sharma	36.1	2	170	6	28.33	3-51	–	4.70
RJ Shastri	92.3	2	389	12	32.41	3-26	–	4.20
L Sivaramakrishnan	17	0	70	1	70.00	1-36	–	4.11
ED Solkar	4	0	28	0	–	–	–	7.00
K Srikkanth	2.1	0	15	0	–	–	–	6.92

Player	Overs	M	Runs	Wi	Ave	BP	4wi	R/O
J Srinath	118.5	6	542	16	33.87	3-34	–	4.56
SR Tendulkar	77	1	329	4	82.25	2-34	–	4.27
S Venkataraghavan	72	7	217	0	–	–	–	3.01

Player Profiles

AGARKAR, Ajit Bhalchandra   RHB/RFM
Born: 4 December 1977, Mumbai   *Bombay*

Agarkar is one of the new boys since the 1996 World Cup, having made his debut against Zimbabwe at Sharjah in the 1998-99 Champions Trophy. Agarkar runs in swiftly and delivers with a smooth action, is capable of moving the ball both ways, and of plotting the batsman's dismissal. His economy is not great but he is a genuine strike bowler with 58 wickets to his name. He can bat reasonably well from the lower order.

AZHAR-UD-DIN, Mohammed   RHB/RM
Born: 8 February 1963, Hyderabad   *Hyderabad*

Despite twice failing to emerge as the potential World Cup Champions and not winning any major tournaments outside the sub-continent and Sharjah, Azhar remains India's best choice at the helm. Having led the national side since 1990, he draws upon his long experience, having made his one day debut in 1984-85. He set a World Record 300th one day international appearance in October of last year. World Records are not new to him – he set one in his debut Tests in 1984-85 when he became the first player to score centuries in his first three Tests. He has won more games as India's captain than any other player. Despite that fact he lost the captaincy in 1997 and was then surprisingly dropped from the team. It was short lived though as he was reinstated last year. A wristy but elegant batsman, he has been at the backbone of India's middle order for years. With a wristy action he flicks and glances the ball off the bat and once settled in can be unstoppable. He is an outstanding bowler offering spin and medium-pace and he is also a top class fielder, possessing a safe pair of hands. After losing the Indian captaincy in 1997, then unaccountably dropped from the national team, he returned to provide experience and class to a young and talented middle order and eventually was reinstated as captain in early 1998. He is fast approaching the 9,000 run mark in one day internationals and, if selected, looks certain to break this barrier during the World Cup. Having played with Derbyshire he is more than aware of the summer conditions in England.

DRAVID, Rahul RHB
Born: 11 January 1973, Indore *Karnataka*

Solid and compact are the first two words that come to mind while describing this young orthodox batsman with immense ability. His two hundreds in New Zealand at the beginning of the year, batting at number three in the limited overs game, makes him a good bet for the team, particularly if a few early wickets do happen to fall. He has a good temperament which can help steady the innings and he blends in nicely with other stroke players in the side.

GANGULY, Saurav Chandidas LHB/RM
Born: 8 July 1972, Calcutta *Bengal*

There is something very calm and serene about Ganguly's batting. Even the most electric of atmospheres fails to make him rush for his strokes which he plays with delightful timing all around the wicket. With his medium pace bowling he has turned into a top class all-rounder in limited overs cricket. Being a left-hander, he makes an ideal opening partner to the more explosive Sachin Tendulkar. It would not surprise anyone if the Indian selectors opt for the same combination in the World Cup.

JADEJA, Ajaysingh RHB/RM
Born: 1 February 1971, Jamnagar *Haryana*

An experienced campaigner, Jadeja first played for his country in one day cricket against Sri Lanka at Mackay in the 1992 World Cup. He is an attractive strokeplayer who has adapted extremely well to his role down the batting order, displaying the ability to both step up the run rate, or shore up the innings – he was once an opener. With over 4,000 runs, at an average of 35, and with four centuries and 23 50s to his name, Jadeja will be looking to cement his place in the history books in this World Cup. His favourite fielding haunt is backward point, where he saves countless runs. His gentle medium pace bowling, though useful, is a bit expensive.

KAMBLI, Vinod Ganpat   LHB/ROB

Born: 18 January 1972, Bombay   *Bombay*

Kambli made his debut against arch rivals Pakistan at Sharjah in the
1991-92 Wills Trophy and came to fame in a manner he wouldn't have
chosen when he was caught on TV celebrating too much with the
crowd during a rain break in the 1996 World Cup. This schoolmate of
Tendulkar and free-stroking left-hander with the high backlift shrugged
off this bad press to score two successive double Test centuries against
England and Zimbabwe. The high of his first seven Tests receded and
Kambli has been in and out of the team but looks to be back to form.
His lightning fast footwork makes him the nemesis of spin bowlers
worldwide, including Shane Warne. An average of 37 and a top score
of 106 can't be ignored and over 2,000 one day runs include 13 50s.

KANITKAR, Hrishikesh Hemant   LHB/ROB

Born: 14 November 1974, Pune   *Maharashtra*

A recent recruit, who debuted against Sri Lanka at Indore in 1997-98,
Kanitkar looks an interesting prospect with ball and bat and stunned the
cricket world when he hit the winning runs as India successfully scaled
the target of 300 plus against Pakistan in a one day contest at Dhaka.
His 17 wickets so far have been bought at 4.75 per over and he has hit
a solid 57 top score and, with eight not outs, has an average over 20.
He comes from a cricketing family, and his father Hemant kept wicket
for India.

KUMBLE, Anil   RHB/LBG

Born: 17 October 1970, Bangalore   *Karnataka*

Kumble is probably the best spin bowler on the world scene and he has
put in a lot of work since his debut against Sri Lanka at Sharjah in the
1989-90 Australasia Cup. His record-breaking play in Tests aside, he
has taken 212 one day wickets with a best performance of 6-12. An
average economy rate over all those overs is a little over four per six
balls. He knows English conditions and players, having played at
Northamptonshire. It is his well concealed googly and flipper, along
with his genuine medium-pace faster balls that are his strike weapons
rather than the leg-break, which he turns little. His batting is ordinary.

LAXMAN, Vangipurappu Venkata Sai   RHB/ROB
Born: 1 November 1974, Hyderabad   *Hyderabad*

Laxman played his debut game against Zimbabwe at Cuttack in the 1997-98 Pepsi Triangular Series and he is still establishing his credentials in one day cricket. A best bat of 23 not out is promising but the World Cup will be a learning experience with both bat and ball.

MONGIA, Nayan Ramlal   RHB/WK
Born: 19 December 1969, Baroda   *Baroda*

Mongia stepped into the shoes of his predecessor Kiran More without much fuss. He is a gritty lower order batsman who has also opened the innings when required. His steady wicket-keeping is accompanied by excessive appealing.

PRASAD, Bapu Krishnarao Venkatesh   RHB/RM
Born: 5 August 1969, Bangalore   *Karnataka*

This fast-medium swing bowler established himself in the Indian side on the 1996 tour of England, where conditions suited his combination of swing and seam. He has developed a superb leg cutter, and a well disguised slower ball. He made his debut against New Zealand at Christchurch in 1993-94 and played back in New Zealand this winter. He has taken 119 one day wickets, striking every 35 balls and with a best performance of 4-17. His economy is good at 4.75 but don't expect anything with the bat.

RAMESH, Sadagoppan   LHB/ROB
Born: 13 October 1975, Chennai   *Tamil Nadu*

Ramesh has been touted as the next opening batsman for his country and he's been getting the chance to prove himself in the Asian Test series. He produced 323 runs in his first three matches, with a 96 top score and an average over 50. He has shown that he has the technique to handle pace bowling, which is what international cricket is all about so watch out for a new star in the Indian batting firmament.

SIDHU, Navjot Singh   RHB
Born: 20 October 1963, Patiala   *Punjab*

Sidhu is a long-serving Indian opener who has made more comebacks than any modern-day cricketer. A Punjabi who made a name for himself by scoring four consecutive half centuries in the 1987-88 World Cup. Not exactly a model of consistency he enjoys a grand reputation on Indian wickets. In limited overs cricket he is more than willing to use his feet against spinners for straight lofted strokes. His innings of 93 in the do-or-die quarter-final against Pakistan at Bangalore in the 1995-96 World Cup was to prove a match-winning effort. Cautious against the new ball, Sidhu hits his stride against spinners. On India's last tour to India, Sidhu left the team after a disagreement with the present captain, Mohammed Azhar-ud-din.

SINGH, Rabindra Ramanarayan   LHB/RMF
Born: 14 September 1963, Princes Town, Trinidad   Tamil Nadu
Robin Singh is a seasoned campaigner with 72 games under his belt in international one day games, having made his debut against the West Indies, back home at Port-of-Spain in 1988-89. He has been dropped and recalled as an all-rounder, only to pick up some crucial wickets (best 5-42) and contribute substantially in the fielding department from the covers. His right-hand medium pace bowling can restrict batsmen in the right conditions but his overall economy is not great. He is a powerful hitter in the latter overs, remaining not out on a number of occasions to help his average towards the 30 mark.

SRINATH, Javagal   RHB/RFM
Born: 31 August 1969, Mysore   Karnataka
In the fourth match of the Coca-Cola Champions Trophy tournament at Sharjah against Sri Lanka on 9th November 1998, Javagal Srinath became the third Indian after Kapil Dev and Anil Kumble to take 200 wickets in one day international cricket. It was Srinath's 147th match and he had bowled 7,663 balls at that moment. He created a new Indian record of taking 200 wickets in the least number of balls, previously held by Kumble and also equalled Kumble's Indian record of achieving this feat in 147 games. Only Dennis Lillee and Waqar Younis have taken 100 wickets in fewer one day matches. Srinath is the spearhead of the Indian pace attack and he is very much the genuine article as a speed merchant. He had a 1995 stint with Goucestershire. He has had injury problems in the last couple of years and India will be hoping he can better his best of 5-23 in this World Cup. He has a one day 50 to his name and is no bunny.

TENDULKAR, Sachin Rumesh   RHB, RM/LB
Born: 24th April 1973, Bombay   Bombay
The little batting genius from Bombay is unarguably the most complete batsman in world cricket at present. At 26 years old, Tendulkar is on his way to breaking all aggregate records in limited overs cricket at

international level. Ever since his promotion to opening the batting he has no less than nineteen one day international hundreds to his name. His 143 against Australia at Sharjah in April 1998 remains his highest. Difficult to recall him having a bad patch and as recent as last year, few of the leading Australian players in the current side did not hesitate in comparing his awesome talent with Sir Donald Bradman. A very quiet individual off the field Tendulkar's bat does all the talking for him. For a man whose each and every move on the cricket field is observed with great detail, he has more than fulfilled the expectations and amazingly stayed clean of any major controversy so far. Very useful partnership-breaker with his medium-paced inswingers and leg-breaks. He made his one day debut in 1989-90.

KENYA

A Professional Approach

This is Kenya's second time in the Finals. A sponsorship deal worth $130,000 a year from local beer firm Kenya Breweries has allowed the team to turn professional before the World Cup as they look to improve on the one win they recorded in 1996. And what a win it was – coming on Leap Year Day when they humiliated the great West Indian side, bowling them out in 35.2 overs to win by 73 runs.

Nowadays their coach is West Indian Alvin Kallicharan – he of the great one-day innings in the first World Cup in 1975 and he has helped to instil a more professional approach into the team which was due to have started its World Cup build-up with a tour of Bangladesh in March. The team's top batsmen, Maurice Odumbe and Steve Tikolo, both play professional cricket in Bangladesh. Spectators are in for a treat if the Kenyan batsmen can come to terms with English conditions but whether another game victory is in their grasp must be doubtful. The West Indies will be happy they are seeded in the other Group!

Team strip: Bright green shirt emblazoned with the shield and spears from the nation's flag. White collar tipped with black.

World Cup Record

	First Year	P	W	L	NR	SR%
Australia	1995-96	1	–	1	–	–
India	1995-96	1	–	1	–	–
Sri Lanka	1995-96	1	–	1	–	–
West Indies	1995-96	1	1	–	–	100.00
Zimbabwe	1995-96	1	–	1	–	–
Total...		*5*	*1*	*4*	*–*	*20.00*

Campaign Performances

Year	Pos	Captain	Result
1995-96	Gp	M Odumbe	Failed to qualify for quarter finals

One-Day Records

	Period	P	W	L	T	NR	SR%
All-Time:	… … 95-96 to 98-99	20	4	15	0	1	21.05
Since Last WC:	… … … … …	14	3	11	0	0	21.42

Highest Innings Totals:

Runs	Overs	R/O	Opponents	Venue	Year
254-7	50 overs	5.08	Sri Lanka	Kandy	1995-96

Lowest Completed Innings:

Runs	Overs	R/O	Opponents	Venue	Year
134	49.4 overs	2.69	Zimbabwe	Patna	1995-96

World Cup Individual Records

Highest Individual Innings

Runs	bp	Player	Opponents	Venue	Year
96	3	S Tikolo	Sri Lanka	Kandy	1995-96
85	1	K Otieno	Australia	Vishakhapatnam	1995-96

No Kenyan player has hit a century in World Cup cricket.

Partnership Record for each Wicket

	Total	Partnership	Opponents	Year
1st	47	D Chudasama (27), K Otieno (14)	Sri Lanka	1995-96
2nd	53	D Chudasama (34), K Otieno (19)	Zimbabwe	1995-96
3rd	102	K Otieno (85), M Odumbe (50)	Australia	1995-96
4th	137	S Tikolo (96), H Modi (41)	Sri Lanka	1995-96
5th	21	E Odumbe (14), D Tikolo (11no)	Australia	1995-96
6th	42	M Odumbe (30), E Odumbe (20)	Zimbabwe	1995-96
7th	44	H Modi (26), T Odoyo (24)	West Indies	1995-96
8th	*8	D Tikolo (*25), M Suji (*2)	Sri Lanka	1995-96
9th	29	T Odoyo (24), AV Karim (11)	West Indies	1995-96
10th	11	AV Karim (11), R Ali (*6)	West Indies	1995-96

Best Bowling Figures

Score	Arm	Player	Opponents	Venue	Year
3-15	RM	M Odumbe	West Indies	Pune	1995-96
3-17	RM	Rajab Ali	West Indies	Pune	1995-96
3-22	RM	Rajab Ali	Zimbabwe	Patna	1995-96
3-45	RM	Rajab Ali	Australia	Vishakhapatnam	1995-96

No Kenyan player has taken four wickets in the World Cup.

Man of the Match Awards

One Award: M Odumbe (1).

World Cup Player Performances

Batting

Player	First Yr	P	I	no	Runs	HS	Ave	100	50	CS
S Tikolo	95-96	5	5	–	196	96	39.20	–	2	3
K Otieno	95-96	5	5	–	147	85	29.40	–	1	1
L Onyango	95-96	1	1	–	23	23	23.00	–	–	1
M Odumbe	95-96	5	5	–	112	50	22.40	–	1	–
D Chudasama	95-96	5	5	–	103	34	20.60	–	–	1
H Modi	95-96	5	5	–	84	41	16.80	–	–	3
E Odumbe	95-96	5	5	1	54	20	13.50	–	–	2
T Odoyo	95-96	4	4	–	42	24	10.50	–	–	–
M Suji	95-96	5	4	2	18	15	9.00	–	–	3
Asif Karim	95-96	5	3	1	17	11	8.50	–	–	–
Tariq Iqbal	95-96	2	2	–	17	16	8.50	–	–	2
D Tikolo	95-96	3	2	2	36	*25	–	–	–	2
Rajab Ali	95-96	5	2	2	6	*6	–	–	–	1

Bowling

Player	Overs	M	Runs	Wi	Ave	BP	4wi	R/O
Rajab Ali	36.2	3	176	9	19.55	3-17	–	4.84
M Odumbe	42.5	6	189	6	31.50	3-15	–	4.41
Asif Karim	48	4	171	4	42.75	1-19	–	3.56
E Odumbe	14	0	87	2	43.50	2-34	–	6.21
M Suji	40.2	3	213	4	53.25	2-55	–	5.28
S Tikolo	10	0	83	1	83.00	1-26	–	8.30
L Onyango	4	0	31	0	–	–	–	7.75
D Tikolo	8	0	55	0	–	–	–	6.87
T Odoyo	16	0	102	0	–	–	–	6.37

CHUDASAMA, Dipak   RHB
Born: 20 May 1963, Mombasa   *Nairobi Gymkhana*

Chudasama is an opening bat who has played for Kenya since 1988. He played in the 1990 and 1994 ICC tournaments and was another member of the team to make Kenyan history in India at the 1996 World Cup. Technically correct, Chudasama's consolidation of the opening batting spot has been a puzzle at times due to his inconsistency with only two innings over 50. Nevertheless, he has been a solid performer in critical situations and has a 25 plus average and an excellent 122 best innings. A medical doctor by profession, Chudasama is known as 'Doc' amongst his team mates.

KARIM, Aasif   RHB/ROB
Born: 15 December 1963, Mombasa   *Jaffery Sports Club*

Karim is a left arm orthodox spinner, and a useful right-handed lower order batsman with a promising highest score of 53, if not a great average of just over 11. He is probably the best spinner Kenya has, with the best cricketing brain, and he restricts batsmen to around the four per over mark. Karim has a good variation of flight and length, and is consistently amongst the wickets in the Kenyan leagues. His best in the international arena is 5-33. With a wealth of experience in three ICC tournaments, he has also captained Kenya, both in cricket, and in the Davis Cup tournament as an excellent tennis player. Another of the class of '96 who debuted in the World Cup of that year in the sub-continent.

MODI, Hitesh   LHB/ROB
Born: 13 October 1971, Kisumu   *Nairobi Gymkhana*

Also in the 1996 World Cup side due to his fielding and batting qualities, Modi normally bats at number six. He has since built up a reasonable international one day record with nearly 500 runs an average in the late 20s and with a highest innings total of 73 not out. Modi occasionally bowls offspin in Kenyan league matches but has only twice turned his arm over for Kenya.

NGOCHE, Lameck Onyango   RHB/RFM

Born: 22 September 1973, Nairobi   Swamibapa Sports Club

A young fast-medium bowler, Ngoche bowls mostly outswing. He came in against Sri Lanka at Kandy in the 1996 World Cup, and he's been part of the touring Kenyan team to Bangladesh and South Africa in recent years but hasn't often found himself in the one day side, something perhaps to do with a record of 96 runs off nine overs. More positively, in one of his three innings he scored a decent 23 and he is an excellent fielder.

OBUYA, Kennedy Otieno   RHB/WK

Born: 11 March 1972, Nairobi   Aga Khan Sports Club

Obuya is the right hand opening batsman and the first choice wicketkeeper for Kenya. He has scored a lot of runs in domestic cricket and made a useful 49 in the ICC Trophy final which took Kenya to the 1996 World Cup. An excellent international one day average of more than 32 means that Kenya can look forward to some decent starts to their innings. A 144 maximum means he is capable of holding together a complete innings. He debuted in the 1996 World Cup against India at Cuttack, Kenya's one day international initiation.

ODOYO, Thomas   RHB/RMF

Born: 12 May 1978, Nairobi   Nairobi Gymkhana

Somewhat of a teenage sensation, Thomas Odoyo is easily the fastest bowler in Kenya currently. He opens the bowling for his Kenyan league side and although his most recent international performances have been satisfactory at best, he is proclaimed to be one of the brightest prospects for the future. His economy of over five per over is a little worrying but if he can pull off some figures like his best 3-25, his captain won't worry too much. Odoyo is a good fielder and can be a useful late order batsman as well with an average in the mid teens and a high score of 41. Like a number of the current Kenyan side, Odoyo's one day debut came about when thrown into the cauldron of the 1996 World Cup, in his case against India at Cuttack.

ODUMBE, Maurice Omondi   RHB/ROB

Born: 15 June 1969, Nairobi   Aga Khan Sports Club

The captain of the Kenyan side, Maurice Odumbe has played for the national Test team for a number of years and his one day international debut was against India at Cuttack in the 1996 World Cup. A technically correct batsman, it is a difficult task for bowlers to dismiss him when he gets going and he has a high score of 83 to prove it. An average of 26 is less promising in a world context but this affable player will be determined to lead his team to a good show on the world stage. Odumbe has also been used occasionally as an off-spinner thanks to the coaching skills of Balwinder Sandhu. A reasonable economy rate well under four per over and a best of 3-14 could mean that Odumbe will be bringing himself on to help the side. Additionally, he is an excellent fielder. He will, in most likelihoods, be batting at number four, and will be heavily relied upon, along with Steve Tikolo, to get the bulk of the runs for Kenya.

ODUOL, Angara Joseph   RM
Born: 8 November 1971, Nairobi   *Swamibapa Sports Club*
Oduol made his one day debut against Zimbabwe at Nairobi (Gymk) in the 1997-98 President's Cup and he played in the Coca-Cola Triangular Series. He has excelled at neither art but his two wickets give hope for his career at international level. He is a right arm medium pace bowler who can use the new ball effectively, and a useful low order batsman and fielder. He once took seven wickets in an innings in a league match.

ONDIK, Anthony Suji   RHB/RM
Born: 5 February 1976, Nairobi   *Aga Khan Sports Club*
Tony Suji embarked on his one day international career against Pakistan at Nairobi (AK) in the 1996-97 KCA Centenary Tournament. He is a promising all-rounder, middle order right-hand batsman and right-arm medium pace bowler, and a good fielder. Although he has only taken three wickets in his eight games, an over economy rate of 4.62 is not bad. His batting also makes a worthwhile contribution to the team's cause as an average of nearly 20 confirms. A high score of 63 perhaps promises more from this young talent.

SHAH, Ravindu   RHB
A promising batsman who made his debut against Bangladesh at Hyderabad (Deccan) in the 1997-98 Coca-Cola Triangular Series and who has built some substantial innings, three over fifty, in his five matches so far. His 213 runs are at a world class average of over 40 so watch out for a new talent during this World Cup.

SUJI, Martin   RHB/RFM
Born: 2 June 1971, Nairobi   *Aga Khan Sports Club*

Another to appear in his country's first international one day game against India in the 1996 World Cup, Martin Suji is one of the few Kenyans with first-class experience (with Transvaal in South Africa). Suji is a middle to lower order bat but has made no impact with a top score of only 15. He is better known for his bowling. He is likely to open the bowling with his fast medium right arm swing and seam. He has taken 14 wickets with an economy rate of around four and a half per over and he is capable of swinging a game Kenya's way. He is also a good fielder.

TIKOLO, Steven Ogomji   RHB/ROB
Born: 25 June 1971, Nairobi   *Border*

One of Kenya's team which made its international debut against India in the 1996 World Cup, Steven Tikolo has playing first class cricket for Border in South Africa and has also played for Swansea in the Welsh cricket league. He often bats at number three and will be expected to make runs if Kenya are to perform respectably. In his early twenties he had an astounding 1994 season in domestic cricket, scoring 1,959 runs in 18 innings. His highest score was 224 off only 108 balls. His current average is in the mid 20s, respectable but not outstanding and his best ever total narrowly missed out on a century with 96. He is also a useful off-spin bowler with 13 wickets and a best of 3-29, and an excellent fielder.

VADER, Alpesh   RHB
Born: 7 September 1974   *Premier Club*

Alpesh Vader is another of the new lads to have made their debut since the last World Cup, his first game against Bangladesh at Nairobi (Gymk) in the 1997-98 President's Cup. He has put together one good innings at 42 not out and three other not out knocks to produce an average of 31. He has been on tour with the squad since 1995 and this World Cup may be breakthrough time.

NEW ZEALAND

Form Strengthens Case

New Zealand are one of the form teams coming into this competition. Their Test record is especially formidable at the moment and a number of players are emerging to lead their World Cup challenge, amongst them all-rounder Cairns and Doull who has bowled himself into the top rankings. Their one day series against India finished tied at 2-2 (the third game had been abandoned) and a tough test of strength against South Africa has prepared them for the top. They will need it in Group B which includes potential whipping boys in Bangladesh and Scotland. Their World Cup record against their other group opponents – Australia, Pakistan and West Indies – isn't great and will need improving if they are to reach the Super Sixes.

Team strip: Panelled with New Zealand's silver fern across the chest and into the collar. Bordered with black piping.

World Cup Record

	First Year	P	W	L	NR	SR%
Australia	1987-88	4	1	3	–	25.00
East Africa	1975	1	1	–	–	100.00
England	1975	6	3	3	–	50.00
Holland	1995-96	1	1	–	–	100.00
India	1975	5	3	2	–	60.00
Pakistan	1983	5	1	4	–	20.00
South Africa	1991-92	2	1	1	–	50.00
Sri Lanka	1979	4	3	1	–	75.00
UAE	1995-96	1	1	–	–	100.00
West Indies	1975	3	1	2	–	33.33
Zimbabwe	1987-88	3	3	–	–	100.00
Grand Total		*35*	*19*	*16*	–	*54.28*

Campaign Performances

Year	Pos	Captain	Result
1975	SF	GM Turner	Lost to West Indies by 4 wickets
1979	SF	MG Burgess	Lost to England by 9 runs
1983	Gp	GP Howarth	Failed to qualify for semi-finals
1987-88	Gp	JJ Crowe	Failed to qualify for semi-finals
1991-92	SF	MD Crowe	Lost to Pakistan by 4 wickets
1995-96	QF	LK Germon	Lost to Australia by 6 wickets

One-Day Records

	Period	P	W	L	T	NR	SR%
All-Time:	… … 72-73 to 98-99	316	130	169	4	13	42.90
Since Last WC:	… … … … …	58	22	30	3	3	46.80

Highest Innings Totals:

Runs	Overs	R/O	Opponents	Venue	Year
309-5	60 overs	5.15	East Africa	Birmingham	1975
307-8	50 overs	6.14	Holland	Baroda	1995-96
286-9	50 overs	5.72	Australia	Madras	1995-96

Lowest Completed Innings:

Runs	Overs	R/O	Opponents	Venue	Year
158	52.2 overs	3.01	West Indies	The Oval	1975
166	48.2 overs	3.43	Pakistan	Christchurch	1991-92

World Cup Individual Records

100 Pluses

Runs	bp	Player	Opponents	Venue	Year
171no	1	GM Turner	East Africa	Birmingham	1975
130	5	CZ Harris	Australia	Madras	1995-96
114no	1	GM Turner	India	Manchester	1975
101	2	NJ Astle	England	Ahmedabad	1995-96
100	4	MD Crowe	Australia	Auckland	1991-92

Partnership Record for each Wicket

	Total	Partnership	Opponents	Year
1st	114	MJ Greatbatch (68), RT Latham (60)	S.Africa	1991-92
2nd	*126	GM Turner (*83), GP Howarth (*63)	Sri Lanka	1979
3rd	149	GM Turner (*171), JM Parker (66)	E.Africa	1975
4th	168	LK Germon (89), CZ Harris (130)	Australia	1995-96
5th	88	CL Cairns (52), AC Parore (55)	Holland	1995-96
6th	46	JV Coney (33), MD Crowe (34)	Pakistan	1983
7th	70	JV Coney (*66), RJ Hadlee (31)	England	1983
8th	48	BJ McKechnie (27), DR Hadlee (20)	England	1975
9th	59	WK Lees (26), JG Bracewell (34)	Pakistan	1983
10th	65	MC Snedden (40), EJ Chatfield (*19)	Sri Lanka	1983

Four Wicket Hauls

Score	Arm	Player	Opponents	Venue	Year
5-25	RF	RJ Hadlee	Sri Lanka	Bristol	1979

Man of the Match Awards

17 Awards: MD Crowe (3), GM Turner (2), MJ Greatbatch (2), GP Howarth (1), BA Edgar (1), RJ Hadlee (1), JV Coney (1), JJ Crowe (1), KR Rutherford (1), AH Jones (1), NJ Astle (1), CM Spearman (1), RG Twose (1)

World Cup Player Performances

Batting

Player	First Yr	P	I	no	Runs	HS	Ave	100	50	CS
NJ Astle	95-96	6	6	–	111	101	18.50	1	–	2
SL Boock	87-88	4	3	2	19	12	19.00	–	–	2
JG Bracewell	83	7	7	2	80	34	16.00	–	–	1
MG Burgess	79	4	2	–	45	35	22.50	–	–	2
BL Cairns	75	11	9	–	43	14	4.77	–	–	4
CL Cairns	91-92	11	9	3	160	52	26.66	–	1	10
EJ Chatfield	79	13	8	7	45	*19	45.00	–	–	2
RO Collinge	75	4	2	–	8	6	4.00	–	–	1
JV Coney	79	10	8	2	244	*66	40.66	–	2	4
JJ Crowe	83	8	8	1	220	*88	31.42	–	1	4
MD Crowe	83	21	21	5	880	*100	55.00	1	8	8
BA Edgar	79	8	8	1	194	*84	27.71	–	1	5

Player	First Yr	P	I	no	Runs	HS	Ave	100	50	CS
SP Fleming	95-96	6	6	–	193	66	32.16	–	1	3
LK Germon	95-96	6	6	3	191	89	63.66	–	1	2/1
MJ Greatbatch	91-92	7	7	–	313	73	44.71	–	3	4
BG Hadlee	75	1	1	–	19	19	19.00	–	–	–
DR Hadlee	75	4	3	1	28	20	14.00	–	–	–
RJ Hadlee	75	13	10	1	149	42	16.55	–	–	3
CZ Harris	91-92	14	10	1	200	130	22.22	1	–	5
BF Hastings	75	4	4	1	76	34	25.33	–	–	3
PA Horne	87-88	1	1	–	18	18	18.00	–	–	–
GP Howarth	75	11	11	1	374	76	37.40	–	4	2
HJ Howarth	75	4	2	1	1	*1	1.00	–	–	2
AH Jones	87-88	13	13	2	416	78	37.81	–	4	3
RJ Kennedy	95-96	3	1	–	2	2	2.00	–	–	1
GR Larsen	91-92	11	3	1	46	37	23.00	–	–	6
RT Latham	91-92	7	7	–	136	60	19.42	–	1	3
WK Lees	79	8	6	1	88	26	17.60	–	–	10
BJ McKechnie	75	8	4	2	45	27	22.50	–	–	2
DK Morrison	87-88	11	4	3	27	12	27.00	–	–	2
JFM Morrison	75	6	5	–	102	55	20.40	–	1	3
DJ Nash	95-96	4	2	1	13	8	13.00	–	–	–
JM Parker	75	4	4	–	71	66	17.75	–	1	–
AC Parore	95-96	5	5	–	144	55	28.80	–	1	1
DN Patel	87-88	17	11	2	97	40	10.77	–	–	3
KR Rutherford	87-88	14	12	2	416	75	41.60	–	4	5
IDS Smith	83	17	13	3	138	29	13.80	–	–	9
MC Snedden	83	9	8	–	218	64	27.25	–	1	2
CP Spearman	95-96	6	6	–	191	78	31.83	–	2	1
LW Stott	79	1	–	–	–	–	–	–	–	1
SP Thomson	95-96	5	5	2	101	*31	33.66	–	–	3
GB Troup	79	3	1	1	3	*3	–	–	–	–
GM Turner	75	14	14	4	612	*171	61.20	2	2	2
RG Twose	95-96	6	6	–	175	92	29.16	–	1	1
KJ Wadsworth	75	4	4	–	68	25	17.00	–	–	3/1
W Watson	87-88	14	5	4	29	*12	29.00	–	–	2
JG Wright	79	18	18	–	493	69	27.38	–	3	4

Bowling

Player	Overs	M	Runs	Wi	Ave	BP	4wi	R/O
NJ Astle	27	1	129	3	43.00	2-10	–	4.77
SL Boock	32.4	2	156	4	39.00	2-42	–	4.77
JG Bracewell	59	2	310	1	310.00	1-66	–	5.25
BL Cairns	115.2	16	436	14	31.14	3-36	–	3.78
CL Cairns	68.5	5	368	4	92.00	2-43	–	5.34
EJ Chatfield	131.3	16	524	14	37.42	2-24	–	3.98
RO Collinge	48	13	137	6	22.83	3-28	–	2.85
JV Coney	89	7	303	12	25.25	3-28	–	3.40
MD Crowe	18	2	116	1	116.00	1-15	–	6.44
SP Fleming	2	0	8	1	8.00	1-8	–	4.00
MJ Greatbatch	1	0	5	0	–	–	–	5.00
DR Hadlee	46	5	162	8	20.25	3-21	–	3.52
RJ Hadlee	146.1	38	421	22	19.13	5-25	1	2.88
CZ Harris	105.1	6	477	21	22.71	3-15	–	4.53
HJ Howarth	40	5	148	5	29.60	3-29	–	3.70
AH Jones	12	0	52	2	26.00	2-42	–	4.33
RJ Kennedy	21	2	88	4	22.00	2-36	–	4.19
GR Larsen	94	9	336	12	28.00	3-16	–	3.57
RT Latham	23	0	136	1	136.00	1-35	–	5.91
BJ McKechnie	89.5	9	304	13	23.38	3-24	–	3.38
DK Morrison	79	2	396	8	49.50	3-42	–	5.01
JFM Morrison	8	0	31	0	–	–	–	3.87
DJ Nash	35	4	153	6	25.50	3-26	–	4.37
DN Patel	140	9	555	13	42.69	3-36	–	3.96
KR Rutherford	1.4	0	11	0	–	–	–	6.60
MC Snedden	81.5	6	455	10	45.50	2-36	–	5.56
LW Stott	12	1	48	3	16.00	3-48	–	4.00
SA Thomson	42.3	2	197	5	39.40	3-20	–	4.63
GB Troup	32	3	104	4	26.00	2-36	–	3.25
RG Twose	13	0	79	0	–	–	–	6.07
W Watson	132	14	571	19	30.05	3-37	–	4.32

ALLOTT, Geoffrey Ian
RHB/FM

Born: 24 December 1971, Christchurch
Canterbury

Allott debuted against England at Napier in their third one day clash of 1996-97, having missed the previous one day series against Zimbabwe and World Cup 1996. A quick left armer in the Richard Collinge mould, he was considered too inaccurate for limited overs. But he built up his strength and a great game for New Zealand 'A' versus England in 1997 earned him a well deserved recall to the Test team and the one day team for the England series in 1997, when he made a complete mockery of the earlier judgements about his accuracy. He bowls a good accurate stock ball, is not put off by left/right combinations, and is prepared to bend his back to generate extra pace. Not a batsman to trouble the scoreboard too often though.

ASTLE, Nathan John
RHB/RM

Born: 15 September 1971, Christchurch
Canterbury

Astle made his one day debut against the West Indies at Auckland, in 1994-95 and he played in the recent New Zealand series against Sri Lanka, India and South Africa. Astle played in the last World Cup and followed up with a season in England with Nottinghamshire so he knows Trent Bridge and the English conditions. He has an outstanding Test record and his one day game isn't far behind with a batting average in the 30s and over 50 wickets at below 4.5 an over. Not only will he get the innings off to a rousing start, but he has shown the ability to carry on well into the accumulation phase with three one day centuries and other big scores. An unorthodox batsman in that he likes to play the cross-batted shots off the front foot. Look particularly for the front foot cut, and a pull/sweep. He has an ability to bowl ten very miserly overs of slow mediums but, not doing much with the ball, finds this harder to do at the top level. He is a safe fielder at third slip, gully, or in the deep.

BELL, Matthew David
RHB/ROB

Born: 25 February 1977, Dunedin
Wellington

Made his debut as recently as against Zimbabwe at Dhaka in the 1998-99 Wills International Cup. He also played against Sri Lanka but made little impression on the scoreboard.

CAIRNS, Christopher Lance   RHB/RFM
Born: 13 June 1970, Picton   *Canterbury*

One of those players with 'ability' written all over him. He played for
New Zealand at the very tender age of 19 against Australia at Perth in
1989 and it seemed a matter of course that he would fulfil his potential
on the international scene. He made his one day debut against England
at Wellington in the second one day game of 1990-91. Injury and
family bereavement slowed down his development, especially on the
bowling front. He got his pace and penetration back but he again gave
up bowling due to a foot injury. His batting has always held up well.
He struck a Test century in 1996 against Zimbabwe which included
nine sixes, and some straight hitting and cleanly struck reverse sweeps.
Retained in both Test and one day teams as a specialist batsman he
played much more responsibly than he did as an all-rounder and
gathered more than 2000 runs. The selectors have retained their faith in
him and his recent form indicates that they will reap their reward.
Cairns hammered the fifth fastest one day century in history to guide
New Zealand to an emphatic 70 run win over India in their fifth one-
dayer during the winter. After surviving a very strong caught behind
appeal on 51, he ended on 115. His bowling is back and good enough
although he probably won't beat his 5-42 best, and his batting average
of 25 doesn't do his current form justice.

DOULL, Simon Blair   RHB/RM
Born: 6 August 1969, Pukekohe   *Northern Districts*

The archetypal swing bowler, but a particularly good exponent of his
craft. Doull made the New Zealand side perhaps a little before his time,
but always looked to be a wicket taker right from the start because of
his ability to swing his briskish fast mediums both ways. He prefers to
mix it up rather than concentrate on a stock ball for a given batsman
and use his variety as a surprise weapon and sometimes his control
isn't the best. He debuted in one day cricket against Zimbabwe at
Bulawayo in 1992-93 but wasn't a regular until recently. Accuracy and
economy are valuable in the one day game of course and Doull has
started to develop consistency of line, length and purpose to get a
regular place in the one day set-up. His Test average has always been
in the high 20s range and this is right up with the best of New Zealand
bowlers except for Richard Hadlee. With the greater accuracy now
being shown, it looks likely he can improve on his one day strike rate

of just under 40 and an over economy rate over five; he has the potential to be remembered as New Zealand's second best bowler. At World Cup level, especially once through the group stage, Doull's ability to turn a match could prove decisive in English swing bowling conditions. Doull is a useful slogger with the bat and a safe fielder in the deep.

FLEMING, Stephen Paul   LHB
Born: 1 April 1973, Christchurch   *Canterbury*

Fleming is a very elegant batsman with great timing and touch who prefers the middle order. His one day debut was against India at Napier in 1993-94. For a couple of seasons he failed to pass three figures under the Silver Fern, but he then achieved centuries at both one day level (in the West Indies, 1996) and Test level (home to England, 1997). Nevertheless his record shows consistency and he plays many of his best innings when they are most needed. An enigma at the crease, he can concentrate, but then may do something silly and he is never boring to watch. He has scored almost 3,000 runs in one day internationals and averages in the 30s with the bat, with a top score of 116 not out. The off side drive is one of his most accomplished strokes. Like most left-handers, he has a weakness against the quicker ball angled across him, often being caught at slip. Off spinners bowling at his leg stump can therefore cause him problems if he remains crease bound. He was promoted to captain on merit for the home Test series against Sri Lanka in 1997 and his team achieved only the third instance of back to back Test victories in New Zealand history. His ability at first slip is a big plus, but at one day level he usually operates as a leg side sweeper in the field.

HARRIS, Chris Zinzan   LHB/RM
Born: 20 November 1969, Christchurch   *Canterbury*

Chris Harris is a specialist one day player, including being the batter with the ability to slog to a purpose at the tail end of an innings. He debuted against Australia at Sydney in the 1990-91 World Series and had the best New Zealand bowling figures in the 1992 World Cup, mainly due to cheap wickets in the slog overs. He performed heroically against Australia in the 1996 World Cup quarter final, scoring 130 of a huge partnership with Lee Germon, not to mention completing ten overs and fielding well. His is now one of the first names on the New Zealand team sheet at one day level, having notched well over 2,000 runs with an average of over 30. His bowling lacks real penetration but he has developed medium paced leg cutters and leg spinners for variety and keeps batsmen to just over four per over. He has taken over 100 wickets with a best of 5-42. A lithe, athletic fieldsman at point or square leg, Harris is lethal with the ball in hand and with the batsman out of his ground.

HORNE, Matthew Jeffery   RHB/RM
Born: 5 February 1970, Takapuna   *Otago*
A stylish middle-order front foot 'left-elbow' player. In 1996-97 he moved to Otago where he was reasonably assured of a spot at first class level and in lower level representative teams. He nearly made a 50 on debut and batted in the second innings after suffering a break in the hand. So his courage, commitment and ability are not in doubt. He has since sought to gain experience and shore up the New Zealand middle order at the same time, with reasonable success. His one day debut was against world champions Sri Lanka at Christchurch, in their second one day game of the 1996-97 season and last year he was again in action in Sri Lanka itself in the Singer-Akai Nidahas Trophy.

LARSEN, Gavin Rolf   RHB/RM
Born: 27 September 1962, Wellington   *Wellington*
The need for five bowlers in limited overs cricket was Rolf Larsen's route to the top. Most teams have a 'fifth' and he worked his way up from that role with Wellington to the class, economical one day international bowler he is today. He is one of those bowlers who comes on to the bat quicker than you think. On a typical slow turner he can make it hard for the batsman to even hit it off the square, but he is at his best on a slow seaming track, very much what he'll find in England in May. Keeping it just short of a drivable length he will get away movement off the seam and be both penetrative and well nigh impossible to hit, as his economy rate of 3.77 per over testifies. Many times in the past he has rescued New Zealand from a wayward start with the new ball. He made his one day debut against India at Dunedin in 1989-90 and took part in the latest six match home series against South Africa. His best performance with the ball is 4-24 and he'll probably bowl his 1,000th international one day over during the World Cup. His batting is second best but he has been known to win a game with the bat at the death and he has a high score of 37. As a reliable

player, a thinker, and a provincial captain, he has a lot to offer his captain in terms of tactical thinking.

MCMILLAN, Craig Douglas   RHB/RM
Born: 13 September 1976, Christchurch   *Canterbury*
McMillan made his one day debut against Sri Lanka at Hyderabad in the 1996-97 Independence Cup competition. He has developed into a handy one day player with a decent batting average in the late 20s and the ability to pick up wickets on a regular basis. He came out of a disciplinary cloud last autumn and will be looking to the World Cup to establish himself firmly in the minds of the selectors again.

NASH, Dion Joseph   RHB/RM
Born: 20 November 1971, Auckland   *Northern Districts*
Dion Nash was always rated as something of an all-rounder, but in the Lord's Test of 1994, after an ordinary start to his Test career, he suddenly bowled out of his skin to take 11 for 169 off 54 overs in the two England innings. Scoring 56 with the bat in his only innings, this was an all-round performance that was very close to being a match winning one. A season with Middlesex was then followed by injury and a loss of form. Nash made his one day debut against Zimbabwe at Bulawayo in 1992-93. His batting ability, with a best of 40 not out, comes in handy and his bowling remains pretty economical. He is a real athlete in the deep, with a strong accurate throw.

PARORE, Adam Craig   RHB/WK
Born: 23 January 1971, Auckland   *Auckland*
Parore is a versatile batsman and one who has made centuries at both Test and one day level and he debuted in one day cricket back in 1992-93 against Zimbabwe at Bulawayo. He is a natural wicket-keeper who was persuaded by coach Glen Turner to specialise in batting to accommodate then captain Lee Germon. At one day level, whether keeping or not, he has alternated between number three – anchoring the innings through the middle stages by rotating the strike – and number six, where his ability to hit at a rate of more than one per ball and his speed between the wickets ensures a good acceleration of the innings in the final ten overs. In over 100 games he has amassed over 2,500 runs and averages in the early 30s. One weakness as a batsman is poor judgement of a run, sometimes forgetting that his partner has to make his ground as well. A pusher and a nudger, with the ability to

concentrate, his style is suited to English conditions and he has often made runs for New Zealand when all around him have failed. He is a good, if at times inconsistent, fielder when not keeping. When the 15 overs is up, look for him sweeping on the cover boundary with sliding saves.

TWOSE, Roger Graham   LHB/RM
Born: 17 April 1968, Torquay, Devon   *Wellington*
Made his one day international debut against India at Jamshedpur in 1995-96, having come straight into the one day side after qualifying for New Zealand citizenship. He now has over 30 games behind him and a batting average in the late 20s. He can also bowl a bit, often acting as an attacking partnership breaker, and has a best of 2-31, although his economy rate is over the five per over mark. Twose waits to play the shots he knows he can, has good concentration and reads the game well. He has occupied the pivotal one day number four position, from where he can pace the innings, pushing the single if his partner is set, hitting out if the run rate needs a boost, and always taking charge whatever his role of the moment.

VETTORI, Daniel Luca   LHB/SO
Born: 27 January 1979, Auckland   *Northern Districts*
The New Zealand selectors regarded Vettori as the best spinner in New Zealand, even at the tender age of 18 and his first four Test matches in 1997 brought 18 wickets averaging in the mid 20s. He is an attacking bowler who can turn the ball, but lacking the variety of delivery that those of greater years have developed. He has a reputation for 'hitting the splice'. He made his one day debut against Sri Lanka at Christchurch in 1996-97 and after early unhappy experiences with accuracy in one day games, he has begun to mature into a useful bowling option with more than 20 wickets now and an under five per over economy rate. He opens the batting for his club side in Hamilton so a handy average of 15 or so is not surprising and could get better. Vettori is a young man who could use the World Cup as a launching pad for his career.

WISEMAN, Paul John   RHB/ROB
Born: 4 May 1970, Auckland   *Otago*
Wiseman made his one day debut as recently as the 1997-98 season against India at Sharjah in the Coca-Cola Cup. He has bowled his off

breaks at an economy rate of five per over but showed no signs of troubling the leading batsmen. His batting has yet to be really tested but he has the potential to put down a reasonable score.

PAKISTAN

Opener the Key

Pakistan's batting is always strong and they currently have three top 20 world bowlers in Younis, Akram and Ahmed, the former two with tremendous records in English conditions. A mentally gruelling series against India has doubtful value as a warm-up for an English early summer but Pakistan will benefit from enthusiastic support. A first game against West Indies could be vital in a strong group also containing Australia and New Zealand. Historically in the competition they have been successful against Australia and New Zealand but their record against the West Indies is in dire need of improvement.

Team strip: Print of the national cricket logo in dark green on a lime green body with the inscription 'Pakistan' in the centre of the nation's star. White piped raglan sleeves.

World Cup Record

	First Year	P	W	L	NR	SR%
Australia	1975	4	2	2	–	50.00
Canada	1979	1	1	–	–	100.00
England	1979	8	4	3	1	57.14
Holland	1995-96	1	1	–	–	100.00
India	1991-92	2	–	2	–	–
New Zealand	1983	5	4	1	–	80.00
South Africa	1991-92	2	–	2	–	–
Sri Lanka	1975	6	6	–	–	100.00
UAE	1995-96	1	1	–	–	100.00
West Indies	1975	6	1	5	–	16.66
Zimbabwe	1991-92	1	1	–	–	100.00
Total		*37*	*21*	*15*	*1*	*58.33*

Campaign Performances

Year	Pos	Captain	Result
1975	Gp	Asif Iqbal	Failed to qualify for semi-finals
1979	SF	Asif Iqbal	Lost to West Indies by 43 runs
1983	SF	Imran Khan	Lost to West Indies by 8wickets
1987-88	SF	Imran Khan	Lost to Australia by 18 runs
1991-92	F	Imran Khan	Won; beat England by 22 runs
1995-96	QF	Wasim Akram	Lost to India by 39 runs

One-Day Records

	Period	P	W	L	NR	SR%	
All-Time: ……	72-73 to 98-99	414	210	189	5	19	53.29
Since Last WC: ……………		95	46	46	0	3	50.00

Highest Innings Totals:

Runs	Overs	R/O	Opponents	Venue	Year
338-5	60 overs	5.63	Sri Lanka	Swansea	1983
330-6	60 overs	5.50	Sri Lanka	Nottingham	1975
297-7	50 overs	5.94	Sri Lanka	Faisalabad	1987-88
286-7	60 overs	4.76	Australia	Nottingham	1983
281-5	50 overs	5.62	New Zealand	Lahore	1995-96

Lowest Completed Innings:

Runs	Overs	R/O	Opponents	Venue	Year
74	40.2 overs	1.83	England	Adelaide	1991-92

World Cup Individual Records

100 Pluses

Runs	bp	Player	Opponents	Venue	Year
119no	2	Rameez Raja	New Zealand	Christchurch	1991-92
114	2	Aamir Sohail	Zimbabwe	Hobart	1991-92
113	1	Rameez Raja	England	Karachi	1987-88
111	1	Aamir Sohail	South Africa	Karachi	1995-96
103no	4	Zaheer Abbas	New Zealand	Nottingham	1983
103	4	Javed Miandad	Sri Lanka	Hyderabad	1987-88
102no	5	Imran Khan	Sri Lanka	Leeds	1983
102no	1	Rameez Raja	West Indies	Melbourne	1991-92
100	3	Salim Malik	Sri Lanka	Faisalabad	1987-88

Partnership Record for each Wicket

	Total	Partnership	Opponents	Year
1st	159	Sadiq Mohammed (74), Majid Khan (84)		
			Sri Lanka	1975
2nd	167	Rameez Raja (113), Salim Malik (88)	England	1987-88
3rd	145	Aamir Sohail (114), Javed Miandad (89)		
			Zimbabwe	1991-92
4th	*147	Zaheer Abbas (*103), Imran Khan (*79)		
			N.Zealand	1983
5th	87	Majid Khan (61), Asif Iqbal (61)	Australia	1979
	87	Javed Miandad (*57), Inzamam-ul-Haq (60)		
			N.Zealand	1991-92
6th	144	Imran Khan (*102), Shahid Mahboob (77)		
			Sri Lanka	1983
7th	52	Asif Iqbal (51), Wasim Raja (21)	England	1979
8th	36	Zaheer Abbas (*83), Sarfraz Nawaz (11)		
			England	1983
9th	*39	Zaheer Abbas (*83), Wasim Bari (18)		
			England	1983
10th	28	Abdul Qadir (*41), Rashid Khan (9)	N.Zeland	1983

Four Wicket Hauls

Score	Arm	Player	Opponents	Venue	Year
5-44	LBG	Abdul Qadir	Sri Lanka	Leeds	1983
4-21	LBG	Abdul Qadir	New Zealand	Birmingham	1983
4-26	RF	Waqar Younis	Holland	Lahore	1995-96
4-31	LBG	Abdul Qadir	England	Rawalpindi	1987-88
4-32	RF	Wasim Akram	New Zealand	Christchurch	1991-92
4-37	RF	Imran Khan	West Indies	Lahore	1987-88
4-37	RF	Imran Khan	England	Karachi	1987-88
4-44	RFM	Sarfraz Nawaz	West Indies	Birmingham	1975
4-56	RM	Asif Iqbal	West Indies	The Oval	1979

Man of the Match Awards

24 Awards: Abdul Qadir (3), Aamir Sohail (3), Zaheer Abbas (2), Imran Khan (2), Javed Miandad (2), Salim Malik (2), Mushtaq Ahmed (2), Sarfraz Nawaz (1), Sadiq Mohammed (1), Asif Iqbal (1), Mohsin Khan (1), Salim Yousaf (1), Inzamam-ul-Haq (1), Wasim Akram (1), Waqar Younis (1).

Batting

Player	First Yr	P	I	no	Runs	HS	Ave	100	50	CS
Aamir Sohail	91-92	16	16	–	598	114	37.37	2	4	4
Aaqib Javed	91-92	15	3	3	8	*6	–	–	–	2
Abdul Qadir	83	13	9	7	118	*41	59.00	–	–	3
Asif Iqbal	75	5	4	–	182	61	45.50	–	3	5
Asif Masood	75	3	1	–	6	6	6.00	–	–	–
Ata-ur-Rehman	95-96	1	1	–	0	0	–	–	–	–
Haroon Rasheed	79	4	4	1	69	*37	23.00	–	–	–
Ijaz Ahmed Sr.	87-88	20	17	3	340	70	24.28	–	3	7
Ijaz Faqih	83	6	5	1	61	*42	15.25	–	–	1
Imran Khan	75	28	24	5	666	*102	35.05	1	4	6
Inzamam-ul-Haq	91-92	16	15	2	370	60	28.46	–	2	4
Iqbal Sikander	91-92	4	1	1	1	*1	–	–	–	–
Javed Miandad	75	33	30	5	1083	103	43.32	1	8	10/1
Majid Khan	75	7	7	–	359	84	51.28	–	5	1
Mansoor Akhtar	83	8	8	–	108	33	13.50	–	–	2
Manzoor Elahi	87-88	1	1	1	4	*4	–	–	–	–
Mohsin Khan	83	7	7	–	223	82	31.85	–	2	3
Moin Khan	91-92	10	5	2	44	*20	14.66	–	–	11/3
Mudassar Nazar	79	12	10	1	149	40	16.55	–	–	6
Mushtaq Ahmed	91-92	15	5	1	27	17	6.75	–	–	5
Mushtaq Mohammed	75	3	3	–	89	55	29.66	–	1	1
Naseer Malik	75	3	1	1	0	*0	–	–	–	–
Parvez Mir	75	2	2	1	8	*4	8.00	–	–	1
Rameez Raja	87-88	16	16	3	700	*119	53.84	3	2	4
Rashid Khan	83	7	1	–	9	9	9.00	–	–	1
Rashid Latif	95-96	6	2	–	26	26	13.00	–	–	7/2
Sadiq Mohammed	75	7	7	1	189	74	31.50	–	2	3
Saeed Anwar	95-96	6	6	2	329	*83	82.25	–	3	–
Salim Jaffer	87-88	5	3	2	9	*8	9.00	–	–	–
Salim Malik	87-88	23	19	5	572	100	40.85	1	4	5
Salim Yousaf	87-88	7	6	3	112	56	37.33	–	1	9
Saqlain Mushtaq	95-96	1	–	–	–	–	–	–	–	–
Sarfraz Nawaz	75	11	8	1	65	17	9.28	–	–	2
Shahid Mahboob	83	5	3	–	100	77	33.33	–	1	1

Player	First Yr	P	I	no	Runs	HS	Ave	100	50	CS
Shoaib Mohammed										
	87-88	1	1	–	0	0	–	–	–	–
Sikander Bakht	79	4	2	1	3	2	3.00	–	–	1
Tahir Naqqash	83	1	1	1	0	*0	–	–	–	1
Tauseef Ahmed	87-88	6	2	–	1	1	0.50	–	–	1
Waqar Younis	95-96	6	1	1	4	*4	–	–	–	2
Wasim Akram	87-88	22	16	4	207	39	17.25	–	–	3
Wasim Bari	75	14	8	4	87	34	21.75	–	–	18/4
Wasim Haider	91-92	3	2	–	26	13	13.00	–	–	–
Wasim Raja	75	8	8	–	154	58	19.25	–	1	4
Zaheer Abbas	75	14	14	2	597	*103	49.75	1	4	7
Zahid Fazal	91-92	2	2	–	13	11	6.50	–	–	1

Bowling

Player	Overs	M	Runs	Wi	Ave	BP	4wi	R/O
Aamir Sohail	86	3	384	8	48.00	2-26	–	4.46
Aaqib Javed	124.2	15	517	18	28.72	3-21	–	4.15
Abdul Qadir	135.4	8	506	24	21.08	5-44	3	3.72
Asif Iqbal	59	5	215	10	21.50	4-56	1	3.64
Asif Masood	30	3	128	2	64.00	1-50	–	4.26
Ata-ur-Rehman	10	0	40	1	40.00	1-40	–	4.00
Ijaz Ahmed Sr.	40	1	170	1	170.00	1-28	–	4.25
Ijaz Faqih	37	2	125	0	–	–	–	3.37
Imran Khan	169.3	18	655	34	19.26	4-37	2	3.86
Iqbal Sikander	35	2	147	3	49.00	1-30	–	4.20
Javed Miandad	22	2	73	4	18.25	2-22	–	3.31
Majid Khan	47	8	117	7	16.71	3-27	–	2.48
Mansoor Akhtar	17	2	75	2	37.50	1-7	–	4.41
Manzoor Elahi	9.4	0	32	1	32.00	1-32	–	3.31
Mohsin Khan	1	0	3	0	–	–	–	3.00
Mudassar Nazar	105	8	397	8	49.62	3-43	–	3.78
Mushtaq Ahmed	135	5	549	26	21.11	3-16	–	4.06
Mushtaq Mohammed	7	0	23	0	–	–	–	3.28
Naseer Malik	30	5	98	5	19.60	2-37	–	3.26
Parvez Mir	15	2	59	2	29.50	1-17	–	3.93
Rashid Khan	71	11	266	8	33.25	3-47	–	3.74
Sadiq Mohammed	6	1	20	2	10.00	2-20	–	3.33
Salim Jaffer	39.4	0	210	5	42.00	3-30	–	5.29
Salim Malik	56	2	282	4	70.50	2-41	–	5.03

Player	Overs	M	Runs	Wi	Ave	BP	4wi	R/O
Saqlain Mushtaq	10	1	38	2	19.00	2-38	–	3.80
Sarfraz Nawaz	119	15	435	16	27.18	4-44	1	3.65
Shahid Mahboob	52	4	224	4	57.00	1-37	–	4.38
Sikander Bakht	41	10	108	7	15.42	3-32	–	2.63
Tahir Naqqash	8	0	49	1	49.00	1-49	–	6.12
Tauseef Ahmed	60	4	230	5	46.00	1-35	–	3.83
Waqar Younis	54	4	253	13	19.46	4-26	1	4.68
Wasim Akram	186.2	7	768	28	27.42	4-32	1	4.12
Wasim Haider	19	1	79	1	79.00	1-36	–	4.15
Wasim Raja	13.4	4	46	1	46.00	1-7	–	3.36
Zaheer Abbas	19.4	2	74	2	37.00	1-8	–	3.76

Player Profiles

AFRIDI, Shahid Khan
RHB/LBG

Born: 1 March 1980, Kohat   *Karachi*

Afridi heads the current list of bright young talent that keeps emerging from Pakistan. He created a sensation by reaching a limited overs 100 against Sri Lanka off a mere 37 balls in his first outing at the crease. In October 1996 Shahid had been summoned to join the side in Kenya to replace the injured leg-spinner, Mushtaq Ahmed. His captain on the day, Saeed Anwar, decided to use him as a pinch-hitter. Since that feat he has been a regular feature in Pakistan's one-day plans. Often asked to open the innings, he has failed miserably through sheer lack of application. Only recently he scored his second 100 against India in Canada. His fastish leg-breaks add strength to his side's bowling resources. He is an excellent all-round fielder. He was voted Man of the Finals in the 1996-97 World Series Cricket.

AKHTAR, Shoaib
RHB/RF

Born: 13 August 1975, Rawalpindi   *Lahore*

The latest bowling sensation to emerge from Pakistan who has come on leaps and bounds since his one day debut in 1997-98. On his first overseas tour with the senior side in South Africa, he was clocked faster than Waqar Younis and Allan Donald. He possesses old-fashioned aggression and hot-headedness which could serve him well, particularly while honing his skills under the guidance of two all-time greats, ie, Wasim Akram and Waqar Younis.

AHMED, IJAZ Sr.   RHB/LM, SLA

Born: 20 September 1968, Sialkot   *Gujranwala*

Having been made redundant for two years, Ijaz in his comeback game scored a run-a-ball 110 against South Africa in the triangular series at Rawalpindi in 1994-95. He has never looked back since, having established himself as a permanent place in the top order. The first six seasons provided him with very few opportunities. A gritty batsman whose strength lies in clever placing of the ball, square of the wicket on both sides. His technique is suited best to pitches with low bounce. His sharp instinct to improvise in the latter stages of the innings is a useful tool both while batting first or in a frenetic run-chase. In the 1991-92 World Cup his medium-pace around-the-wicket version was used quite frequently by Imran Khan. He survived that tournament on his ability for a quick-fire burst in the lower middle order and excellent throwing arm in the deep. He is still a formidable outfielder with an excellent catching record. One of his nine limited over hundreds includes a whirlwind unbeaten 139 off 84 balls against India at Lahore in the 1997-98 Wills Challenge Series. Opening the innings he hit no less than ten fours and nine sixes in one of the most brutal displays of batting seen on the subcontinent, that enabled Pakistan to reach 219 in 26.2 overs

AHMED, Mushtaq   RHB/LBG

Born: 28 June 1970, Sahiwal   *United Bank*

A match-winning leg spinner he was a huge success in the last World Cup taking over from leg spin wizard, Abdul Qadir. In the Final at Melbourne he snapped up Graeme Hick with a classic wrong 'un and later had Graham Gooch top-edging a sweep to be caught in the fine-leg region. Accurate, although in the past he has been accused of overdoing his variety. He is a confident and cheerful character who can bat a bit if needed. In the last three years he has not been an automatic choice for the limited overs side. His experience of English conditions might strengthen his case for inclusion.

AKRAM, Wasim   LHB/LF

Born: 3 June 1966, Lahore   *Lahore*

Arguably the best left arm new ball bowler in the history of the game. During the winter tour to India, Wasim was reinstated as captain of Pakistan for the fourth time. Since August 1994, he heads the table of most one-day international wickets with 363 wickets at 23.10 with an economy rate of 3.83. He made his one day debut in 1984-85 and will be appearing in his fourth World Cup this year. Always lifts himself for the big occasion – no more so than in the 1991-92 World Cup Final against England at Melbourne, when he hit 33 off 18 balls and took the wickets of Botham, Lamb and Lewis to help secure the trophy. In the 1989-90 final of the Austral-Asia Cup against Australia at Sharjah, he hit 49 off 35 balls and finished the match with a hat-trick. Wasim's clever use of pace and deceptive wristy action makes him a formidable bowler in any conditions. Although he never quite fulfilled his potential with the bat, Wasim is a useful late order batsman who is at his best when attacking. His highest innings of 86 came off 76 balls in the World Series Cricket final against Australia at Melbourne in 1989-90.

ANWAR, Saeed   LHB/SLA
Born: 6 September 1968, Karachi   *United Bank*

High-scoring left-hand batsman, Saeed in his first four years was only considered good enough for limited overs cricket. He uses short back-lift and relies on his exquisite timing and ability to find gaps with precision, particularly on the off-side, to give his side a positive start. His 194 against India at Chennai in the Independence Cup in 1997-98 remains the highest individual score in a limited overs international match. It was all the more remarkable for he employed a runner when suffering from dehydration. Capable of breathtaking brilliance without adopting violence his tally of 15 centuries, which includes three successive in the 1993-94 Pepsi Champions Trophy in Sharjah, is behind only Sachin Tendulkar (19) and Desmond Haynes (17). Even in the present fifteen-overs rule, Saeed would rarely be seen going for the lofted strokes. His one problem has been maintaining full fitness whenever away on tours due to dietary problems. He made his one day debut in 1988-89 but his only tour with the Pakistan side to date was to England in 1996.

INZAMAM-UL-HAQ   RHB/SLA
Born: 3 March 1970, Multan   *Multan*

Often regarded as a sleeping giant, he played one of the most spectacular innings in the history of the one day game in the 1991-92 World Cup semi-final against New Zealand at Auckland. When all seemed lost he scored 60 off 37 balls to enable Pakistan to score 123 in the last 15 overs to clinch a Final berth. Despite not fulfilling his undoubted potential, Inzamam is one of the premier stroke players in the present world of cricket. Perhaps his best years are ahead of him. With more application and will to reach the top he would have reached greater heights. A natural striker of the ball Inzamam has a wide range of powerful dismissive strokes executed with alarming ease. His figures confirms him as the most consistent Pakistani middle order batsman since Javed Miandad. The most productive of his five limited overs hundreds is 137 not out that he scored against New Zealand in the 1993-94 semi-final of the Austra-Asia Cup in Sharjah. Inzamam is a more than capable slip fieldsman and also a safe bet in the deep. He has been beset with weight problems that have also triggered knee complaints in the last three years.

KHAN, Moin   RHB/WK
Born: 23 September 1971   *Karachi*

Moin was drafted into the side after an injury to Salim Yousuf in the 1990-91 home series against the West Indies. The following season he won a spot in the World Cup. In the semi-final against New Zealand at Auckland his unbeaten 20 off 11 balls calmed the nerves of the entire nation. His steady work behind the stumps very often goes unnoticed for it lacks the element of spectacularity. Very busy character in terms of co-ordinating verbally with his bowlers and has a reputation of excessive appealing. Very good fitness record over the years, although he returned home from Sharjah due to chicken-pox during the 1994-95 Asia Cup matches while leading the side for the first time. He is an unorthodox lower middle order batsman who has so often picked up his side from shambles to respectability. He is a tough character who never gives an inch away. Moin's highest score in limited overs matches is 69 not out scored against India at Canada in the 1998-99 Sahara Cup. He made his one day debut in 1990-91.

MAHMOOD, Azhar   RHB/RFM
Born: 28 February 1975, Rawalpindi   *Islamabad*

Azhar Mahmood is a very fine prospect for an all-round spot. A vibrant cricketer whose aggressive medium-fast bowling could prove vital in English conditions, particularly as it is being held in the early part of the summer. He is a highly talented cricketer who has yet to show any form of consistency with either bat or ball in the limited overs internationals. His highest innings with the bat, 65 not out, came against Australia at Peshawar in 1998-99.

MALIK, Salim **RHB/LB**
Born: 16 April 1963, Lahore *Lahore City*
The most senior member of the the side and a former Indian captain,
Malik is now better known for his alleged role in the betting scandal
which linked him with Waugh and Warne. He knows England from his
time at Essex and from a number of tours. He made his debut against
West Indies at Sydney in the World Series Cup way back 1981-82. He
has amassed over 7,000 runs in the intervening years, including five
100s and 46 50s. Pakistan still rely on his silky batting skills in the
middle order so look out for his swan song in this World Cup. He has
bowled over 500 one day overs and has a best performance of 5-35, but
his economy rate is now over five per over.

MUSHTAQ, Saqlain **RHB/OB**
Born: 27th November 1976 *Islamabad*
Probably the best off spinner in modern cricket. In the last three and a
half years he has picked up 176 wickets in 88 limited overs matches.
He has a modest background having learned his cricket on the street
and his rich variety of well disguised deliveries owes much to his infant
years. Despite his relative youth he has an excellent temperament and
is particularly cool in the final overs of a game where he is almost
unplayable for the tail-enders. In the last three years he has taken the
most wickets for Pakistan. He played a pivotal role in his side's success
in the WSC 1996-97. He was picked for only one game in the previous
World Cup. He has the potential to become one of the all-time greats.

RAZA, Hasan **RHB/LB**
Born: 11 March 1982, Karachi *Karachi*
A young prodigy who made his mark with the Pakistan Under-15 side,
not least by scoring a stylish 80 against India at Lord's in the final of
the Lombard Under-15 World Cup. He promises to be another wristy
player in the league of Zaheer Abbas and Salim Malik. Has only been
drafted in when one of the senior batsmen is missing. Has an outside
chance of being picked for the World Cup.

SOHAIL, Aamir **LHB/SLA**
Born:14 September 1966, Lahore *Sargodha*
Out of favour for the recent tour of India, having stepped down as a
skipper, Aamir has an outside chance of being picked once again to
open the batting with Saeed Anwar. On and off the two left-handers

have enjoyed a fruitful opening partnership in the last four to five years. Sohail appeared in the winning side of the 1991-92 World Cup. His reputation as an aggressive left-hand opening batsman was established in that very tournament. An out and out team man he has worn the label of the angry young man of Pakistan cricket. Not the most technically correct player, he has a tendency of loose strokes outside the off stump. Aamir relies a lot on his sharp eye and reflexes while entrenching himself for a long stay at the crease. His highest score of 134 came in the semi-final of the 1993-94 Austral-Asia Cup against New Zealand in Sharjah. His slow left-arm is a useful commodity in the limited overs version and he has often been employed for a full quota of overs. Made his one day debut 1990-91.

YOUHANNA, Yousuf   RHB
Born: 27 August 1974, Lahore   *Bahawalpur*
A recent batting success in the middle order. Youhana was first spotted and picked for the Pakistan team to South Africa when he played beautifully against the visiting English Team, in Lahore, for some pre-Sharjah Cup warm up games. He is another one of Pakistan's rising stars and this World Cup will offer a first chance for many to see his gritty defence and dazzling stroke play. He made his debut against Zimbabwe at Harare in 1997-98 and played in the return series. In his 11 innings, he averages 53.22 with a high score of exactly 100. He is one of the few Pakistani players of Christian descent and the first since Khalid Ibadullah in 1967.

YOUNIS, Waqar   RHB/RF
Born:16 November 1971, Vehari   *Multan*
In his very first season of international cricket, Waqar dominated the Austral-Asia Cup in Sharjah like nobody's business. Coming in as a change bowler he ran through strong batting sides such as India and Sri Lanka by developing a lethal late inswing at a very high speed. Now though a much more mature and experienced bowler, old habits die hard. Waqar is an all-time great by any yardstick but his attacking nature that overlooks the fact that a dot ball is an achievement in limited overs cricket can prove costly. His tendency to over pitch the ball has sometimes made him an expensive commodity. His World Cup squad inclusion would depend on how selectors think of his form, fitness and suitability on English wickets. At the death his inswinging yorkers in which he specialises with the semi old ball, are definite wicket-taking missiles.

SCOTLAND

Amateur Debuts

This is the Scots' first finals following their deserved qualification from the ICC Trophy tournament in 1997. Theoretically the weakest side in the competition, they nevertheless have a chance of winning their game at home in Edinburgh against Bangladesh although the Bangladeshis defeated the Scots by 73 runs in the semi finals of the ICC Trophy competition in 1997. Scotland finished third in that competition – which was high enough to ensure this year's debut. They may well look towards James Brinkley for experience – a player on Hampshire's books who played in the 1998 Benson & Hedges Cup, his bowling could cause some of the opposition batsmen problems. Whether it is enough to upset Australia, Pakistan, New Zealand and West Indies is doubtful though.

Team strip: Stylised St Andrew's Cross, tartan collar and embroidered thistle.

Player Profiles

ALLINGHAM, Mike   RHB/RM
Born: 6 January 1965, Inverness   *Heriot's FP*
A genuine all-rounder, Allingham first appeared for the Scottish side in 1991 and was immediately successful, scoring a 50 in his first game (against the England Amateur XI). Since that time he has played 19 times for his country with a top score of 64 not out against Transvaal Under-23s during Scotland's tour of 1992 to Johannesburg. His best bowling was the man of the match winning performance of four for 35 against Netherlands last season. A noted all-round athlete Allingham has represented the Scotland 'B' XI at rugby, playing scrum half, and could well have made progress to the full Scotland side but for a severe knee injury. He is a school master at Fettes College, Edinburgh.

BLAIN, John   RHB/RFM
Born: 4 January 1979, Edinburgh   *Dunfermline*
John Blain was first capped in 1996 against Nottinghamshire in the Benson & Hedges Cup when he became Scotland's youngest capped

cricketer for 106 years. An opening bowler, who has also yet to show his full prowess with the bat for Scotland, Blain had a particularly successful series of games during the 1996 European Championship until he was injured in the last game of the tournament. He achieved his best figures of four for 34 against the England Amateur XI during the tournament and also recorded the figures of 10-3-12-2 against Israel. A footballer of some note, Blain was signed for the Scottish senior club Falkirk FC but elected to try for a career as a professional cricketer by signing for Northamptonshire for the 1997 season.

BRINKLEY, James Edward   RHB/RFM
Born: 13 March 1974, Helensburgh, Strathclyde   *Hampshire*
Played four times in the Benson & Hedges in 1998 and scored a 30 not out but only got eight runs in the other three times at the crease. He bowled 38.3 overs at an economical 3.5 an over so Scotland will look to him to pin down some of the more well-known opposition batsmen.

BUTT, Asim   RHB/RMF
Born: 2 May 1968, Lahore   *Heriot's*
Butt is another of Scotland's players who have benefited from their country's participation in the Benson & Hedges domestic one day tournament, providing valuable experience against professional teams. He took five wickets for 32 in one of his three games in 1998 and ended with five for 114 from 26.3 overs. He bowled very tightly in two games in the Nat West Trophy and kept the batsmen pinned down to 2.77 an over. His batting was nothing exceptional but he did manage to stay not out on a couple of occasions.

COWAN, David   LHB/RFM
Born: 30 March 1964, St. Andrews   *Freuchie*
Cowan first played for Scotland in 1989 and he has since been in and out of the side since that time, gaining a total of 25 caps. Destroying all the bowling in club cricket 'The Cool', as he is known, has had little opportunity to show his prowess while batting for the national side. However, he has contributed many vital spells of bowling, with the best being five for 45 against MCC in 1994. He works as a tradesman with Fife Council, Building Operations.

CRAWLEY, Stephen Thomas   RHB/RFM

Born: 16 September 1962, Bebington   *Grange*

Crawley didn't play for Scotland in the domestic one day games last season so he will rely on a trip to Sharjah to get any experience he can prior to the World Cup.

DAVIES, Alec   RHB/WK

Born: 18 April 1962, Rawalpindi, Pakistan   *West Lothian*

Davies will play at his home ground in Edinburgh if he makes the team for Scotland's two home World Cup Group B games. He first appeared for Scotland (against MCC) in 1993 but made only one more appearance for the national side before establishing himself as number one wicket keeper in the latter half of the 1995 season and he now has 39 caps. He performed extremely well during the 1996 season in taking 20 catches and five stumpings in 16 representative games, and had two match winning performances against Ireland in limited overs matches in 1995. A stylish right hand batsman, his top score is 45 not out against Netherlands in 1995. The holder of qualifications in Physical Education, he is a Sports Development Officer with West Lothian Council.

GOURLAY, Scott   RHB/RM

Born: 8 January 1971, Kirkaldy   *Freuchie*

An all-rounder, Gourlay is a useful later order bat and medium pace bowler. Capped for the first time during the 1995 Triple Crown Tournament against Ireland, he had acquired 18 caps by the end of 1998, with a top score of 23 against Netherlands in 1995 and best bowling figures of two for 27 in the second game against Ireland during the same season. He works as a storeman.

LOCKHART, Douglas   RHB

Born: 19 January 1976, Glasgow   *Glasgow Academicals*

An extremely promising opening batsman, Lockhart captained the Scotland Under-19 team during a surprisingly successful inaugural appearance in the International Youth Tournament in Amsterdam in 1995 when he won the Player of The Tournament award. He first appeared for the full Scotland side later in the same season scoring 31 against MCC and he did even better in his second appearance, scoring 119 not out against the Earl of Arundel's XI in 1996. He now has a number of caps and an impressive batting average. He has also studied at, and played for, Oxford University.

LOCKIE, Bryn   RHB

Born: 5 June 1968, Alloa   *Carlton*

First capped in 1995, Bryn Lockie has now got some experience behind him at international level. His top score is 74 against MCC at Lord's in 1996 and he also featured in a match winning first wicket partnership of 198 against Ireland in 1996. A senior rugby player before injury cut short his career, Lockie is a school master at Daniel Stewart's Melville College in Edinburgh.

PARSONS, Robert Andrew   LHB/M

Born: 26 February 1975, Irvine   *Prestwick*

Drew Parsons played in the Benson & Hedges and Nat West one day domestic tournaments in 1998, scoring two decent innings from four games, a 37 and a 30. However, he didn't get to bowl.

PATTERSON, Brian Matthew Winston   RHB

Born: 29 January 1965, Ayr   *Ayr*

Brian Patterson played in the Benson & Hedges preliminaries in 1998 and achieved a highest score of 33 in one of four innings, averaging just over 15. In his two Nat West games he scored 71 and 0 – the fortunes of cricket!

PHILIP, Ian   RHB/SLA/WK

Born: 9 June 1958, Falkirk   *Stenhousemuir*

Ian Philip is a very experienced player with over 120 caps in his international career which spans 13 years from 1986. He has played for Poloc and Selkirk, as well as Stenhousemuir. Philip was born in Stenhousemuir but moved to Perth, Western Australia when 11. In recent years he has spent six months in either country playing continuous cricket while operating as a professional for various Scottish clubs. However, his first love has always been his home town club of Stenhousemuir. He first played for Scotland in 1986 and has been an outstandingly successful performer for his country having made more appearances for his country than any other player, scored more runs than any other Scotland batsman, scored more centuries than any other batsman and made the highest score ever by a Scotland player (234 against MCC in 1991). An elegant batsman, he has been the corner stone of the Scottish side throughout his career. He has also kept wicket a number of times for Scotland in one day games. However, his bowling is most definitely of the friendly variety.

SALMOND, George   RHB/RM
Born: 1 December 1969, Dundee   *Grange*

Salmond is an exciting stroke player and brilliant fielder who took over the Scotland captaincy during the 1995 season. He has played and captained Scotland at Under-16, Under-19 and 'B' XI levels. He is now one of the more experienced players for the full Scotland side with a top score of 181 in the 1996 three-day first-class match against Ireland. His two previous highest scores were attained in the corresponding fixture in 1992, just missing out on the distinction of two centuries in one first-class game. He works as a primary school teacher at George Watson's College in Edinburgh. He's another Grange Club player who will be in familiar surroundings in the dressing room when Scotland play Bangladesh and New Zealand at home.

SHERIDAN, Keith   LHB/SLA
Born: 26 March 1971, Bellshill, Glasgow   *Poloc*

Sheridan was one of Scotland's youngest ever caps when he played his first match for his country in 1989 (against MCC) after having been the prodigy of the previous national coach Omar Henry. He has now gained over 50 caps, with a best bowling performance of five for 48 against Transvaal University during the national side's tour of Johannesburg in 1992. An opening bat in club cricket, he is more usually asked to bring up the tail for the national side thereby accounting for a top score of only 16. A civil engineer by profession.

SMITH, Mike   RHB/RM
Born: 30 March 1966, Edinburgh   *Aberdeenshire*

A cultured early order bat, Smith made his debut for Scotland in 1987, scoring 79 in his first innings against Ireland. However, he fell out of favour with the selectors in 1990 and did not regain his place in the national side until 1994. He now has a totalled more than 50 caps with a top score of 100 not out against MCC at Lord's in 1994. An entertaining stroke player he has also bowled in several games for Scotland although with less frequency in recent seasons. He has played a fair amount of senior rugby in Scotland. He resigned from his job as a sales representative in order to play cricket during the northern hemisphere winter months in Australia so that he could make a big impact on the ICC Trophy competition.

STANGER, Ian Michael RHB/RFM

Born: 5 October 1971, Glasgow *Clydesdale*

Another Scotsman with some first class experience, with Leicestershire, and who can bat and bowl a bit. In last year's Nat West Trophy he scored 67 runs in two steady innings and bowled 14.2 overs at just 4.32 per over.

TENNANT, Andy LHB/SLC

Born: 17 February 1966, Ayr *Prestwick*

After many years as a successful bowler with his club side, Andy Tennant made the breakthrough to the national side in 1994 when he appeared against both Denmark and Netherlands during the Triangular Tournament in Holland. He bowled exceptionally well last year at Headingley, recording figures of 10-1-29-2 against Yorkshire in the Benson & Hedges Trophy but his best figures are three for 28 against Ireland (also in 1996). He also had a five wicket haul while opening the bowling in a non-capped game against Ireland.

THOMSON, Kevin RHB/RMF

Born: 24 December 1971, Dundee *Aberdeenshire*

A strong right arm opening bowler, Thomas first appeared for Scotland in 1992, having previously played at Under-15, Under-16, Under-19 and 'B' XI levels. He now has a total of 39 caps, a total that would have undoubtedly been higher but for injury. His best bowling figures are three for 24 against Wales in 1995. He had several trial matches with Durham County. He is, by trade, a plumber.

WILLIAMSON, Greig RHB/RM

Born: 20 December 1968, Glasgow *Clydesdale*

A seam bowler, a stylish and aggressive batsman and brilliant fielder, Williamson won his first cap in 1989 but then fell out of the international scene until 1993. He re-established himself as a regular player thereafter. He was a particularly key member of the side during 1996, when he was one of Scottish Cricket's 'Players of the Year'. He has now gained 61 caps for Scotland with the highlight undoubtedly being his match against West Indies in 1995. He scored a splendid aggressive 57 after taking three wickets for 68 runs. His best bowling figures are four for 19 against the Earl of Arundel's XI in 1996. He is both a qualified accountant and lawyer and now works as a solicitor in Glasgow.

WRIGHT, Craig McIntyre   **RHB/RM**
Born: 28 April 1974, Paisley   *West of Scotland*
Another player with Benson & Hedges and Nat West experience in
1998, Wright bowled 26.5 overs in four B&H matches at 4.84 per over,
grabbing five wickets and a best performance of 2-37. His 20 overs in
two Nat West games were bowled at a grudging 2.45 runs per over and
Wright excelled with one set of figures of 5-23.

SOUTH AFRICA

Camp Woolmer Could Pay Dividends

Under Bob Woolmer's tutelage, South Africa have enjoyed a period of success and the recent one day clobbering of West Indies will have given them any confidence back, if it needed a boost after a less than convincing tour of England in the summer of 1998. Allan Donald is without peer among current fast bowlers while his new ball partner, Shaun Pollock, looks to have regained the sharpness that was missing on South Africa's tour of England. Kallis has emerged as a second formidable all-rounder.

Woolmer, with assistance from Eddie Barlow at a camp in Bloemfontein, has been working on the team's objectives and attitudes in the middle and this professional attitude is paying off. Consistent team selection, a formidable batting line-up and experience amongst the players of the English conditions should make South Africa strong World Cup favourites. Taking this all into account the players probably have the temperament to turn their form into an appearance in the final at the very least.

Team strip: Green and gold, inspired by the colours and shapes featured in the national flag of South Africa.

World Cup Record

	First Year	P	W	L	NR	SR%
Australia	1991-92	1	1	–	–	100.00
England	1991-92	3	1	2	–	33.33
Holland	1991-92	1	1	–	–	100.00
India	1991-92	1	1	–	–	100.00
New Zealand...	1991-92	2	1	1	–	50.00
Pakistan	1991-92	2	2	–	–	100.00
Sri Lanka	1991-92	1	–	1	–	–
UAE	1991-92	1	1	–	–	100.00
West Indies	1991-92	2	1	1	–	50.00
Zimbabwe	1991-92	1	1	–	–	100.00
Grand Total		*15*	*10*	*5*	*–*	*66.66*

Campaign Performances

Year	Pos	Captain	Result
1991-92	SF	KC Wessels	Lost to England by 19 runs
1995-96	QF	WJ Cronje	Lost to West Indies by 19 runs

One-Day Records

	Period	P	W	L	NR	T	SR%
All-Time:	…… …91-92 to 98-99	157	98	56	0	3	63.63
Since Last WC:	………………	69	54	14	0	1	79.41

Highest Innings Totals:

Runs	Overs	R/O	Opponents	Venue	Year
328-3	50 overs	6.56	Holland	Rawalpindi	1995-96
321-2	50 overs	6.42	UAE	Rawalpindi	1995-96

Lowest Completed Innings:

Runs	Overs	R/O	Opponents	Venue	Year
195	50 overs	3.90	Sri Lanka	Wellington	1991-92
190-7	50 overs	3.80	New Zealand	Auckland	1991-92

World Cup Individual Records

100 Pluses

Runs	bp	Player	Opponents	Venue	Year
188no	2	G Kirsten	UAE	Rawalpindi	1995-96
161	2	AC Hudson	Holland	Rawalpindi	1995-96

Partnership Record for each Wicket

	Total	Partnership	Opponents	Year
1st	186	G Kirsten (83), AC Hudson (161)	Holland	1995-96
2nd	116	G Kirsten (*188), WJ Cronje (57)	UAE	1995-96
3rd	*145	G Kirsten (*188), DJ Cullinan (*41)	UAE	1995-96
4th	79	PN Kirsten (90), DJ Richardson (28)	N.Zealand	1991-92
5th	78	DJ Cullinan (65), WJ Cronje (*45)	Pakistan	1995-96
6th	71	WJ Cronje (*47), BM McMillan (33)	Pakistan	1991-92
7th	41	PN Kirsten (90), BM McMillan (*33)	N.Zealand	1991-92
8th	29	DJ Cullinan (69), PL Symcox (24)	West Indies	1995-96
9th	21	BM McMillan (*18), O Henry (11)	Sri Lanka	1991-92
10th	17	CR Matthews (*8), PR Adams (10)	West Indies	1995-96

Four Wicket Hauls

Score	Arm	Player	Opponents	Venue	Year
4-11	RFM	MW Pringle	West Indies	Christchurch	1991-92

Man of the Match Awards

10 Awards: AC Hudson (2), PN Kirsten (2), WJ Cronje (2); KC Wessels (1), MW Pringle (1), G Kirsten (1), JN Rhodes (1).

World Cup Player Performances

Batting

Player	First Yr	P	I	no	Runs	HS	Ave	100	50	CS
PR Adams	95-96	2	1	–	10	10	10.00	–	–	–
T Bosch	91-92	1	–	–	–	–	–	–	–	–
WJ Cronje	91-92	14	12	4	378	78	47.25	–	2	6
DJ Cullinan	95-96	6	6	2	255	69	63.75	–	2	3
PS deVilliers	95-96	1	1	–	12	12	12.00	–	–	–
AA Donald	91-92	13	1	–	3	3	3.00	–	–	1
O Henry	91-92	1	1	–	11	11	11.00	–	–	–
AC Hudson	91-92	12	12	–	571	166	47.58	1	4	2
JH Kallis	95-96	5	4	2	63	26	31.50	–	–	1
G Kirsten	95-96	6	6	1	391	*188	78.20	1	1	2
PN Kirsten	91-92	8	8	2	410	90	68.33	–	4	2
AP Kuiper	91-92	9	8	1	113	36	16.14	–	–	3
CR Matthews	95-96	6	2	2	17	*9	–	–	–	1
BM McMillan	91-92	15	9	4	145	*33	29.00	–	–	8
SJ Palframan	95-96	6	3	–	45	28	15.00	–	–	8
SM Pollock	95-96	6	3	1	38	*20	19.00	–	–	2
MW Pringle	91-92	7	1	1	5	*5	–	–	–	1
JN Rhodes	91-92	13	11	1	191	43	19.10	–	–	5
DJ Richardson	91-92	9	5	2	66	28	22.00	–	–	14/1
MW Rushmere	91-92	3	3	–	49	35	16.33	–	–	1
RP Snell	91-92	9	4	2	24	*11	12.00	–	–	1
PL Symcox	95-96	4	2	–	25	24	12.50	–	–	–
KC Wessels	91-92	9	9	2	313	85	44.71	–	3	7

Bowling

Player	Overs	M	Runs	Wi	Ave	BP	4wi	R/O
PR Adams	18	0	87	3	29.00	2-45	–	4.83
T Bosch	2.3	0	19	0	–	–	–	7.60
WJ Cronje	42	2	172	4	43.00	2-17	–	4.09
DJ Cullinan	2	0	7	0	–	–	–	3.50
PS de Villiers	7	1	27	2	13.50	2-27	–	3.85
AA Donald	112	5	455	21	21.66	3-21	–	4.06
O Henry	10	0	31	1	31.00	1-31	–	3.10
JH Kallis	13	0	57	0	–	–	–	4.38
G Kirsten	3	1	9	0	–	–	–	3.00
PN Kirsten	18	1	87	5	17.40	3-31	–	4.83
AP Kuiper	41	0	235	9	26.11	3-40	–	5.73
CR Matthews	59.3	2	226	7	32.28	2-30	–	3.80
BM McMillan	116	12	433	17	25.47	3-11	–	3.73
SM Pollock	53	4	219	6	36.50	2-16	–	4.13
MW Pringle	57	6	236	8	29.50	4-11	1	4.14
PR Snell	72.5	10	310	8	38.75	3-42	–	4.25
PL Symcox	40	2	149	6	24.83	2-22	–	3.72

BACHER, Adam Marc   RHB/RM
Born: 29 October 1973, Johannesburg   *Gauteng*

A right-handed batsman with little experience behind him, Bacher has developed into a superb attacking opening batsman, especially in limited overs matches. His made his one day debut against India at Port Elizabeth in 1996-97. He started the 1998 Standard Bank limited overs programme with two fine centuries and more than 400 runs in seven innings. This included a top score of 140 against North West at Fochville. Bacher toured Sri Lanka with the South African Under-24 side in 1995. He was selected for the South African 'A' team to play Zimbabwe and in the same season he played against the visiting England team, scoring 116 runs in the four day match in Kimberley. He averages in the 20s for international one day games but averaged over 40 in the South African Super Sports series in 1998.

BENKENSTEIN, Dale Martin   RHB/ROB/RM
Born: 9 June 1974, Salisbury, Rhodesia   *Natal*

One of South Africa's new boys, Benkenstein made his one day international debut against England at Dhaka in the Wills International Cup. Against West Indies in the winter he showed what he is capable of, with a crucial 69 in the fifth game in the series. He has played for Natal since the 1993-94 season and is a member of a cricketing family with a father and two brothers involved in top class cricket. He is relatively inexperienced but has found his feet quickly. To his advantage in the World Cup, he knows English conditions from a period playing in the Lancashire League.

BOJE, Nico   LHB/LS
Born: 20 March 1973, Bloemfontein   *Free State*

Nicky Boje is a tidy left-arm slow bowler and capable left-handed batsman, having recently established himself following good performances in a couple of one day series at home. He doesn't normally get many wickets but is economical and he recently bamboozled the West Indies tailenders. His batting holds together the lower order nicely. He first came on the South Africa 'A' tour of Zimbabwe at the start of the 1994-95 season, during which he made his maiden first-class century. He toured Zimbabwe with the full national team in 1995-96, playing in one limited overs international. He gained a second cap during England's tour of South Africa in the same season. Boje, who captained South Africa schools in 1991, continued to make good progress on the 'A' tour of England in 1996 and was rewarded with a place in the senior squad which played in a limited overs tournament in Kenya at the start of the 1996-97 season.

BOUCHER, Mark Verdon   RHB/WK

Born: 3 December 1976, East London   *Border*

Boucher debuted against New Zealand at Perth in the 1997-98 series but he has yet to put together a big one day innings. The time is coming though and he struck the first Test century of his career to rescue South Africa on the opening day of the fifth and final Test against West Indies. Boucher, who before this match had gone 17 Test innings without a half-century and had scored just 68 runs in the series, faced 183 balls and hit 16 fours. A fine keeper, Boucher gets plenty of catching practice working with Donald and Pollock. His batting can't be relied upon but he is capable of getting his team out of a scrape.

CRONJE, Wessel Johannes   RHB/RM

Born: 25 September 1969, Bloemfontein   *Leicestershire, Free State*

Hansie Cronje is an outstanding cricketer in all respects. Leading from the front, Cronje's athletic frame houses an astute cricketing brain. The captain and his coach make detailed studies of their opposition, especially batsmen, and Cronje sets fields to work them out. He remains phlegmatic when events take a turn for the worse so don't ever assume South Africa are down and out.

An outstanding young leader, Cronje captained Free State at the age of 21 and first led his country at 24 when he deputised for the injured Kepler Wessels in Australia. He was 25 when he was officially appointed captain against New Zealand in 1994-95. He turned back to back losses into five successive Test victories, a record for a South African. The victory over the West Indies in the fifth game of the series was Cronje's 76th in 100 limited overs internationals as captain. He is the sixth player in one day international cricket to have led his country 100 times but none of the others has achieved a comparable success rate.

A member of a cricketing family with father and brother involved at the top level, Cronje made his international one day debut against Australia at Sydney in the 1992 World Cup. In one-day cricket he allows his attacking instincts full rein. He had a particularly prolific sequence against Australia in South Africa in 1993-94, making 12, 97, 45 and 50 not out in successive one day internationals, 44 and a career best 251 for Free State against the tourists and 21 and 122 in the first Test match. A total of 742 runs at an average of 106 in 17 days. Today he averages in the high 30s with the bat and bowls more than you might imagine in one day games and is pretty economical, with a best performance of 5 for 32.

CULLINAN, Daryll John   RHB/ROB
Born: 4 March 1967, Kimberley   *Derbyshire, Gauteng*

Cullinan began his career with Border in 1983-84 and scored a first-class century at the age of 16 to supplant Graeme Pollock as the youngest South African player to achieve this mark. In the third game of the winter's South Africa v West Indies series, he became only the second one day batsman to be given out hand ball. Cullinan emulated India's Mohinder Amarnath when he cut at Keith Arthurton and then caught the ball as it headed towards his stumps. After earning his spurs, he has established himself as a fixture in the South African Test team at number four. With an excellent technique, he has shown an ability to handle both fast and spin bowling. He made his one day international debut against Pakistan at Durban back in 1992-93. On the tour of Sri Lanka in 1993 he made his maiden Test century in the third Test but he lost his way through illness before recovering his place against England in 1994, making 94 and being the only South African to withstand the nine wicket onslaught of Devon Malcolm. Since then he has been a model of consistency at Test level and he averaged more than 50 against England during the 1995-96 series. He has played for Derbyshire so knows English conditions. His one day average is in the high 30s and he has just had an impressive domestic season.

DONALD, Allan Anthony   RHB/RF
Born: 20 October 1966, Bloemfontein   *Warwickshire, Free State*

Donald played with Warwickshire between 1987 and 1995 (where he will return after the World Cup), so knows English conditions and how to take advantage of them. He made an immediate impact on South Africa's return to international cricket in 1991-92, taking 5-29 against India in Calcutta, also the scene of his first one day international. After taking a career best 8-71 against Zimbabwe, he won one of a number of man of the series awards for his efforts against England in 1995-96. He keeps batsmen down to around four an over. He has the skill, aggression and speed to make important breakthroughs and, with his natural action, can bring the ball into the right-hander as well as moving the ball away late. He has an alarming bouncer but in England he will know to concentrate on bowling a good line and length. He is a good fielder with a strong arm but has not improved his adequate batting. He is a little more injury prone these days, which could hurt his and South Africa's chance of grabbing the one day cricket crown.

ELWORTHY, Steven   RHB/RFM
Born: 23 February 1965, Bulawayo   *Northern Transvaal*
One of South Africa's new pace bowler finds, Elworthy debuted against Pakistan at Durban in the 1997/98 series. He has a good strike rate but isn't the most economic of the bowlers. His batting has yet to be tested at international level but, like many of the South African bottom order, he's capable of hanging around for a few runs. Known as 'Shots' to his Northerns and Test team-mates, Elworthy took over the role of South Africa's main strike bowler for the ICC knock-out event in Dhaka, Bangladesh when Pollock was out injured. He was player of the year in the first two consecutive seasons of the limited overs Standard Bank series in South Africa.

GIBBS, Herschelle Herman   RHB/RMF, LB
Born: 23 February 1974, Green Point, Cape Province   *Western Province*
This right-handed opener/middle order batsman has been playing for the senior Western Province team since he made his debut, at the age of 16, in 1990-91. This attacking stroke-player has the ability to play all the text-book shots (the straight drive being particularly impressive) but has in the past suffered from impatience early on in his innings. Gibbs has managed to lift his fielding to a level of excellence to the degree that he equals Jonty Rhodes in the point position in all aspects but crowd support and reputation. He made his one day debut against Kenya at Nairobi in 1996-97 and he now has 22 innings and over 400 runs under his belt.

HALL, Andrew James   RHB/RFM
Born: 31 July 1975, Johannesburg   *Gauteng*
A one day international novice, Hall made his debut this winter in the third one day clash with the West Indies at Durban. It's difficult to judge on these performances in a winning side but in domestic one day

cricket he has proved an effective bowler and a moderately successful batsman.

KALLIS, Jacques Henry   RHB/RM
Born: 16 October 1975, Pinelands, Cape Town   Western Province
Kallis is an immensely talented top-order batsman, who showed promise from his high school days. Kallis stands tall and hits well through the line of the ball, while being very comfortable against pace bowling off either the front or back foot. Despite adjusting to provincial cricket smoothly, and playing a number of dominant innings for Western Province, Kallis has found the transition to Test cricket rather difficult. Making his debut against England in 1995-96, Kallis' introduction to Test cricket was harsh, dismissed by Peter Martin for just one run. However, in the one day international innings that he has played to date, he oozes class. His one day debut was as recent as against England at Cape Town during the 1995-96 tour. He has a tremendous first class average around the 50 mark and is up over 40 for his country in one day cricket. He gets a few wickets too with a best of 5-30 and giving away not much more than four an over. After the World Cup, Kallis goes to Glamorgan to play in English cricket for the first time.

KIRSTEN, Gary   RHB/ROB
Born: 23 November 1967, Cape Town   Western Province
Made his one day debut against Australia at Sydney in the 1993-94 series but, having been one of the senior players for some time, he has been out of form during the past year. Over 3,500 runs and an average of over 40 can't be overlooked however. If he does get back then Kirsten's traditional weapons of concentration, determination and technique will suit English conditions. Excellent reflexes, speed over the ground and a strong arm make Kirsten a valuable fielder.

KLUSENER, Lance   LHB/RFM
Born: 4 September 1971, Durban   Natal
Klusener's debut was against England at East London in the sixth of the one day games of the 1995/96 series and he featured in the latest games against West Indies. He claims that he wants to be entertaining and exciting to watch, which bodes well for crowds at this year's event. On an 'A' tour of England Klusener took 31 wickets, more than double the tally of any of his team-mates. He played in eight of the team's nine first-class matches, and averaged 34.2 with the bat to emphasise his

claim as a possible successor to McMillan as an all-rounder. He has now got over 1,000 runs under his belt at an average over 35 and including eight half centuries. His bowling isn't the most economical but a 6-49 best performance proves his match-winning capability. He proved himself with both bat and ball in the fifth game against West Indies when hitting 54 off 36 balls and taking two wickets.

MPITSANG, Victor   RHB/RFM
Born: 28 March 1980   *Free State*
New boy on the block and all-round athlete, Mpitsang was part of the Under-19 World Cup team and he also plays basketball for Free State. His one day international debut took place this winter against the West Indies at Bloemfontein in the sixth rubber when, after a nervous start, he took 2-49 in seven overs and batted for 1 not out. At 18 years and 314 days Mpitsang thus became the youngest player to represent South Africa in an international match.

POLLOCK, Shaun Maclean   RHB/RFM
Born: 16 July 1973, Port Elizabeth   *Natal*
The son of former Test pace man Peter and nephew of batting great Graeme, the young Pollock has embarked on what promises to be an illustrious international career. A loose-limbed fast bowler with an awkward bouncer, Pollock is always a threat. He has the ability to seam the ball and get bounce even on flat wickets. Pollock has a good slower ball and sometimes bowls a delivery that comes into the right-hander and then moves away off the pitch. He and Allan Donald have become one of the most formidable new ball attacks in the world. As well as taking wickets, he keeps the toll from his bowling down below four. As a batsman, he is aggressive, and averages in the 30s. Pollock is also a wonderful fielder, who has a beautifully strong and accurate throwing arm. Pollock played county cricket for Warwickshire in 1996 and confirmed the opinion of those who believe that he has the potential to become a top-quality all-rounder by making his first two first-class centuries. He had to cut his English season short to have an operation to remove a bone spur from his left ankle and was subsequently unfit for the tours to Kenya and India. He made his one day debut against England at Cape Town in the first match of the 1995-96 series.

RHODES, Jonathan Neil   RHB/RM
Born: 26 July 1969, Pietermaritzburg   *Natal*
Jonty Rhodes' exuberance and acrobatic fielding during the 1992
World Cup made him a South African hero. He remains a fielder of
extraordinary ability, commanding the field from his favourite
backward point position. Although fewer questions are now asked
about his batting ability, he is both able to produce a telling
performance at a crucial time and fail to establish a decent innings.
Like his captain, he first played in one day cricket for South Africa
against Australia at Sydney in the 1992 World Cup. In one day cricket
his fielding ability and improvisation with the bat keep him in a
winning team. He has scored over 3,000 runs in one day internationals
and averages over 30. Of many remarkable fielding exploits, his world
record of five catches against the West Indies in Bombay in 1993-94
remains a highlight, with each catch a feat of athleticism. If you get to a
game early you may enjoy the sight of Jonty practising his throws on
the run, hitting a single stump from all angles.

RINDEL, Michael John Raymond   LHB/RMF
Born: 9 February 1963, Durban   *Northern Transvaal*
Rindell made his one day international debut against New Zealand at
Cape Town, in the Mandela Trophy in 1994-95. He joined his
Northerns Titans team mate Steve Elworthy for the game against
England in Dhaka in autumn 1998 as a replacement for an injured Gary
Kirsten and played against the West Indies this winter. His 22 one day
internationals have yielded up over 500 runs at an average in the late
20s. He has also done a fair amount of bowling but without much
success.

SYMCOX, Patrick Leonard   RHB/ROB
Born: 14 April 1960, Kimberley   *Natal*
One of the remarkable success stories of South African cricket,
Symcox was not even a member of the Natal provincial squad in the
season before he made his international debut at the age of 33. His one
day debut was against Sri Lanka at Kandy in the first one day game of
1993-94 series. He is an economical off-spinner with over 70 wickets
and a best performance of 4-28. His height helps provide dangerous
bounce and turn. His batting is worth having at an average in the late
teens in over 50 innings and he looked good in his 1998 performances.
At the start of his career, Symcox was an opening batsman. He is a

fierce striker of the ball and in a successful experiment he was used as a top-order 'pinch-hitter' in Sharjah at the end of the 1995-96 season. Symcox has worked hard on his fitness and agility in order to keep up with his younger colleagues in the field.

TERBRUGGE, David John   RHB/RFM
Born: 31 January 1977, Ladysmith   *Gauteng*
Terbrugge has bowled very effectively in domestic cricket and a couple of Test matches, pinning down the opposition batsmen at times. His batting is untried but doesn't promise anything special.

WILLIAMS, Henry Smith   RHB/RFM
Born: 11 June 1967, Pniel, near Stellenbosch
Williams made his one day international debut against the West Indies at East London in the second round during the winter. Neither bowling nor batting have been anything to write home about but perhaps Woolmer and company think of him as a good squad player to have waiting in the wings.

SRI LANKA

Holders Almost Intact

Things didn't look good for the world one-day champions at the beginning of their tour to Australia, when they crashed to an eight-wicket defeat by Australia 'A' in Perth after being routed for only 89. Coming third to England and Australia in the triangular tournament confirmed that some of the sparkle was missing from Ranatunga's side. Watch out for off-spinner Muttiah Muralitharan, who destroyed England with a 16-wicket haul in a one-off test at The Oval last August. The Sri Lankan slow bowler has been controversially no-balled for throwing though his action has subsequently been cleared by the International Cricket Council (ICC). As defending world champions, Sri Lanka will play the opening game of the '99 World Cup at Lord's against England on May 14th. Sri Lanka's 30-man squad included all the players from the triumphant 1996 team apart from Asanka Gurusinghe but after Australia, the team line-up was in for a shake-up.

Team strip: Traditional blue colour and a bold, golden print of the nation's lion.

World Cup Record

	First Year	P	W	L	NR	SR%
Australia	1975	4	2	2	–	50.00
England	1983	6	1	5	–	16.66
India	1979	4	3	–	1	100.00
Kenya	1995-96	1	1	–	–	100.00
New Zealand	1979	4	1	3	–	25.00
Pakistan	1975	6	–	6	–	–
South Africa	1991-92	1	1	–	–	100.00
West Indies	1975	6	1	4	1	20.00
Zimbabwe	1991-92	2	2	–	–	100.00
Total		*34*	*12*	*20*	*2*	*37.50*

Campaign Performances

Year	Pos	Captain	Result
1975	Gp	APB Teenekoon	Failed to qualify for semi-finals
1979	Gp	B Warnapura	Failed to qualify for semi-finals
1983	Gp	LRD Mendis	Failed to qualify for semi-finals
1987-88	Gp	LRD Mendis	Failed to qualify for semi-finals
1991-92	Gp	PA deSilva	Failed to qualify for semi-finals
1995-96	F	A Ranatunga	Won – beat Australia by 7 wickets

One-Day Records

	Period	P	W	L	T	NR	SR%
All-Time:	… … … … … 75-98-99	297	114	169	1	13	40.14
Since Last WC:	… … … … … …	77	43	30	1	3	58.10

Highest Innings Totals:

Runs	Overs	R/O	Opponents	Venue	Year
398-5	50 overs	7.96	Kenya	Kandy	1995-96
313-7	49.2 overs	6.34	Zimbabwe	New Plymouth	1991-92
288-9	60 overs	4.80	Pakistan	Swansea	1983
286	58 overs	4.93	England	Taunton	1983

Lowest Completed Innings:

Runs	Overs	R/O	Opponents	Venue	Year
86	37.2 overs	2.30	West Indies	Manchester	1975
136	50.4 overs	2.67	England	Leeds	1983
138	50.1 overs	2.75	Pakistan	Nottingham	1975

World Cup Individual Records

100 Pluses

Runs	bp	Player	Opponents	Venue	Year
145	4	PA de Silva	Kenya	Kandy	1995-96
107no	4	PA de Silva	Australia	Lahore	1995-96

Partnership Record for each Wicket

	Total	Partnership	Opponents	Year
1st	128	RS Mahanama (59), MA Samarasekera (75)		
			Zimbabwe	1991-92
2nd	101	ST Jayasuriya (82), AP Gurusinha (45)		
			England	1995-96
3rd	183	AP Gurusinha (84), PA de Silva (145)		
			Kenya	1995-96
4th	*97	PA de Silva (*107), A Ranatunga (*47)		
			Australia	1995-96
5th	*131	A Ranatunga (*46), HP Tillekeratne (*70)		
			India	1995-96
6th	61	A Ranatunga (*88), HP Tillekeratne (18)		
			Zimbabwe	1991-92
7th	36	A Ranatunga (*88), RS Kalpage (11))		
			Zimbabwe	1991-92
8th	54	DS de Silva (35), RG deAlwis (*59)	Pakistan	1983
	54	DS de Silva (28), RG deAlwis (*58)	England	1983
9th	35	RG deAlwis (*58), ALF deMel (27)	England	1983
10th	33	RJ Ratnayake (*20), VB John (15)	England	1983

Four Wicket Hauls

Score	Arm	Player	Opponents	Venue	Year
5-32	RFM	ALF deMel	New Zealand	Derby	1983
5-39	RFM	ALF deMel	Pakistan	Leeds	1983
4-57	RM	UC Hathurusinghe			
			West Indies	Berri Oval	1991-92

Man of the Match Awards

Nine Awards: PA de Silva (4), ST Jayasuriya (2), LRD Mendis (1), ALF deMel (1), A Ranatunga (1).

Player of the Tournament Award

ST Jayasuriya (1) v India/Pakistan/Sri Lanka – 1995-96.

Batting

Player	First Yr	P	I	no	Runs	HS	Ave	100	50	CS
SD Anurasiri	87-88	11	5	2	21	11	7.00	–	–	3
HDP K Dharmasena	95-96	6	1	–	9	9	9.00	–	–	1
RG deAlwis	83	6	6	3	167	*59	55.66	–	2	5
ALF deMel	83	9	7	–	66	27	9.42	–	–	–
DLS deSilva	79	2	1	–	10	10	10.00	–	–	1
DS deSilva	75	11	10	1	148	35	16.44	–	–	2
GRA deSilva	75	2	2	1	2	*2	2.00	–	–	–
PA de Silva	87-88	20	19	3	724	145	45.25	2	3	7
RL Dias	79	10	10	1	310	80	34.44	–	3	5
ER Fernando	75	3	3	–	47	22	15.66	–	–	–
FRM Goonatillake	79	1	–	–	–	–	–	–	–	–
AP Gurusinha	87-88	18	17	–	488	87	28.70	–	3	3
UC Hathurusinghe	91-92	4	3	–	26	16	8.66	–	–	1
PD Heyn	75	2	2	–	3	2	1.50	–	–	1
SA Jayasinghe	79	2	1	–	1	1	1.00	–	–	1
ST Jayasuriya	91-92	12	11	–	295	82	26.81	–	2	9
S Jeganathan	87-88	3	3	1	24	*20	12.00	–	–	1
VB John	83	11	9	7	46	15	23.00	–	–	1
RS Kalpage	91-92	7	6	2	67	14	16.75	–	–	3
LWS Kaluperuma	75	3	2	2	19	*13	–	–	–	–
RS Kaluwitharana	95-96	6	6	–	73	33	12.16	–	–	2/3
DSBP Kuuruppu	83	11	11	–	251	72	22.81	–	2	4/1
GF Labrooy	91-92	1	1	–	19	19	19.00	–	–	–
RS Madugalle	79	11	10	–	193	60	19.30	–	1	4
RS Mahanama	87-88	20	19	3	460	89	28.75	–	5	5
LRD Mendis	75	16	16	2	412	64	29.42	–	3	2
M Muralitharan	95-96	6	1	1	5	*5	–	–	–	2
ARM Opatha	75	5	3	–	29	18	9.66	–	–	3
SP Pasqual	79	2	2	1	24	*23	–	–	–	–
HS M Pieris	75	3	3	1	19	16	9.50	–	–	–
KR Pushpakumara	95-96	2	–	–	–	–	–	–	–	–
CPH Ramanayake	91-92	8	6	2	25	12	6.25	–	–	4
AN Ranasinghe	75	3	3	1	23	*14	11.50	–	–	–
A Ranatunga	83	25	24	8	835	*88	52.18	–	6	6

Player	First Yr	P	I	no	Runs	HS	Ave	100	50	CS
RJ Ratnayake	83	9	8	2	81	*20	13.50	–	–	3
JR Ratnayeke	87-88	6	5	–	52	22	10.40	–	–	–
MAR Samarasekera	83	8	8	–	224	75	28.00	–	1	1
APB Tennekoon	75	4	4	–	137	59	34.25	–	1	3
HP Tillekeratne	91-92	14	12	4	207	*70	25.87	–	1	6/1
MH Tissera	75	3	3	–	78	52	26.00	–	1	–
WPUJC Vaas	95-96	6	1	–	23	23	23.00	–	–	–
B Warnapura	75	5	5	–	79	31	15.80	–	–	3
S Wettimuny	83	6	6	–	128	50	21.33	–	1	–
SR de S Wettimuny	75	3	3	1	136	67	68.00	–	2	–
GP Wickremasinghe										
	91-92	12	4	4	34	*21	–	–	–	2
KIW Wijegunawardene										
	91-92	3	–	–	–	–	–	–	–	–

Bowling

Player	Overs	M	Runs	Wi	Ave	BP	4wi	R/O
SD Anurasiri	105	4	455	9	50.55	3-41	–	4.33
HDPK Dharmasena	56	1	250	6	41.66	2-30	–	4.46
ALF deMel	90.2	13	449	18	24.94	5-32	2	4.97
DLD deSilva	20	2	54	2	27.00	2-36	–	2.70
DS deSilva	110	12	463	10	46.30	3-29	–	4.20
GRA deSilva	19	2	85	1	85.00	1-39	–	4.47
PA de Silva	60	0	310	7	44.28	3-42	–	5.16
FRM Goonatillake	9	1	34	0	–	–	–	3.77
AP Gurusinha	53	0	307	7	43.85	2-67	–	5.79
UC Hathurusinghe	17	0	97	5	19.40	4-57	1	5.70
ST Jayasuriya	57	1	275	7	39.28	3-12	–	4.82
S Jeganathan	29	2	123	4	30.75	2-45	–	4.24
VB John	99.2	10	477	4	119.25	1-49	–	4.80
RS Kalpage	50	0	241	4	60.25	2-33	–	4.82
LWS Kaluperuma	27.4	2	102	1	102.00	1-50	–	3.68
GF Labrooy	10	1	68	1	68.00	1-68	–	6.80
M Muralitharan	57.1	3	216	7	30.85	2-37	–	3.77
ARM Opatha	42.1	1	180	5	36.00	3-31	–	4.26
SP Pasqual	4.4	0	20	0	–	–	–	4.28
HSM Pieris	22	0	135	2	67.50	2-68	–	6.13
KR Pushpakumara	15	0	99	1	99.00	1-53	–	6.60
CPH Ramanayake	64.4	6	265	5	53.00	2-37	–	4.09

Player	Overs	M	Runs	Wi	Ave	BP	4wi	R/O
AN Ranasinghe	10	0	65	0	–	–	–	6.50
A Ranatunga	81.1	2	460	6	76.66	2-26	–	5.66
RJ Ratnayake	89	6	437	12	36.41	2-18	–	4.91
JR Ratnayeke	54	2	313	10	31.30	3-41	–	5.79
MAR Samarasekera	16.2	2	71	0	–	–	–	4.34
HP Tillekeratne	1	0	4	0	–	–	–	4.00
WPUJC Vaas	49	6	193	6	32.16	2-30	–	3.93
B Warnapura	36	0	159	4	39.75	3-42	–	4.41
S Wettimuny	3	0	15	0	–	–	–	5.00
GP Wickremasinghe								
	87.1	5	417	7	59.57	2-29	–	4.78
KIW Wijegunawardene								
	17	1	88	0	–	–	–	5.17

Player Profiles

ATAPATTU, Marvan Samson RHB/ROB
Born: 22 November 1970, Kalutara   *Sinhalese Sports Club*
Marvan Atapattu made his one day debut against India at Nagpur in
1990-91 and his career has been spent playing one day games rather
than Tests. His 66 games have brought nearly 2,000 runs at an average
of 34.59. An exceptional high score of 132 not out (against England in
the Emirates Triangular Final at Lord's in 1998) and 14 one day 50s
shows the strength of the Sri Lankan batting line-up.

CHANDANA, Umagiliya Durage Upul RHB/LB
Born: 5 July 1972, Galle   *Tamil Union Cricket and Athletic Club*
Upul Chandana is one of the successful group of players who won the
1996 World Cup and is purely a one day international. He brings both
steady leg-spin and steady late/middle order batting to the side. Since
his debut against Australia at Sharjah in the 1993-94 Australasia Cup,
he has bowled 290 overs at an economy rate of 4.85 per over, with a
best performance of 4-31. His batting is useful but not match winning
with a best performance of 50 and an average of 16. He is a fringe
player these days but has the advantage of experience of the big day.

DE SILVA, Pinnaduwage Aravinda   RHB/ROB

Born: 17 October 1965, Colombo   Nondescripts Cricket Club

A powerful striker of the ball, Aravinda's masterful display with the bat was the highlight of Sri Lanka's grand success in the 1995-96 World Cup. His 107 not out in the final against Australia at Lahore was a masterpiece of an innings that could not have arrived at a better time. Earlier in the tournament he had plundered 145 against Kenya at Kandy, which remains his best effort with the bat in the limited overs internationals. Predominately a leg-side player in the early part of his career, his repetoire of strokes has flourished over the years. His pull stokes off good length balls are a treat to watch and often prove demoralising for his opponents. Played only a couple of matches in the recently concluded World Series Cricket in Australia due to an injury. His full fitness will enhance his nation's chances of retaining the title. Useful off break bowler who comes on to break partnerships.

DHARMASENA,
Handunettige Deepthi Priyantha Kumara   RHB/ROB

Born: 24 April 1971, Colombo   Tamil Union

Dharmasena's medium-paced off-breaks suited well in the sub-continent conditions for him to play a vital role in the success of the Sri Lankans in the last World Cup. He keeps a good length without without quite getting into the miser category. Useful tail-end batsman.

JAYASURIYA, Sanath Teran   LHB/SL

Born: 30 June 1969, Matara

Has turned the role of pinch-hitting opener into an art form in the last three years of devastating batting displays in every part of the world. For a strong bottom-hand player, he displays an amazing array of stright driven lofted boundaries from the very word go. The first five years of Jayasuriya's career were spent in the lower middle order with a regular spell with the ball. The transformation in his career took place in the one-day tournaments prior to the last World Cup, in which his opening partnership with wicket-keeper Kaluwitharana was formed.

JAYAWARDENE,
Denagamage Proboth Mahela de Silva   **RHB/RM**
Born: 27 May 1977, Colombo   *Sinhalese Sports Club*
Jayawardene debuted against Zimbabwe at Colombo (RPS) in 1997-98 and he was part of the squad in Australia this winter. A promising high score of 120 is not supported by an average of 22.78. He can also turn over his arm but once again it's early days and this World Cup may have come to soon for this all-rounder.

KALPAGE, Ruwan Senani   **LHB/ROB**
Born: 19 February 1970, Kandy   *Nondescripts Cricket Club*
Ruwan Kalpage is an experienced all-rounder with 65 innings behind him with an average of 21 and a healthy 27 not out performances. His 626 overs have brought a harvest of 71 wickets at an excellent economy rate of 4.44. He debuted against Pakistan at Sargodha in 1991-92 and his best bowling performance is 4-36.

KALUWITHARANA, Romesh Shantha   **RHB/WK**
Born: 24 November 1969, Colombo
Despite a period in and out of the side, Kaluwitharana is a stalwart of the World Cup winning team. Kaluwitharana debuted against India at Margao in 1990-91 and he has since played 112 matches. His wicket-keeping has featured in key moments in Sri Lanka's success, most notably when he stumped Tendulkar in the 1996 semi-final against India. A fair average of 18.92 has been maintained and a more significant figure is perhaps the 12 50s which he has scored in amongst his 1,930 overall total. His exuberant, dashing style has won the hearts of many a fan.

MAHANAMA, Roshan Siriwardene   **RHB**
Born: 31 May 1966, Colombo   *Colombo Cricket Club*
Roshan Mahanama made his one day debut against Pakistan at Kandy in 1985-86 and he's been a regular ever since. In 193 innings he has managed to hold down an average of 29.36 with a 119 not out high contributing to a total of over 5,000 runs. One of the Sri Lankan batters who secured the World Cup, the jury is out on whether this group of players has had their day, or not. Originally an opening batsman, he now bats down the order, driving magically off the front foot and with a scintillating cover drive. He brings the same level of natural talent to his fielding.

MURALITHARAN, Muttiah   RHB/LOB

Born: 17 April 1972, Kandy   Tamil Union Cricket and Athletic Club
A prodigious spinner of the ball and an exciting fielder to watch, Muralitharan debuted back in 1993-94 against India at Colombo (RPS). He has bowled almost 1,000 overs in his international career and taken 151 wickets, with a best of 5-23. With a decent economy rate of 4.23, he is undoubtedly in the top bracket of spinners. Unfortunately Muralitharan is going to have to work hard if he wants to be remembered for his exploits rather than just the controversy over his bowling action. Let's hope the silliness of the winter Triangular tournament is left behind and the public get to see this spinner at his best. One thing is for sure: no-one is going to be talking about his batting average of 5.8.

PERERA, Anhettige Suresh Asanka   RHB/RM

Born: 16 February 1978, Colombo   Sinhalese Sports Club
Perera debuted against India at Colombo (RPS) in the Singer-Akai Nidahas Trophy in 1997-98 and he was seen at Lord's in the Emirates Triangular Tournament in 1998. His six matches have brought eight wickets and a best of 2-25. His economy rate is over five at the moment but he remains an excellent prospect. His batting is untried as yet.

PUSHPAKUMARA,
Karuppiahyage Ravindra   RHB/RFM

Born: 21 July 1975, Panadura
Pushpakumara made his debut against India at Hyderabad (Deccan) in 1993-94 and his bowling has resulted in the taking of 24 wickets at an economy rate of just over five per over. He is probably the fastest bowler in the Sri Lankan side and he can move the ball both ways through the air. A best performance of 3-25 is the sort of strike bowling his captain needs from him on a more regular basis and as he learns extra control, Pushpakumara is likely to deliver. His batting is ordinary low order with a best of 14 not out.

RANATUNGA, Arjuna   LHB/RM

Born: 1 December 1963, Colombo   Sinhalese Sports Club
Ranatunga's name is synonymous with the recent Sri Lankan success. Once again this stockily built left-hand batsman will be the cornerstone of any success Sri Lanka are to have, both as captain, most experienced player, and as the mainstay of the middle order. He uses deft placement

on both sides of the wicket, combined with fluent driving through the offside in particular, to earn his runs. He has put together over 7,000 runs at a consistent average of 36.42 with an outstanding top score of 131 not out. He is also a deceptive and useful medium pace bowler with an economy rate of 4.78 per over and 79 wickets and a best of 4-14. His debut was against England at Colombo (SSC) almost in another era of cricket, back in 1981-82.

TILLAKARATNE, Hashan Prasantha   LHB/RM
Born: 14 July 1967, Colombo   *Nondescripts Cricket Club*
Tillakaratne made his one day debut against India at Sharjah in the 1986-87 Champions Trophy. He is an extremely stylish batsman and he is capable of stepping up the run rate extremely well and has been involved in some of the most thrilling chases in the limited overs matches. He is also an extremely agile close in fielder. He, in fact, started off his career as a wicket-keeper. His average of 29.23 typifies the strength of batting in the Sri Lankan side. The thirty overs in his career have resulted in six wickets but it's not part of the game he has developed.

VAAS, Warnakulasuriya Patabendige
Ushantha Joseph Chaminda   LHB/LFM
Born: 27 January 1974, Colombo   *Colts Cricket Club*
Chaminda Vaas' incisive left arm pace bowling brought extra bite to Sri Lanka's attack and he became the first Sri Lankan to take 10 wickets in a Test match. Vaas made his debut against India at Rajkot in 1993-94 and he has now bowled over 800 overs and taken 132 wickets, one batsman down every 27 runs. His best performance is 4-20 and his economy is very good at 4.17 per over conceded to the batting side. His batting record includes a top score of 33 and average of 12.97.

WICKREMASINGHE,
Gallage Pramodya   RHB/RFM
Born: 14 August 1971, Matara   *Sinhalese Sports Club*
Pramodya Wickremasinghe has been a mainstay in the Sri Lankan attack for many years now. Although not as pacy as either Vaas or Pushpakumara, he lends the attack a blend of experience and control and he has retained a clinical accuracy. Since his debut against Bangladesh at Calcutta in the 1990-91 Asia Cup he has taken 79

wickets and kept the batsmen down to 4.48 runs per over. His best performance is 3-20. Hs batting can't be relied on and his average is only 7.8, with a best of 21 not out.

WEST INDIES

Good Days Gone?

West Indies, who began the year brightly enough with a 3-1 Test series win at home over England, have relied too much and too long on its superb but ageing strike pair of Curtly Ambrose and Courtney Walsh. With its batting failing miserably in the South African Tests and one day games, even its fast bowlers have been unable to save it from humiliating defeats. The West Indies holds the record for the most consecutive wins in the World Cup finals with nine between 7th June 1975 and 23rd June 1979. Even if Lara returns to form, it's unlikely that this current side can come close to emulating the performances of previous teams. They will need to show some form though if they are going to oust one of Australia, New Zealand and Pakistan from Group B to make it to the Super Six stage.

Team strip: Palm and sun design from the West Indies cricket logo, coupled with traditional burgundy and silver grey.

World Cup Record

	First Year	P	W	L	NR	SR%
Australia … … … … … …	1975	7	5	2	–	71.42
England … … … … … …	1979	4	1	3	–	25.00
India … … … … … … …	1979	6	3	3	–	50.00
Kenya … … … … … …	1995-96	1	–	1	–	–
New Zealand … … … … …	1975	3	2	1	–	66.66
Pakistan … … … … … …	1975	6	5	1	–	83.33
South Africa … … … …	1991-92	2	1	1	–	50.00
Sri Lanka … … … … …	1975	6	4	1	1	80.00
Zimbabwe … … … … …	1983	4	4	–	–	100.00
Total … … … … … … … …		*39*	*25*	*13*	*1*	*65.78*

Campaign Performances

Year	Pos	Captain	Result
1975	F	CH Lloyd	Won – beat Australia by 17 runs
1979	F	CH Lloyd	Won – beat England by 92 runs

1983	F	CH Lloyd	Lost to India by 43 runs
1987-88	Gp	IVA Richards	Failed to qualify for semi finals
1991-92	Gp	RB Richardson	Failed to qualify for semi finals
1995-96	SF	RB Richardson	Lost to Australia by 5 runs

One-Day Records

	Period	P	W	L	T	NR	SR%
All-Time:	… … … 73 to 98-99	356	220	126	4	6	62.85
Since Last WC:	… … … … …	39	19	20	0	0	48.71

Highest Innings Totals:
Runs	Overs	R/O	Opponents	Venue	Year
360-4	50 overs	7.20	Sri Lanka	Karachi	1987-88
293-6	60 overs	4.88	Pakistan	The Oval	1979
291-8	60 overs	4.85	Australia	Lord's	1975
286-9	60 overs	4.76	England	Lord's	1979
282-9	60 overs	4.70	India	The Oval	1983

Lowest Completed Innings:
Runs	Overs	R/O	Opponents	Venue	Year
93	35.2 overs	2.63	Kenya	Pune	1995-96
136	38.4 overs	3.51	South Africa	Christchurch	1991-92
140	52 overs	2.69	India	Lord's	1983

World Cup Individual Records

100 Pluses
Runs	bp	Player	Opponents	Venue	Year
181	4	IVA Richards	Sri Lanka	Karachi	1987-88
138no	3	IVA Richards	England	Lord's	1979
119	3	IVA Richards	India	The Oval	1983
111	3	BC Lara	South Africa	Karachi	1995-96
110	3	RB Richardson	Pakistan	Karachi	1987-88
110	3	PV Simmons	Sri Lanka	Berri Oval	1991-92
106no	1	CG Greenidge	India	Birmingham	1979
105no	1	CG Greenidge	Zimbabwe	Worcester	1983
105	1	DL Haynes	Sri Lanka	Karachi	1987-88
102	5	CH Lloyd	Australia	Lord's	1975

Partnership Record for each Wicket

	Total	Partnership	Opponents	Year
1st	*175	DL Haynes (*93), BC Lara (88no)	Pakistan	1991-92
2nd	138	S Chanderpaul (56), BC Lara (111)	South Africa	1995-96
3rd	*195	CG Greenidge (*105), HA Gomes (*75)	Zimbabwe	1983
4th	149	RB Kanhai (55), CH Lloyd (102)	Australia	1975
5th	139	VA Richards (*138), CL King (86)	England	1979
6th	*83	KL Arthurton (*58), CL Hooper (*34)	India	1991-92
7th	52	CH Lloyd (102), BD Julien (*26)	Australia	1975
8th	*40	CH Lloyd (*73), J Garner (*9)	New Zealand	1979
9th	41	SFA Bacchus (47), WW Daniel (*16)	Australia	1983
10th	71	AME Roberts (*37), J Garner (37)	India	1983

Four Wicket Hauls

Score	Arm	Player	Opponents	Venue	Year
7-51	RFM	WW Davis	Australia	Leeds	1983
5-38	RFM	J Garner	England	Lord's	1979
4-20	LFM	BD Julien	Sri Lanka	Manchester	1975
4-27	LFM	BD Julien	New Zealand	The Oval	1975
4-33	RF	MA Holding	India	Birmingham	1979
4-33	RFM	AC Cummins	India	Wellington	1991-92
4-40	RF	CA Walsh	Pakistan	Lahore	1987-88
4-47	OB	RA Harper	South Africa	Karachi	1995-96
4-50	RFM	KD Boyce	Australia	Lord's	1975

Man of the Match Awards

24 Awards: IVA Richards (5), CG Greenidge (3), BC Lara (3), AI Kallicharran (2), CH Lloyd (2), PV Simmons (2), RB Richardson (2), BD Julien (1), WW Davis (1), SFA Bacchus (1), AC Cummins (1), CEL Ambrose (1).

Batting

Player	First Yr	P	I	no	Runs	HS	Ave	100	50	CS
JC Adams	95-96	4	4	2	41	*17	20.50	–	–	6/1
CEL Ambrose	91-92	13	8	2	46	*15	7.66	–	–	1
KLT Arthurton	91-92	13	12	1	235	*58	21.36	–	2	2
SFA Bacchus	83	8	5	1	157	*80	39.25	–	1	–
EAE Baptiste	87-88	1	1	–	14	14	14.00	–	–	1
WKM Benjamin	87-88	13	10	5	69	*24	13.80	–	–	4
CA Best	87-88	2	2	–	23	18	11.50	–	–	1
IR Bishop	95-96	6	4	1	35	17	11.66	–	–	1
KD Boyce	75	5	2	–	41	34	20.50	–	–	–
CR Browne	95-96	5	4	–	64	26	16.00	–	–	3/2
SL Campbell	95-96	4	4	–	57	47	14.25	–	–	–
S Chanderpaul	95-96	6	6	–	211	80	35.16	–	2	1
CEH Croft	79	4	1	1	0	*0	–	–	–	–
CE Cuffy	95-96	1	1	–	1	1	1.00	–	–	1
AC Cummins	91-92	6	2	1	11	6	11.00	–	–	–
WW Daniel	83	3	1	1	16	*16	–	–	–	–
WW Davis	83	5	1	1	0	*0	–	–	–	–
PJL Dujon	83	14	9	1	112	46	14.00	–	–	19/1
RC Fredricks	75	5	5	–	116	58	23.20	–	1	2
J Garner	79	8	5	3	52	37	26.00	–	–	4
LR Gibbs	75	1	–	–	–	–	–	–	–	–
HA Gomes	83	8	7	3	258	78	64.50	–	3	3
OD Gibon	95-96	3	2	–	7	6	3.50	–	–	1
CG Greenidge	75 to 83	15	15	2	591	*106	45.46	2	4	1
RA Harper	87-88	14	13	2	118	24	10.72	–	–	6
DL Haynes	79	25	25	2	854	105	37.13	1	3	12
RIC Holder	95-96	2	2	–	5	5	2.50	–	–	–
VA Holder	75	5	2	1	22	16	22.00	–	–	2
MA Holding	79	11	5	–	36	20	7.20	–	–	5
CL Hooper	87-88	14	12	3	162	63	18.00	–	1	8
BD Julien	75	5	3	2	48	*26	48.00	–	–	–
AI Kallicharran	75	9	8	1	251	78	35.85	–	2	6
RB Kanhai	75	5	4	2	109	55	54.50	–	1	3
CL King	79	4	3	–	132	86	44.00	–	1	2
BC Lara	91-92	14	14	2	602	111	50.16	1	5	4

Player	First Yr	P	I	no	Runs	HS	Ave	100	50	CS
CH Lloyd	75	17	11	2	393	102	43.66	1	2	12
AL Logie	83	15	13	2	282	*65	25.63	–	2	4
MD Marshall	83	11	7	–	40	18	5.71	–	–	–
DL Murray	75	9	5	2	122	618	40.66	–	1	16
BP Patterson	87-88	7	2	2	4	*4	–	–	–	2
IVA Richards	75	23	21	5	1013	181	63.31	3	5	9
RB Richardson	87-88	20	20	3	639	110	37.58	1	4	6
AME Roberts	75	16	8	3	85	*37	17.00	–	–	–
PV Simmons	87-88	8	8	–	323	110	40.37	1	2	1
CA Walsh	87-88	12	6	2	31	*9	7.75	–	–	3
D Williams	91-92	8	6	2	52	*32	13.00	–	–	11/3

Bowling

Player	Overs	M	Runs	Wi	Ave	BP	4wi	R/O
JC Adams	22	0	110	3	36.66	3-53	–	5.00
CEL Ambrose	124.3	17	405	17	23.82	3-28	–	3.25
KLT Arthurton	35	0	178	3	59.33	2-40	–	5.08
EAE Baptiste	8	1	33	0	–	–	–	4.12
WKM Benjamin	123	10	515	14	36.78	3-27	–	4.18
IR Bishop	49	6	194	3	64.66	2-35	–	3.95
KD Boyce	52	3	185	10	18.50	4-50	1	3.55
CEH Croft	43	3	140	8	17.50	3-29	–	3.25
AC Cummins	59	1	246	12	20.50	4-33	1	4.16
CE Cuffy	8	0	31	1	31.00	1-31	–	3.87
WW Daniel	24	6	84	3	28.00	3-28	–	3.50
WW Davis	54.3	6	206	8	25.75	7-51	1	3.77
J Garner	90	12	289	13	22.23	5-38	1	3.21
LR Gibbs	4	0	17	0	–	–	–	4.25
OD Gibson	19.4	1	90	1	90.00	1-27	–	4.57
HA Gomes	74	4	304	9	33.77	2-46	–	4.10
RA Harper	132	10	488	18	27.11	4-47	1	3.21
VA Holder	43.2	4	184	5	36.80	3-30	–	4.24
MA Holding	115.5	16	341	20	17.05	4-33	1	2.94
CL Hooper	121	2	493	15	32.86	3-42	–	4.07
BD Julien	60	11	177	10	17.70	4-20	2	2.95
CL King	32	2	128	2	64.00	1-36	–	4.00
CH Lloyd	36	4	125	3	41.66	1-31	–	3.47
MD Marshall	113	13	349	14	24.92	3-28	–	3.08
BP Patterson	66	2	278	15	18.53	3-31	–	4.21

Player	Overs	M	Runs	Wi	Ave	BP	4wi	R/O
IVA Richards	83	2	345	10	34.50	3-41	–	4.15
RB Richardson	4	0	24	0	–	–	–	6.00
AME Roberts	170.1	29	552	26	21.23	3-32	–	3.24
PV Simmons	20	1	91	3	30.33	2-40	–	4.55
CA Walsh	111	15	439	16	27.43	4-40	–	3.95

Player Profiles

ADAMS, James Clive   LHB/SLA
Born: 9 January 1968, Port Maria, Jamaica   *Nottinghamshire*
After a great success in the early part of his career, Jimmy Adams is
looking to make his comeback in this World Cup. An all-rounder and
reserve wicket-keeper, he has been giving solid performances as
captain of the West Indies 'A' team. He first came to the fore in 1993-
94 in India when his performances took him to the top of the batting
rankings. Injury hindered further development and he has had to call on
his undoubted talent to pull him out of a slump. He made his one day
debut in 1992-93 in the World Series against Pakistan at Sydney.
Despite having scored over 1,000 runs in the one day game he still
awaits his first century – 81 not out being his best score to date – with
an average of under 30 a game, which compares poorly with his Test
average of over 50 a game. With the ball he bowls at an economy rate
of 4.80 with 5-37 being his best match performance.

AMBROSE, Curtly Elconn Lynwall   LHB/RF
Born: 21 September 1963, Swetes Village   *Leeward Islands*
A giant among the present-day West Indian pacemen, 'King Curtly' as
he is lovingly referred to, is in the very twilight of his distinguished
career. On wickets that offer him assistance, he would still at the ripe
old age of thirty-five be considered as the most dangerous bowler to
face. Ambrose has never been known to swing the ball but he makes
things awkward by keeping a nagging length and making the odd ball
jump from a good length. In his era as the leading strike bowler, West
Indies have not won a worthwhile one day tournament in the past six
years.

ARTHURTON, Keith Lloyd Thomas   LHB/SLO

Born: 21 February 1965, Charlestown, Nevis   Leeward Islands
The 1992 World Cup was the stage for Arthurton to make his mark on
the international scene with 25 runs and a match-winning 53 against
India. He started out with the Leeward islands and made the natural
progression to the West Indian side. Not the most graceful of players,
he does not ruffle easily and his favourite shot is the powerful drive
square of the wicket, especially now he has eradicated his tendency to
shuffle along the crease. He has established himself as a middle order
batsman and has gained a reputation as a fighting player – largely
because of a staunch 157 he scored at the Gabba in 1992-93. Suffered a
dip in form last year which put his position in the side under threat.
However, his form in Sharjah seems to indicate he is back to his best.

BISHOP, Ian Raphael   RHB/RF

Born: 24 October 1967, Port-of-Spain, Trinidad   Trinidad & Tobago
But for a two-year lay-off due to back problems Ian Bishop might have
established himself alongside the likes of past greats from the
Caribbean Islands. Bishop delivers the ball fast and with pace off the
pitch. He is highly successful, reaching the 100 Test wicket landmark
quicker than any other Caribbean in history. After that came the back
injury which has dogged his career ever since. He made his one day
debut against England at Headingley in 1988 and has moved past the
100 wicket mark in the one day game with an economy rate of 4.33 and
a best of 5-25. A lower order batsman, he is closing on his 500th run
while averaging 16.2 runs per innings with 33 not out being his best
performance. He has been playing with Derbyshire in recent times so
will have no excuses regarding the English style wickets, as long as his
back and selection hold up.

CAMPBELL, Sherwin   RHB/ROB

Born: 1 November 1970, Barbados   Durham, Barbados
An opener for the West Indies in the Test arena in the past he has been
unable to bring his Test consistency into the one day game. That said,
his steadfast approach at the wicket can provide a base from which
large totals can be built especially if he is given the time to settle in.
The fast nature of the one day game though doesn't always allow this.
His highest score in the one day game is 86 which doesn't compare
well to the double century he hit at Test level in 1996-97. He made his

one day debut at Madras against India in 1994-95. He has experience with Durham so has a good knowledge of English conditions.

CHANDERPAUL, Shivnarine   LHB/LBG
Born: 18 August, 1974, Unity Village, Guyana   *Guyana*
Although originally a middle order batsman, Chanderpaul's success in limited overs cricket has come in a role as an opener. A man of small but athletic frame, he has made rapid strides in the world rankings due to his great powers of concentration. Not the most aesthetically pleasant to watch because of his crouched stance, his effectiveness stems from an admirable selection of strokes, making him an ideal limited overs cricketer. His leg breaks are rarely used at the highest level. He is an outstanding fieldsman at any position. Made his one day debut in 1994-95.

DILLON, Mervyn   RHB/RFM
Born: 5 June 1974, Mission Village, Trinidad   Trinidad & Tobago
A pace bowler who once took five Pakistani wickets at Karachi in 1997 and followed this up last year in the Wills Cup semi-final when he demolished India's line-up. He made his one day debut in the Wills Quadrangular in 1997-98 against South Africa at Lahore and may have passed the 100 overs mark by the time of the World Cup – his best performance being 3-32, although at 5.20 his economy rate is a little high, especially when compared to his 3.16 average for Test cricket. Primarily a bowler, Dillion's top score in one day cricket is five not out.

GANGA, Daren   RHB
Born: 14 January 1979, Trinidad   Trinidad & Tobago.
He came to the fore at the right time – that's Daren Ganga who made his Test and one day debuts against South Africa in the winter tour of 1998. Just 19 years old, Ganga is captain of Trinidad and Tobago's Under-19 team. In South Africa he had six Test innings, making 75 runs with a high score of 28. For the one day side his two innings brought just one run.

HOOPER, Carl Llewellyn   RHB/ROB
Born: 15 December 1966, Georgetown   *Guyana*
An enigmatic character, who despite possessing huge talents as an all-round cricketer has been an under-achiever at the highest level. He simply caresses the ball and is a very delicate placer of the ball on both

sides of the wicket. A wonderful player to watch. His very unpredictability makes him a dangerous commodity. He is more than likely to bowl ten overs of his off spin. Varies his pace cleverly. He is an outstanding slip catcher.

LAMBERT, Clayton Benjamin Lambert   LHB/ROB
Born: 10 February 1962, New Amsterdam, Berbice, Guyana   Guyana
Made his debut in both Test and one day games against England. Since his Test start in 1991 at the Oval Lambert was ignored by the West Indian selection committee for over six years until a succession of consistent performances in domestic play made his return almost inevitable. Curiously it was against England and his century of runs made him, at 36, the third oldest West Indian to reach the ton mark. His physical size makes him easy to recognise and his power with the bat comes from his quick footwork. In the one day game he averages over 30 per innings.

LARA, Brian   LHB/LB
Born: 2 May 1969, Santa Cruz, Trinidad   Warwickshire
One of the most prolific batsmen of our times, Lara has achieved a variety of records in recent years including a highest ever innings score in first class cricket (501 not out for Warwickshire against Durham 1994) and the equivalent in international Test cricket. Having the West Indian captainship for the World Cup will surely be a major boost to his confidence and, given a good run in the competition, he could score his 6,000th run in the one day game. Lara made his first class debut with Trinidad & Tobago in 1988 and took over the skipper's role just a year later at the age of 20. He was elevated to the West Indies team following the retirements of Richards, Greenidge and Dujon in 1992, and he has been the mainstay of their batting line up ever since. He is small, left handed, and has no apparent weaknesses in his wide array of strokes. When he is in-form the runs come quickly and for bowlers he can be almost impossible to contain. Having played extensively for Warwickshire he is more than familiar with English conditions and the West Indies will be looking for him to improve on his 43.73 batting average.

MCLEAN, Nixon Alexei McNamara   LHB/RF
Born: 28 July 1973, St Vincent   Windward Islands
Lack of match practice has been one of the problems plaguing McLean in the lead up to the World Cup. A double groin injury sidelined him

for much of last season. Nevertheless he was back for the winter tour to South Africa. He made his one day debut in 1996-97 at Melbourne against the Australians and has an economy rate of five when bowling – his best performance being 3-41. A low order batsman, his highest one day international score is just 16. McLean has plenty of experience in England as a player with Hampshire having taken part in the Sunday League, Benson & Hedges Cup and the NatWest Trophy, the latter bringing his best performances with bat (36 high score) and ball (2-23 and 3.95 economy).

MURRAY, Junior Randalph   RHB/WK
Born: 20 January 1968, St George's, Grenada   Windward Islands
Murray was excluded from the squad that toured Bangladesh late last year and that may place his selection for this World Cup in some doubt. He made his one day debut in 1992-93 against Pakistan in the World Series at Perth and has averaged over 22 runs per innings with his highest score of 86 coming against England at the Oval in 1995.

ROSE, Franklyn Albert   RHB/RF
Born: 1 February 1972, St Anns Bay, Jamaica   Jamaica
A fast bowler who is another West Indian with experience of the one day game in England. As a youth he worked his way through the Jamaican national sides where he had great success before progressing to the Under-23 side where he suffered a severe drop in form. So bad did the slump affect him that he gave up cricket for two years only to come back and win a place in the West Indies side to play India in Kingston in 1997. It marked his Test debut and allowed him to set a record when he became the first West Indian to take six wickets on a Test debut! He made his one day international debut at the same time against India and his best bowling figures remain at 3-25.

SIMMONS, Philip Verant   RHB/RM
Born: 18 April 1963, Arima, Trinidad   Leicestershire, Trinidad & T.
Simmons made his one day debut in 1987-88 against Pakistan in Lahore. He has been playing one day international cricket for over ten years, including the recent tournament in Bangladesh. In his career he has amassed over 3,500 runs, averaging close to 30 per innings and he is approaching his 100th wicket. His best performance with the ball includes 4-3 against Pakistan in Sydney in 1992-93. He has experience of cricket in England with Leicestershire.

WALLACE, Philo Alphonso   RHB/RM
Born: 2 August 1970, Around-the-town, Barbados   *Barbados*
Philo Wallace made an unspectacular Test debut in Pakistan last year
but Pakistan's let off was to be England's headache. Having scored just
13 against the Pakistanis, he fired 198 runs in three innings against the
English. He made his one day debut in the 1991-92 season at Karachi
against Pakistan. Confidence is the key for Wallace – when he has it in
abundance he uses the bat to great and powerful effect, offering a
variety of strokes to keep the bowler and fielders on their toes.

WILLIAMS, Stuart Clayton   RHB
Born: 12 August 1969, Nevis   *Leeward Islands*
Made his one day debut at Fariadad against India in 1994-95. He has
maintained a batting average of around 35 in some 45 internationals.
His best performance is 105 not out.

ZIMBABWE

Super Sixes in Sight

Zimbabwe, the youngest of Test-playing nations, came into 1998 with only one win behind them – at home against Pakistan in 1995 – since they entered the Test arena in 1992, but chalked up two successes before the year was out. In October they beat India in Harare in a one-off Test and capped that the following month by comfortably beating Pakistan by seven wickets for their first Test win abroad and first series win. Zimbabwe find themselves in Group A which includes their recent Indian scalps. Another success against them and a win against Kenya could see them move into the second stage of the competition for the first time.

Team strip: Vivid red and colours from the nation's cricket logo with a central print of Zimbabwe's national bird.

World Cup Record

	First Year	P	W	L	NR	SR%
Australia … … … … …	1983	6	1	5	–	16.66
England … … … …	1991-92	1	1	–	–	100.00
India … … … … …	1983	6	–	6	–	–
Kenya … … … … …	1995-96	1	1	–	–	100.00
New Zealand… … …	1987-88	3	–	3	–	–
Pakistan … … … …	1991-92	1	–	1	–	–
South Africa … … …	1991-92	1	–	1	–	–
Sri Lanka … … … …	1991-92	2	–	2	–	–
West Indies … … … …	1983	4	–	4	–	–
Total… … … … … … … … …		25	3	22	–	12.00

Campaign Performances

Year	Pos	Captain	Result
1983	Gp	DAG Fletcher	Failed to qualify for semi-finals
1987-88	Gp	AJ Traicos	Failed to qualify for semi-finals
1991-92	Gp	DL Houghton	Failed to qualify for semi-finals
1995-96	Gp	A Flower	Failed to qualify for quarter-finals

	Period	P	W	L	T	NR	SR%
All-Time:	... ... 83 to 98-99	115	26	83	4	2	23.00
Since Last WC:	... ...	55	19	34	1	0	34.54

Highest Innings Totals:

Runs	Overs	R/O	Opponents	Venue	Year
312-4	50 overs	6.24	Sri Lanka	New Plymouth	1991-92

Lowest Completed Innings:

Runs	Overs	R/O	Opponents	Venue	Year
134	46.1 overs	2.90	England	Albury	1991-92
135	44.2 overs	3.04	India	Bombay	1987-88
137	41.4 overs	3.28	Australia	Hobart	1991-92
139	42.4 overs	3.25	Australia	Madras	1987-88

World Cup Individual Records

100 Pluses

Runs	bp	Player	Opponents	Venue	Year
142	3	DL Houghton	New Zealand	Hyderabad-I	1987-88
115no	1	A Flower	Sri Lanka	New Plymouth	1991-92

Partnership Record for each Wicket

	Total	Partnership	Opponents	Year
1st	79	AH Shah (31), A Flower (*43)	India	1991-92
2nd	81	AH Shah (41), RJ Arnott (51)	N.Zealand	1987-88
3rd	51	DL Houghton (142), AJ Pycroft (12)	N.Zealand	1987-88
4th	85	A Flower (*115), KJ Arnott (52)	Sri Lanka	1991-92
5th	*145	A Flower (*115), AC Waller (*83)	Sri Lanka	1991-92
6th	103	DL Houghton (84), KM Curran (35)	Australia	1983
7th	*75	DAG Fletcher(*69), IP Buchart (*34)		
			Australia	1983
8th	117	DL Houghton (142), IP Butchart (54)	N.Zealand	1987-88
9th	55	KM Curran (62), PWE Rawson (19)	West Indies	1983
10th	36	AJ Pycroft (61), MP Jarvis (*8)	India	1987-88

Four Wicket Hauls

Score	Arm	Player	Opponents	Venue	Year
5-21	LBG	PA Strang	Kenya	Patna	1995-96
4-21	RFM	EA Brandes	England	Albury	1991-92
4-40	LBG	PA Strang	West Indies	Hyderabad-I	1995-96
4-42	RFM	DAG Fletcher	Australia	Nottingham	1983

Man of the Match Awards

Six Awards: DL Houghton (2), DAG Fletcher (1), A Flower (1), EA Brandes (1), PA Strang (1)

World Cup Player Performances

Batting

Player	First Yr	P	I	no	Runs	HS	Ave	100	50	CS
KJ Arnott	87-88	9	8	1	206	60	29.42	–	3	2
EA Brandes	87-88	14	10	3	99	23	14.14	–	–	4
RD Brown	83	7	7	–	110	38	15.71	–	–	5
MG Burmester	91-92	4	3	1	17	12	8.50	–	–	1
IP Butchart	83	17	14	2	240	54	20.00	–	1	4
ADR Campbell	91-92	9	8	–	128	76	16.00	–	1	6
KM Curran	83	11	11	–	287	73	26.09	–	2	1
SG Davies	95-96	1	1	–	9	9	9.00	–	–	–
KG Duers	91-92	6	2	1	7	*5	7.00	–	–	2
CN Evans	95-96	5	5	2	92	*39	30.66	–	–	–
DAG Fletcher	83	6	6	2	191	*71	47.75	–	2	–
A Flower	91-92	13	13	2	295	*115	26.81	1	–	6/2
GW Flower	95-96	5	5	–	125	45	25.00	–	–	3
JG Heron	83	6	6	–	50	18	8.33	–	–	1
VR Hogg	83	2	1	1	7	*7	–	–	–	–
DL Houghton	83	20	19	–	567	142	29.84	1	4	14/2
WR James	91-92	4	3	–	35	17	11.66	–	–	1
MP Jarvis	87-88	10	5	3	37	17	18.50	–	–	1
AIC Lock	95-96	5	3	2	8	5	8.00	–	–	–
MA Meman	87-88	1	1	–	19	19	19.00	–	–	–
GA Paterson	83	10	10	–	123	27	12.30	–	–	2
SG Peall	95-96	4	2	–	9	9	4.50	–	–	1
GE Peckover	83	3	3	1	33	*16	16.50	–	–	–
AJ Pycroft	83	20	19	2	295	61	17.35	–	2	6

Player	First Yr	P	I	no	Runs	HS	Ave	100	50	CS
PWE Rawson	83	10	8	3	80	*24	16.00	–	–	4
AH Shah	83	16	16	1	266	60	17.73	–	1	3
BC Strang	95-96	3	2	–	3	3	1.50	–	–	2
PA Strang	95-96	5	4	3	52	*22	52.00	–	–	1
HH Streak	95-96	5	5	1	80	30	20.00	–	–	1
AJ Traicos	83	20	12	5	70	19	10.00	–	–	2
AC Waller	87-88	19	19	–	476	*83	25.05	–	2	3
GJ Whittall	95-96	5	5	–	71	35	14.20	–	–	–

Bowling

Player	Overs	M	Runs	Wi	Ave	BP	4wi	R/O
EA Brandes	118.1	11	586	16	36.62	4-21	1	4.95
MG Burmester	21.5	0	138	4	34.50	3-36	–	6.32
IP Butchart	117	6	640	12	53.33	3-57	–	5.47
ADR Campbell	3	0	13	0	–	–	–	4.33
KM Curran	84.2	3	398	9	44.22	3-65	–	4.71
KG Duers	50	2	256	3	85.33	1-17	–	5.12
DAG Fletcher	50.1	5	221	7	31.57	4-42	1	4.40
GW Flower	11	1	54	0	–	–	–	4.90
VR Hogg	15	4	49	0	–	–	–	3.26
DL Houghton	2	0	19	1	19.00	1-19	–	9.50
MP Jarvis	83.1	5	384	7	54.85	1-21	–	4.61
AIC Lock	32	3	141	3	47.00	2-57	–	4.40
MA Meman	6.5	0	34	0	–	–	–	4.97
SG Peall	23	1	101	1	101.00	1-23	–	4.39
PWE Rawson	95.1	10	427	12	35.58	3-47	–	4.48
AH Shah	104.3	9	456	11	41.45	2-17	–	4.36
BC Strang	18	1	66	3	22.00	2-24	–	3.66
PA Strang	42.1	4	192	12	16.00	5-21	1	4.55
HH Streak	44	8	175	4	43.75	3-60	–	3.97
AJ Traicos	188	13	673	16	42.06	3-35	–	3.57
GJ Whittall	14	0	79	0	–	–	–	5.64

BRANDES, Eddo Andre   RHB/RFM

Born: 5 March 1963, Port Shepstone, Natal, South Africa

Eddo Brandes is celebrating 11 years in one day internationals this
season, having made his debut against New Zealand at Hyderabad
(Deccan) in the 1988 World Cup. His first class debut was for his
country against Cleethorpes in England so he is returning to a familiar
scene. Thirty six is often considered old these days for a spin bowler or
batsman, let alone a fast bowler. Despite the passing of the years
Brandes is still lethal at times, as his best bowling performance of 5-28
demonstrates. On the other hand he can be very expensive as a spell of
six overs for 57 against New Zealand recently confirmed, although his
overall economy rate remains respectable at well below five an over.
Back in March 1992 Brandes was man of the match when he skittled
out England at Albury in the World Cup, including the wicket of
school friend Graeme Hick for a duck. He's also capable of hitting a
few late order runs when his luck is in and he's bagged over 300 runs
in his 38 innings.

CAMPBELL, Alistair Douglas Ross   LHB/ROB

Born: 23 September 1972, Salisbury

Campbell made his one day debut against West Indies at Brisbane in
the 1992 World Cup and he's been a stalwart of the Zimbabwe side
since, and now its captain. A batsman of great skill, he is capable of
taking an attack apart with well timed drives and cut shots. His highest
score of 131 not out proves the point but his average of 28 or so per
innings demonstrates that he doesn't always last long enough to pull
off the big knock. One to watch for an entertaining time at the crease.
Campbell, who is about to reach his 100th one day international, can
also turn his arm over very occasionally and he has four Test wickets
with a best of 2-22.

EVANS, Craig Neil   RHB/RM

Born: 29 November 1969, Salisbury   *Mashonaland*

After a promising early career, including a spell playing in the
Lancashire League, Evans made his one day debut against India at
Harare in 1992-93 and he's still trying to justify the selectors' early
confidence in him. There's a single 96 not out highlight amongst his
innings and he has taken 18 wickets with an economy rate just under

the five per over mark. He has struggled against fast bowling but a renewed dedication to the game could pay off. A return to early form would help his side no end.

FLOWER, Andrew   LHB/ROB/WK
Born: 28 April 1968, Cape Town, South Africa   *Mashonaland*
Flower made his debut against Sri Lanka at New Plymouth in the 1992 World Cup and he has since reached his 100th one day international and amassed nearly 3,000 runs. He is a stylish left hand bat, with wonderful timing, a pure striker of the ball. His captaincy has occasionally been criticised, but with a team usually on the back foot, it is a difficult job. He also has the same problem as England's Alec Stuart, expected to captain, lead the batting and keep wicket. A one day average of over 30 shows he has great ability.

FLOWER, Grant William   RHB/SLO
Born: 20 December 1970, Salisbury   *Mashonaland*
Grant Flower is a solid opening bat, dependable and a good anchor for the faster batsmen. He made his one day debut against India at Harare in 1992-93. He has batted the full 50 overs in one day games, although not at great speed, and in more than a quarter of his innings he goes over the half century mark. Nearly 3,000 runs at an average of over 35, and a high score of 112, make Flower a vital cog in the Zimbabwe batting mechanism. His double century in a recent Test win over Pakistan will long be remembered. He is also a useful off spinner, with over 200 overs in one day matches, who can prove hard to get away although his economy per over is five.

GOODWIN, Murray William   RHB/RM, LB
Born: 11 December 1972, Salisbury   *Mashonaland*
A promising batsman who made his debut against Sri Lanka at Colombo (SSC) in 1997-98 and who has since put together over 700 runs and an average in the late 20s. His 111 top score must give Zimbabwe hope that this will be Goodwin's, and their, World Cup breakthrough. He has also bowled 30 or so overs but his economy is around five per over. Goodwin learned his cricket in Australia and in the 1994-95 season he made his debut for Western Australia against the England tourists, before returning to the team of the land of his birth. He has also spent time playing in England, for Streetly in Sutton

Coldfield and for Guisborough, in the North Yorkshire-South Durham league, scoring 1,700 runs for an average of about 89 in the latter.

HUCKLE, Adam George   RHB/LBG
Born: 21 September 1971, Bulawayo
Huckle's international one day debut was against Bangladesh at Nairobi (Gymk) in the 1997-98 President's Cup and, although he hasn't yet broken any records, he did grab a 2-27 best performance. In his first six innings he didn't manage to get into double figures from low down in the order so the jury is out on this young man from a cricketing family.

JOHNSON, Neil Clarkson   LHB/RFM
Born: 24 January 1970, Salisbury   *Eastern Province*
Johnson played in England, for Leicestershire, in 1997 and 1998 and made his one day debut for his country against New Zealand at Dhaka in the 1998-99 Wills International Cup. He got a 53 and not much more in three Benson & Hedges games last year, bowling too little to be judged. His international record is short but impressive with a 103 top score and a 39 average. He has captured five wickets but economy is not good. In the Test arena Johnson recently completed a maiden Test century off just 117 balls, including 16 fours, in his first Test against Pakistan. He is another Zimbabwean who can pull off a bit of an innings. The question facing supporters is can he do it consistently?

MBANGWA, Mpumelelo   RHB/RFM
Born: 26 June 1976, Plumtree   *Matabeleland*
'Pom' played his first international one day game against Pakistan at Lahore in 1996-97 and is still learning his trade. Over 100 overs now has harvested seven wickets at an economy rate just under five. Mbangwa played at an English school in his youth but missed out on the last Zimbabwe tour of England. He is a line and length bowler rather than possessing top pace and is a prospect for the future rather than a definite hit this time around, although English conditions will suit his style. He has only made it to the crease seven times in 13 games with a highest knock of 11.

OLONGA, Henry Khaaba   RHB/RF

Born: 3 July 1976, Lusaka, Zambia   *Matabeleland*

Henry Olonga made his debut against India at Sharjah as recently as
the 1998-99 Champions Trophy. Olonga has come back from being
called for throwing in a Test match in early 1995 and rebuilt his action
completely. Now no longer 'suspect', he is still in and out of the side
because his wicket taking ability (best 4-46) is offset by his very
expensive, indeed unacceptable, economy (nearly seven per over). He
might seem a long shot but the 22-year-old cricketer was declared
player of the Test series after getting nine wickets in the recent victory
over Pakistan, including a match-winning burst of 4-42 in the first Test
at Peshawar which Zimbabwe won by seven wickets. He is an
ambitious young man and may see the World Cup as a launchpad. He
was a member of the Zimbabwean World Cup team in 1995-96 but did
not play a match. When selected for the final game he asked to stand
down, humbly explaining that he was out of practice and did not feel
able to give of his best.

RENNIE, Gavin James   LHB/SLO

Born: 12 January 1976, Fort Victoria   *Mashonaland*

His one day debut was against Pakistan at Quetta in 1996-97 and his 16
innings have produced 332 runs at an average of just over 25. His high
score of 76 indicates a talent in the making and the World Cup should
provide an excellent stage for this left-hander's emerging talent. He
started his career as an all-rounder, turning more into a batsman who
can bowl. He has struggled to balance work and sport, missing out on
the Zimbabwe tour of England because of job commitments, but he
remains a promising prospect.

STRANG, Paul Andrew   RHB/LBG

Born: 28 July 1970, Bulawayo   *Mashonaland*

Strang, a regular in the Zimbabwe team since his debut against
Australia at Perth in the 1994-95 World Series, has played with Kent
and Nottinghamshire and his 1998 experience of English conditions
with Notts will stand him in good stead. A wily leg spinner who is very
dangerous on the right track, Strang's control is excellent and his
wrong-un can be hard to pick. He has the potential of a long career
with Zimbabwe, based on some very consistent performances so far.
His economy rate of just over four is accompanied by a wicket every
31 balls and a best of 5-21. His consistency shone through in the one

day domestic knockout tournaments last year, with economy rates well below four and a 6-32 performance in the Sunday League. Batting at eight or below, he has provided some good runs at important times in both Tests and one day games. He is nearing 1,000 runs and averages over 25 although he only has a top score of 47.

STREAK, Heath Hilton   RHB/RFM
Born: 16 March 1974, Bulawayo   *Matabeleland*

An experienced campaigner, Streak debuted against South Africa at Bangalore in the Hero Cup back in 1993-94 and has an excellent bowling record. He is very fast and moves the ball both in the air and off the pitch, resulting in danger for all who face him. Streak's class was recently confirmed at Test level when he became the first Zimbabwe player to get 100 Test wickets. His 85 wickets in one day internationals (end of 1998) were grabbed every 30 balls or so and he has only given away 4.47 runs per over, although he has a bit of a reputation of being generous with extras. A best of 5-32 indicates that Streak is a world class fast bowler. A large number of not outs help his batting average of nearly 20 but his top score of 59 means he is capable of hitting important late runs for his side and his record includes a match-winning hit against New Zealand.

WHITTALL, Andrew Richard   RHB/ROB
Born: 28 March 1973, Mutare   *Matabeleland*

Whittall made his one day debut against Sri Lanka at Colombo (SSC), in the 1996-97 Singer World Series, having never before played for a first class side. His experience came from playing at youth level and for Cambridge University. His off breaks have kept batsmen to a pretty meagre four and a bit an over. His batting experience has been minimal but a high score of 29 means he could play a useful innings. His 32 wickets in one day internationals have come every 40 or so balls so he's mainly in for his ability to contain the opposition.

WISHART, Craig Brian   RHB/RM
Born: 9 January 1974, Salisbury   *Mashonaland*

Another natural all-round sportsman, like so many of the Zimbabwe team, Craig Wishart debuted against Australia at Colombo (RPS) in the Singer World Series of 1996-97. In 39 games up to the end of 1998 he put together over 600 runs at an average of 20. It's not yet world class but it includes a best of 102, so Wishart has the ability to make his mark on this World Cup. Although an occasional bowler at club level, he is unlikely to get much of a chance in the World Cup.

WORLD CUP FORM

Records in the World Cup

England have played the most games in the World Cup finals – 40 – which has brought 25 wins and 14 defeats and, despite having reached the Final on three occasions, they await their first title. South Africa make their second appearance in the World Cup finals this time around and their 10 wins from 15 games in the 1996 competition give them the highest success rate with a figure of 66.66%. Hot on their heels though are the West Indies who have a success rate of 65.78% and 25 wins from 39 games. England and South Africa hold the record for most wins in the competition with 25 successes. Zimbabwe have lost the most games in the finals – 22 in all. Kenya have one victory while newcomers Bangladesh and Scotland will be looking to add their own records to the history books.

Country	P	W	L	NR	SR%
Australia	38	22	16	–	57.89
England	40	25	14	1	64.10
India	36	18	17	1	51.42
Kenya	5	1	4	–	20.00
New Zealand	35	19	16	–	54.28
Pakistan	37	21	15	1	58.33
South Africa	15	10	5	–	66.66
West Indies	39	25	13	1	65.78
Zimbabwe	25	3	22	–	12.00

All-Time Records

Of the ten Test playing nations listed below, Australia have played the most one day international games since their inception in the 1970-71 season. They have also won the most games – 229 from 418. However, they lie third in the success rate (SR%) standings, with both South Africa and the West Indies having a better results percentage. South Africa come out top in the SR stakes but they have played less than half the games of both Australia and the West Indies.

Country	Period	P	W	L	T	NR	SR%
Australia	70-71 to 98-99	418	229	175	3	11	56.26
England	70-71 to 98-99	292	147	135	2	8	51.76
India	74 to 98-99	390	175	195	3	17	46.91
Kenya	95-96 to 98-99	20	4	15	0	1	21.05
New Zealand	72-73 to 98-99	316	130	169	4	13	42.90
Pakistan	72-73 to 98-99	414	210	189	5	19	53.29
South Africa	91-92 to 98-99	157	98	56	0	3	63.63
Sri Lanka	75 to 98-99	297	114	169	1	13	40.14
West Indies	73 to 98-99	356	220	126	4	6	62.85
Zimbabwe	83 to 98-99	115	26	83	4	2	23.00

Including results up to 20th February 1999.

Records Since Last World Cup

India have been the most active of the World Cup finalists since the competition was last held in 1996, having played 109 one day internationals. They haven't been as successful as they might have wished though, winning less than half the games. The most successful team has been one of the favourites to take the 1999 crown – South Africa. They have achieved a staggering 79.41% success rate, winning 54 of their 69 games and losing just 14. Current holders Sri Lanka have maintained a 58% success rate while Pakistan join Australia as the only four teams to achieve 50% or more success.

Country	P	W	L	T	NR	SR%
Australia	64	33	31	0	0	51.56
England	45	21	22	1	1	47.72
India	109	45	54	1	9	45.00
Kenya	14	3	11	0	0	21.42
New Zealand	58	22	30	3	3	46.80
Pakistan	95	46	46	0	3	50.00
South Africa	69	54	14	0	1	79.41
Sri Lanka	77	43	30	1	3	58.10
West Indies	39	19	20	0	0	48.71
Zimbabwe	55	19	34	1	0	34.54

Including results up to 20th February 1999.

Australia in the World Cup

Australia are in Group B for the 1999 World Cup. They will meet Bangladesh and Scotland for the first time in the competition but will encounter New Zealand, Pakistan and the West Indies in their other group games. The battle for one of the three spots in the Super Sixes might well hinge on how each team does in its game with New Zealand. If they qualify for the Super Sixes Australia are likely to be facing the likes of England, India, Sri Lanka and South Africa.

England

Year	Stage	Result
1975	Semi Final	Australia won by 4 wickets
1979	Group A	England won by 6 wickets
1987	Final	Australia won by 7 runs
1992	Group	England won by 8 wickets

India

Year	Stage	Result
1983	Group B	Australia won by 162 runs
1983	Group B	India won by 118 runs
1987	Group A	Australia won by 1 run
1987	Group A	India won by 56 runs
1992	League	Australia won by 1 run
1996	Group A	Australia won by 16 runs

Kenya

Year	Stage	Result
1996	Group A	Australia won by 97 runs

New Zealand

Year	Stage	Result
1987	Group A	Australia won by 3 runs
1987	Group A	Australia won by 17 runs
1992	League	New Zealand won by 37 runs
1996	Quarter Final	Australia won by 6 wickets

Pakistan

Year	Stage	Result
1975	Group B	Australia won by 73 runs
1979	Group A	Pakistan won by 89 runs
1987	Semi Final	Australia won by 18 runs
1992	League	Pakistan won by 48 runs

South Africa

Year	Stage	Result
1992	League	South Africa won by 9 wickets

Sri Lanka

Year	Stage	Result
1975	Group B	Australia won by 52 runs
1992	League	Australia won by 7 wickets
1996	Final	Sri Lanka won by 7 wickets
1996	Group A	Sri Lanka won by default

Zimbabwe

Year	Stage	Result
1983	Group B	Zimbabwe won by 13 runs
1983	Group B	Australia won by 32 runs
1987	Group A	Australia won by 96 runs
1987	Group A	Australia won by 70 runs
1992	League	Australia won by 128 runs
1996	Group A	Australia won by 8 wickets

West Indies

Year	Stage	Result
1975	Group B	West Indies won by 4 wickets
1975	Final	West Indies won by 17 runs
1983	Group B	West Indies won by 101 runs
1983	Group B	West Indies won by 7 wickets
1992	League	Australia won by 57 runs
1996	Group A	West Indies won by 4 wickets
1996	Semi Final	Australia won by 5 runs

England in the World Cup

England have played more games in the World Cup Finals than any other team in the competition. They start the competition in Group A and would expect to take full points from Kenya and Zimbabwe, although the Zimbabweans would point out that they won the only encounter between the two sides in the competition which took place in 1992. England will meet Kenya for the first time in the Finals. Interestingly England have only lost one game against each of their other opponents in the Group.

Australia

Year	Stage	Result
1975	Semi Final	Australia won by 4 wickets
1979	Group A	England won by 6 wickets
1987	Final	Australia won by 7 runs
1992	League	England won by 8 wickets

India

Year	Stage	Result
1975	Group A	England won by 202 runs
1983	Semi Final	India won by 6 wickets
1987	Semi Final	England won by 35 runs
1992	League	England won by 9 runs

New Zealand

Year	Stage	Result
1975	Group A	England won by 80 runs
1979	Semi Final	England won by 9 runs
1983	Group A	England won by 106 runs
1983	Group A	New Zealand won by 2 wickets
1992	League	New Zealand won by 7 wickets
1996	Group B	New Zealand won by 11 runs

Pakistan

Year	Stage	Result
1979	Group A	England won by 14 runs
1983	Group A	England won by 8 wickets
1983	Group A	England won by 7 wickets
1987	Group B	Pakistan won by 18 runs
1987	Group B	Pakistan won by 7 wickets
1992	League	No result

| 1992 | Final | Pakistan won by 22 runs |
| 1996 | Group B | Pakistan won by 7 wickets |

South Africa

Year	Stage	Result
1992	League	England won by 3 wickets
1992	Semi Final	England won by 19 runs
1996	Group B	South Africa won by 78 runs

Sri Lanka

Year	Stage	Result
1983	Group A	England won by 47 runs
1983	Group A	England won by 9 wickets
1987	Group B	England won on faster scoring rate
1987	Group B	England won by 8 wickets
1992	League	England won by 106 runs
1996	Quarter Final	Sri Lanka won by 5 wickets

West Indies

Year	Stage	Result
1979	Final	West Indies won by 92 runs
1987	Group B	England won by 2 wickets
1987	Group B	England won by 34 runs
1992	League	England won by 6 wickets

Zimbabwe

Year	Stage	Result
1992	League	Zimbabwe won by 7 runs

India in the World Cup

India play in Group A of the World Cup where they will encounter England, Kenya, Sri Lanka, South Africa and Zimbabwe. The games against Sri Lanka will be closely watched as there has been a great deal of bad blood between the teams. Indeed the two met in the 1996 semi final and problems broke out in the crowd which overflowed onto the pitch and caused the game to be awarded to Sri Lanka who went on to beat Australia in the final. The record books show that in the four meetings with Sri Lanka, India have lost. India also lost to South Africa in their only World Cup encounter. Their record against their other group opponents is well balanced.

Australia

Year	Stage	Result
1983	Group B	Australia won by 162 runs
1983	Group B	India won by 118 runs
1987	Group A	Australia won by 1 run
1987	Group A	India won by 56 runs
1992	League	Australia won by 1 run
1996	Group A	Australia won by 16 runs

England

Year	Stage	Result
1975	Group A	England won by 202 runs
1983	Semi Final	India won by 6 wickets
1987	Semi Final	England won by 35 runs
1992	League	England won by 9 runs

Kenya

Year	Stage	Result
1996	Group A	India won by 7 wickets

New Zealand

Year	Stage	Result
1975	Group A	New Zealand won by 4 wickets
1979	Group B	New Zealand won by 8 wickets
1987	Group A	India won by 16 runs
1987	Group A	India won by 9 wickets
1992	League	New Zealand won by 4 wickets

Pakistan

Year	Stage	Result
1992	League	India won by 43 runs
1996	Quarter Final	India won by 39 runs

South Africa

Year	Stage	Result
1992	League	South Africa won by 6 wickets

Sri Lanka

Year	Stage	Result
1979	Group B	Sri Lanka won by 47 runs
1992	League	No result
1996	Group A	Sri Lanka won by 6 wickets
1996	Semi Final	Sri Lanka won by default

West Indies

Year	Stage	Result
1979	Group B	West Indies won by 9 wickets
1983	Group B	India won by 34 runs
1983	Group B	West Indies won by 66 runs
1983	Final	India won by 43 runs
1992	League	West Indies won by 5 wickets
1996	Group A	India won by 5 wickets

Zimbabwe

Year	Stage	Result
1983	Group B	India won by 5 wickets
1983	Group B	India won by 31 runs
1987	Group A	India won by 8 wickets
1987	Group A	India won by 7 wickets
1992	League	India won by 55 runs
1996	Group A	India won by 40 runs

Kenya in the World Cup

Kenya come into the 1999 Finals, having won only one game in the Finals. That came in the 1996 competition when they sensationally beat the West Indies in what is regarded as the greatest ever upset in one day international cricket. Curiously it happened on Leap Year Day! They beat the two times World Champions by 73 runs having bowled them out in just 35.2 overs. Kenya had scored 166 runs from 49.3 overs. Odumbe and Ali were the heroes of the day taking 3-17 and 3-15 respectively. Ali's wickets included the great Brian Lara for just eight runs! Kenya are in Group A where they will face England, India, Sri Lanka, South Africa and Zimbabwe and it is doubtful if they will add to their 'wins' column, but you never know – just ask the West Indians!

Australia

Year	Stage	Result
1996	Group A	Australia won by 97 runs

India

Year	Stage	Result
1996	Group A	India won by 7 wickets

Sri Lanka

Year	Stage	Result
1996	Group A	Sri Lanka won by 144 runs

West Indies

Year	Stage	Result
1996	Group A	Kenya won by 73 runs

Zimbabwe

Year	Stage	Result
1996	Group A	Zimbabwe won by 5 wickets

New Zealand in the World Cup

On paper New Zealand will have a tough time qualifying for the Super Sixes. While they should overcome both Bangladesh and Scotland in their Group B games they will need to produce some good performances to take one of the three Super Sixes spots from opponents Australia, Pakistan and the West Indies. In 17 games in total against these opponents they have won seven and lost ten.

Australia

Year	Stage	Result
1992	League	New Zealand won by 37 runs
1987	Group A	Australia won by 3 runs
1987	Group A	Australia won by 17 runs
1996	Quarter Final	Australia won by 6 wickets

England

Year	Stage	Result
1975	Group A	England won by 80 runs
1979	Semi Final	England won by 9 runs
1983	Group A	England won by 106 runs
1983	Group A	New Zealand won by 2 wickets
1992	League	New Zealand won by 7 wickets
1996	Group B	New Zealand won by 11 runs

India

Year	Stage	Result
1979	Group B	New Zealand won by 8 wickets
1987	Group A	India won by 16 runs
1987	Group A	India won by 9 wickets
1992	League	New Zealand won by 4 wickets

Pakistan

Year	Stage	Result
1983	Group A	New Zealand won by 52 runs
1983	Group A	Pakistan won by 11 runs
1992	League	Pakistan won by 7 wickets
1992	Semi Final	Pakistan won by 4 wickets
1996	Group B	Pakistan won by 46 runs

South Africa

Year	Stage	Result
1992	League	New Zealand won by 7 wickets
1996	Group B	South Africa won by 5 wickets

Sri Lanka

Year	Stage	Result
1979	Group B	New Zealand won by 9 wickets
1983	Group A	New Zealand won by 5 wickets
1983	Group A	Sri Lanka won by 3 wickets
1992	League	New Zealand won by 6 wickets

West Indies

Year	Stage	Result
1975	Semi Final	West Indies won by 5 wickets
1979	Group B	West Indies won by 32 runs
1992	League	New Zealand won by 7 wickets

Zimbabwe

Year	Stage	Result
1987	Group A	New Zealand won by 3 runs
1987	Group A	New Zealand won by 4 wickets
1992	League	New Zealand won by 48 runs

Pakistan in the World Cup

Australia, Bangladesh, New Zealand, Scotland and the West Indies provide the Group B opposition for Pakistan in the World Cup. The Pakistanis have yet to meet the newcomers Bangladesh and Scotland in the competition but anything but two wins from two against them would be considered a national disaster in the sub-continent. They have a 50% record against the Australians in the competition and have only lost one in five against the New Zealand team. It is the West Indies that historically have proved the real obstacle with just one win from six games.

Australia

Year	Stage	Result
1975	Group B	Australia won by 73 runs
1979	Group A	Pakistan won by 89 runs
1987	Semi Final	Australia won by 18 runs
1992	League	Pakistan won by 48 runs

England

Year	Stage	Result
1979	Group A	England won by 14 runs
1983	Group A	England won by 8 wickets
1983	Group A	England won by 7 wickets

1987	Group B	Pakistan won by 18 runs
1987	Group B	Pakistan won by 7 wickets
1992	League	No result
1992	Final	Pakistan won by 22 runs
1996	Group B	Pakistan won by 7 wickets

India

Year	Stage	Result
1992	League	India won by 43 runs
1996	Quarter Final	India won by 39 runs

New Zealand

Year	Stage	Result
1983	Group A	New Zealand won by 52 runs
1983	Group A	Pakistan won by 11 runs
1992	League	Pakistan won by 7 wickets
1992	Semi Final	Pakistan won by 4 wickets
1996	Group B	Pakistan won by 46 runs

South Africa

Year	Stage	Result
1992	League	South Africa won by 20 runs
1996	Group B	South Africa won by 5 wickets

Sri Lanka

Year	Stage	Result
1975	Group B	Pakistan won by 192 runs
1983	Group A	Pakistan won by 50 runs
1983	Group A	Pakistan won by 11 runs
1987	Group B	Pakistan won by 15 runs
1987	Group B	Pakistan won by 113 runs
1992	League	Pakistan won by 4 wickets

West Indies

Year	Stage	Result
1975	Group B	West Indies won by 1 wicket
1979	Semi Final	West Indies won by 43 runs
1983	Semi Final	West Indies won by 8 wickets
1987	Group B	Pakistan won by 1 wicket
1987	Group B	West Indies won by 28 runs
1992	League	West Indies won by 10 wickets

Zimbabwe

Year	Stage	Result
1992	League	Pakistan won by 53 runs

South Africa in the World Cup

With ten wins from 15 games, South Africa boasts the best success rate percentage of all the World Cup finalists. However two of their Group A opponents, England and Sri Lanka, have managed to inflict three of those four defeats, England being victors in two of their three games. Nevertheless such is the form of the South Africans that it will be a major surprise if they do not progress into the Super Sixes. Their other Group A opponents are India, Kenya, and Zimbabwe.

Australia

Year	Stage	Result
1992	League	South Africa won by 9 wickets

England

Year	Stage	Result
1992	League	England won by 3 wickets
1992	Semi Final	England won by 19 runs
1996	Group B	South Africa won by 78 runs

India

Year	Stage	Result
1992	League	South Africa won by 6 wickets

New Zealand

Year	Stage	Result
1992	League	New Zealand won by 7 wickets
1996	Group B	South Africa won by 5 wickets

Pakistan

Year	Stage	Result
1992	League	South Africa won by 20 runs
1996	Group B	South Africa won by 5 wickets

Sri Lanka

Year	Stage	Result
1992	League	Sri Lanka won by 3 wickets

West Indies

Year	Stage	Result
1992	League	South Africa won by 64 runs
1996	Quarter Final	West Indies won by 19 runs

Zimbabwe

Year	Stage	Result
1992	League	South Africa won by 7 wickets

Sri Lanka in the World Cup

The only time that Sri Lanka managed to get beyond the Group stage of the World Cup they won the competition. That happened in India in 1996 so they arrive in England as the reigning World Cup holders. They start their defence of the trophy in Group A where they are paired with England, India, Kenya, South Africa and Zimbabwe. On past form in the Finals only England have had the spell over the Sri Lankans – winning five of their previous six encounters. The Sri Lankans' record against the other teams in the competition is such that they will feel confident of progressing to the Super Sixes.

Australia

Year	Stage	Result
1975	Group B	Australia won by 52 runs
1992	League	Australia won by 7 wickets
1996	Group A	Sri Lanka won by default
1996	Final	Sri Lanka won by 7 wickets

England

Year	Stage	Result
1983	Group A	England won by 47 runs
1983	Group A	England won by 9 wickets
1987	Group B	England won on faster scoring rate
1987	Group B	England won by 8 wickets
1992	League	England won by 106 runs
1996	Quarter Final	Sri Lanka won by 5 wickets

India

Year	Stage	Result
1979	Group B	Sri Lanka won by 47 runs
1992	League	No result
1996	Group A	Sri Lanka won by 6 wickets
1996	Semi Final	Sri Lanka won by default

Kenya

Year	Stage	Result
1996	Group A	Sri Lanka won by 144 runs

New Zealand

Year	Stage	Result
1979	Group B	New Zealand won by 9 wickets
1983	Group A	New Zealand won by 5 wickets
1983	Group A	Sri Lanka won by 3 wickets
1992	League	New Zealand won by 6 wickets

Pakistan

Year	Stage	Result
1975	Group B	Pakistan won by 192 runs
1983	Group A	Pakistan won by 50 runs
1983	Group A	Pakistan won by 11 runs
1987	Group B	Pakistan won by 15 runs
1987	Group B	Pakistan won by 113 runs
1992	League	Pakistan won by 4 wickets

South Africa

Year	Stage	Result
1992	League	Sri Lanka won by 3 wickets

West Indies

Year	Stage	Result
1975	Group B	West Indies won by 9 wickets
1979	Group B	No Result – rain
1987	Group B	West Indies won by 191 runs
1987	Group B	West Indies won by 25 runs
1992	League	West Indies won by 91 runs
1996	Group A	Sri Lanka won by default

Zimbabwe

Year	Stage	Result
1992	League	Sri Lanka won by 3 wickets
1996	Group A	Sri Lanka won by 6 wickets

West Indies in the World Cup

Looking at results from previous World Cup encounters would suggest that the West Indies will breeze through their Group B games and make it readily into the Super Six stage of the competition. Wins against Bangladesh and Scotland in the first games against these countries look assured – but complacency will not enter the West Indian camp as they will recall that they were sensationally embarrassed by the Kenyan team in the 1996 competition. Against Australia, New Zealand and Pakistan the West Indians have played a total of 18 times and won 12 of them.

Australia

Year	Stage	Result
1975	Group B	New Zealand won by 4 wickets
1975	Final	West Indies won by 17 runs
1983	Group B	West Indies won by 101 runs
1983	Group B	West Indies won by 7 wickets
1992	League	Australia won by 57 runs
1996	Group A	West Indies won by 4 wickets
1996	Semi Final	Australia won by 5 runs

England

Year	Stage	Result
1979	Final	West Indies won by 92 runs
1987	Group B	England won by 2 wickets
1987	Group B	England won by 34 runs
1992	League	England won by 6 wickets

India

Year	Stage	Result
1979	Group B	West Indies won by 9 wickets
1983	Group B	India won by 34 runs
1983	Group B	West Indies won by 66 runs
1983	Final	India won by 43 runs
1992	League	West Indies won by 5 runs
1996	Group A	India won by 5 wickets

Kenya

Year	Stage	Result
1996	Group A	Kenya won by 73 runs

New Zealand

Year	Stage	Result
1975	Semi Final	West Indies won by 5 wickets
1979	Group B	West Indies won by 32 runs
1992	League	New Zealand won by 7 wickets

Pakistan

Year	Stage	Result
1975	Group B	West Indies won by 1 wicket
1979	Semi Final	West Indies won by 43 runs
1992	League	West Indies won by 10 wickets
1983	Semi Final	West Indies won by 8 wickets
1987	Group B	Pakistan won by 1 wicket
1987	Group B	West Indies won by 28 runs

South Africa

Year	Stage	Result
1992	League	South Africa won by 64 runs
1996	Quarter Final	West Indies won by 19 runs

Sri Lanka

Year	Stage	Result
1975	Group B	West Indies won by 9 wicket
1979	Group B	No Result – rain
1987	Group B	West Indies won by 191 runs
1987	Group B	West Indies won by 25 runs
1992	League	West Indies won by 91 runs
1996	Group A	Sri Lanka won by default

Zimbabwe

Year	Stage	Result
1983	Group B	West Indies won by 8 wickets
1983	Group B	West Indies won by 10 wickets
1992	League	West Indies won by 75 runs
1996	Group A	West Indies won by 6 wickets

Zimbabwe in the World Cup

With just three wins from 25 World Cup games the portents don't look too good for Zimbabwe. However, as an international side they are starting to contest more one day international games and this will bear its own fruit in the years to come. Of those three wins one came against Kenya whom they will face in Group A of the competition and which should also bring another victory. They also face an England side they beat in the 1992 competition in the only match-up between the sides at this stage to date. The other win came against Australia who are in the other group. Games against their other Group A opponents India, Sri Lanka and South Africa have resulted in nine defeats from nine games.

Australia

Year	Stage	Result
1983	Group B	Zimbabwe won by 13 runs
1983	Group B	Australia won by 32 runs
1987	Group A	Australia won by 96 runs
1987	Group A	Australia won by 70 runs
1992	League	Australia won by 128 runs
1996	Group A	Australia won by 8 wickets

England

Year	Stage	Result
1992	League	Zimbabwe won by 7 runs

India

Year	Stage	Result
1983	Group B	India won by 5 wickets
1983	Group B	India won by 31 runs
1987	Group A	India won by 8 wickets
1987	Group A	India won by 7 wickets
1992	League	India won by 55 runs
1996	Group A	India won by 40 runs

Kenya

Year	Stage	Result
1996	Group A	Zimbabwe won by 5 wickets

New Zealand

Year	Stage	Result
1987	Group A	New Zealand won by 3 runs
1987	Group A	New Zealand won by 4 wickets
1992	League	New Zealand won by 48 runs

Pakistan

Year	Stage	Result
1992	League	Pakistan won by 53 runs

South Africa

Year	Stage	Result
1992	League	South Africa won by 7 wickets

Sri Lanka

Year	Stage	Result
1992	League	Sri Lanka won by 3 wickets
1996	Group A	Sri Lanka won by 6 wickets

West Indies

Year	Stage	Result
1983	Group B	West Indies won by 8 wickets
1983	Group B	West Indies won by 10 wickets
1992	League	West Indies won by 75 runs
1996	Group A	West Indies won by 6 wickets

QUALIFYING TOURNAMENT

Carlsberg ICC Trophy

The sixth ICC Trophy – held from 24th March to 12th April 1997 – was the largest international cricket tournament ever staged. Hosted in Asia for the first time, 22 teams participated, including every ICC associate member except for Nepal. Italy and Scotland made their appearances for the first time.

The teams played for a variety of incentives: the Trophy itself to the tournament winners, places in the following year's inaugural Commonwealth Games cricket contest (also in Malaysia) for the four best eligible teams, and a place in the first division of the anticipated two-tier structure for the 2001 ICC Tournament. Plus the most lucrative incentive of all: one of three places in the 1999 World Cup in England, together with all the prestige, sponsorship and developmental opportunities which that brings. Changes to residential qualifications meant that defending champions the United Arab Emirates were considered outsiders in their bid to repeat their victory.

Despite the threat of rain, play began unhindered on 24th March. East and Central Africa were dismissed for 26 by Holland who overhauled their total in just 5.3 overs for one of the quickest ever wins. Azam Khan grabbed seven wickets for nine runs.

USA defeated Singapore by 106 runs on day one and Gibraltar by 189 on day two. Kenya, the giant-killers of the West Indies in 1996, stuttered up to Singapore's 89 all out with just two wickets to spare. Scotland notched up an 87 run victory over fancied Hong Kong, whilst fellow newcomers Italy lost by 101 runs to Papua New Guinea.

The first American defeat, on day four, was in a last-over thriller at the hands of Mike Hendrick's Irish team. Kenya were still shaky in winning over Gibraltar. Bangladesh meanwhile won convincingly over Denmark to make it three out of three. Bangladesh came close to World Cup qualification in the 1990 ICC tournament and were pushed out of the final four in 1994. Could they be another Sri Lanka about to emerge from the subcontinent to surprise the cricketing world?

The Duckworth-Lewis rain rule was invoked to determine victories by Malaysia and Gibraltar on day five. This is a complicated rule which may find itself in regular use unless the English climate behaves. The United Arab Emirates' hopes of a place in the second round crashed as Bangladesh bowled them out for 95. Kenya played much more confidently with a 119 run victory over Ireland, Maurice Odumbe 99 not out. Scotland soundly defeated Italy 273 to 142.

The final eight was settled on the final day of the first round, day seven. UAE didn't make it, nor did Bermuda, coached by former Australian manager Bob Simpson. USA didn't make it. Kenya scored 243 for 7 and 19 overs later, the USA's World Cup dreams were all out for 32. Israel, who had been granted permission to enter Malaysia (a Muslim country) to compete, were scheduled to play Gibraltar at the PKNS ground but the Israeli side were driven under tight security to a new ground to avoid a demonstration. Canada and the Netherlands, who had swapped grounds, had to abandon their match without a ball being bowled, due to mistaken identity as the demonstrators burned placards.

The top eight grouped into two sections of four each. The first day of the second round saw Kenya murder Canada as Maurice Odumbe's 148 not out (seven sixes) was more than the North Americans' total. The Duckworth-Lewis formula was in constant use as the rain began to interfere. The officials' calculators finally displayed that Bangladesh, Kenya, Scotland and Ireland were through to the semi-finals. The Dutch bid for their second consecutive World Cup entry, and an opportunity to play at home in Amstelveen, was gone.

As the rain continued to intervene, all of the last week's finals became two-day fixtures, the tournament regulations permitting the continuation of matches across to a reserve day. Odumbe scored 67 for Kenya as they put out Ireland by just seven runs. Bangladesh, looking for their first World Cup place, ended the first day of their clash with Scotland at 243 for seven. This target proved too much for the Scottish on the second evening as they fell to 171 all out.

Scotland versus Ireland in Kuala Lumpur was the line-up in the play-off for the third and final World Cup place. Rain reduced the match to 45 overs a side, and the Duckworth-Lewis formula saw Ireland chasing 192 after Scotland had scored 187 for 8. The gallant Irish fell short at 141 all out. Scotland, the first-timers of the ICC Trophy tournament, were now qualified for cricket's most important limited-over competition.

Overnight rain ensured a late start and a two-day final. Kenya were 15 for two but a partnership of 138 by Steve Tikolo and Maurice Odumbe saw Kenya on their way to 241 for seven from their 50 overs. Tikolo played the innings of the tournament to finish with 147 from 152 deliveries. Bangladesh used nine bowlers.

Persistent rain delayed the second day's start for six hours, reducing Bangladesh's innings to 25 overs. The Duckworth-Lewis-adjusted target was 166, at a run rate just over 6.5 runs per over. Martin Suji clean bowled Naimur Rahman first ball but then Mohammad Rafique and Minjahul Abedin blasted 50 runs in less than seven overs. The batsmen who followed kept up the pace and with five overs remaining Bangladesh needed 45 to win with five wickets in hand. It came down to the last over. Bangladesh were 155 for eight. Khaled Mashud hit a powerful shot straight down the ground for six. Then came a miss, a vital wide, a sharp single, a second dot ball and then two runs from Hasibul Hussain. All the Kenyan players came in to save the single off the last ball and the Bangladeshis won it with a leg bye.

Bangladesh secured the 1997 ICC Trophy championship with a fine team performance under manager Ghazi Ashraf Lipu and the coaching of West Indian legend Gordon Greenidge, who was subsequently awarded Bangladeshi nationality. The man of the tournament was Maurice Odumbe, the leading run-scorer with 493 runs at an average of 98.60 and a strike-rate of 86.94.

Final Rankings

Rank	Team	Honours
1	Bangladesh	ICC Trophy Champions and 1999 World Cup qualification
2	Kenya	1999 World Cup qualification
3	Scotland	1999 World Cup qualification
4	Ireland	
5	Denmark	
6	Netherlands	
7	Canada	
8	Hong Kong	
9	Bermuda	Philip Snow Plate
10	United Arab Emirates	
11	Fiji	
12	United States of America	
13	Papua New Guinea	
14	Singapore	
15	Namibia	
16	Malaysia	
17	East & Central Africa	
18	West Africa	
19	Gibraltar	
20	Argentina	
21=	Israel	
21=	Italy	

Malaysia: 24th March - 12th April 1997

Group A

	P	W	L	NR	Pts
Kenya †	5	5	–	–	10
Ireland †	5	4	1	–	8
USA	5	3	2	–	6
Singapore	5	2	3	–	4
Gibraltar	5	1	4	–	2
Israel	5	–	5	–	0

Match	Result
USA v Singapore	USA won by 106 runs
Ireland v Gibraltar	Ireland won by 192 runs
Kenya v Israel	Kenya won by 7 wickets
Kenya v Singapore	Kenya won by 2 wickets
USA v Gibraltar	USA won by 189 runs
Ireland v Israel	Ireland won by 10 wickets
Kenya v Gibraltar	Kenya won by 7 wickets
Singapore v Israel	Singapore won by 65 runs
USA v Ireland	Ireland won by 2 wickets
Gibraltar v Singapore	Singapore won on higher comparative score after rain stopped play
Kenya v Ireland	Kenya won by 119 runs
USA v Israel	USA won by 7 wickets
Kenya v USA	Kenya won by 211 runs
Gibraltar v Israel	Gibraltar won by 2 wickets
Ireland v Singapore	Ireland won by 10 wickets

Group B

	P	W	L	NR	Pts
Bangladesh †	5	5	–	–	10
Denmark †	5	4	1	–	8
UAE	5	3	2	–	6
Malaysia	5	2	3	–	4
West Africa	5	1	4	–	2
Argentina	5	–	5	–	0

Match	Result
Malaysia v Denmark	Denmark won by 31 runs
Bangladesh v Argentina	Bangladesh won by 5 wickets
UAE v West Africa	UAE won by 7 wickets
Bangladesh v West Africa	Bangladesh won by 9 wickets
Malaysia v Argentina	Malaysia won by 81 runs
UAE v Denmark	Denmark won by 1 wicket
Bangladesh v Denmark	Bangladesh won by 5 wickets
UAE v Malaysia	UAE won by 2 wickets
West Africa v Argentina	West Africa won by 5 wickets
Malaysia v West Africa	Malaysia won on higher comparative score after rain stopped play
Denmark v Argentina	Denmark won by 150 runs
Bangladesh v UAE	Bangladesh won by 100 runs
Bangladesh v Malaysia	Bangladesh won by 59 runs
Denmark v West Africa	Denmark won by 8 wickets
UAE v Argentina	UAE won by 8 wickets

Group C

	P	W	L	NR	Pts	RR
Holland †	4	3	–	1	7	2.94
Canada †	4	3	–	1	7	0.86
Fiji	4	2	2	–	4	
Namibia	4	1	3	–	2	
East & Central Africa	4	–	4	–	0	

Match	Result
Holland v East & C.Africa	Holland won by 8 wickets
Canada v Fiji	Canada won by 4 wickets
Holland v Namibia	Holland won by 10 wickets
Canada v Namibia	Canada won by 60 runs
Fiji v East & C.Africa	Fiji won by 35 runs
Namibia v East & C.Africa	Namibia won by 1 wicket
Holland v Fiji	Holland won by 6 wickets
Namibia v Fiji	Fiji won by 105 runs
Canada v East & C.Africa	Canada won by 4 wickets
Holland v Canada	No result. Drawn game Crowd invaded pitch – match abandoned

Group D

	P	W	L	NR	Pts
Scotland †	4	4	–	–	8
Hong Kong †	4	3	1	–	6
Bermuda	4	2	2	–	4
Papua New Guinea	4	1	3	–	2
Italy	4	–	4	–	0

Match	Result
Bermuda v Italy	Bermuda won by 7 wickets
Bermuda v Hong Kong	Hong Kong won by 3 wickets
Scotland v PNG	Scotland won by 6 wickets
PNG v Italy	Papua New Guinea won by 101 runs
Scotland v Hong Kong	Scotland won by 87 runs
Bermuda v PNG	Bermuda won by 121 runs
Hong Kong v Italy	Hong Kong won by 145 runs
Hong Kong v PNG	Hong Kong won by 81 runs
Scotland v Italy	Scotland won by 131 runs
Bermuda v Scotland	Scotland won by 57 runs

Second Round – Group E

	P	W	L	NR	Pts
Kenya †	3	2	–	1	5
Scotland †	3	1	1	1	3
Denmark	3	1	1	1	3
Canada	3	–	2	1	1

Match	Result
Kenya v Canada	Kenya won on higher comparative score after rain stopped play
Scotland v Denmark	Scotland won by 45 runs
Scotland v Canada	No result. Match abandoned due to rain
Kenya v Denmark	No result. Match abandoned due to rain
Kenya v Scotland	Kenya won on higher comparative score after rain stopped play
Denmark v Canada	Denmark won by 7 runs

Second Round – Group F

	P	W	L	NR	Pts
Bangladesh †	3	2	–	1	5
Ireland †	3	2	–	1	5
Hong Kong	3	–	2	1	1
Holland	3	–	2	1	1

Match	*Result*
Holland v Ireland	Ireland won on higher comparative score after rain stopped play
Bangladesh v Hong Kong	Bangladesh won by 7 wickets
Holland v Hong Kong	No result. Match abandoned due to rain
Bangladesh v Ireland	No result. Match abandoned due to rain
Bangladesh v Holland	Bangladesh won by 15 runs
Ireland v Hong Kong	Ireland won by 51 runs

Semi-Finals

Kenya v Ireland	Kenya won by 7 wickets
Bangladesh v Scotland	Bangladesh won by 72 runs

Consolation Match

Ireland v Scotland	Scotland won on higher comparative score after rain stopped play

† = *qualified for next stage*

The Final

Venue: Kuala Lumpur, Malaysia   Date: 12th - 13th April, 1997
Toss: Bangladesh
Umpires: DB Hair (A) and S Venkataraghavan (I)
Man of the Match: S Tikolo
Bangladesh won on run-rate basis, chasing reduced target

Kenya			Runs
Asif Karim		b Saif-ul-Salam	0
SK Gupta	c and b Khalid Mahmood		16
K Otieno +	lbw	b Saif-ul-Salam	2
S Tikolo	c Saif-ur-Rehman	b Khalid Mahmood	147
M Odumbe *	st Khalid Masood	b Mohammed Rafiq	43
T Odoyo		b Mohammed Rafiq	1
Hitesh Modi	Not Out		12

184

A Suji	st Khalid Masood	b Mohammed Rafiq	1
D Tikolo			
M Suji			
B Patel			
Extras	(b1, lb9, w9)		19
Total	*(50 overs – for seven wickets)*		*241*

Bangladesh	O	M	R	W	Fall of wickets
Saif-ul-Islam	9	0	39	2	0, 15, 58, 196, 212
Hasib-ul-Hassan	6	0	15	0	230, 241
Athar Ali Khan	5	0	22	0	
Khalid Mahmood	7	1	31	2	
Enam-ul-Haque	10	0	41	0	
Naim-ur-Rehman	4	0	21	0	
Mohammed Rafiq	6	1	40	3	
Akram Khan	3	0	22	0	

Bangladesh			Runs
Naim-ur-Rehman		b M.Suji	0
Mohammed Rafiq	c Odumbe	b A.Suji	26
Minhaz-ul-Abedin	c Patel	b Odoyo	26
Amin-ul-Islam		b Asif Karim	37
*Akram Khan	c Odoyo	b Odumbe	22
Enam-ul-Haque	c Gupta	b Asif Karim	5
Saif-ul-Islam	c Odumbe	b Asif Karim	14
+Khalid Masood	Not Out		15
Khalid Mahmood	st Otieno	b Odumbe	5
Hasib-ul-Hasan	Not Out		4
Athar Ali Khan			
Extras	(b3, lb4, w5)		12
Total	*(25 overs – for eight wickets)*		*166*

West Indies	O	M	R	W	Fall of wickets
M Suji	4	0	28	1	0, 50, 63, 116
S Tikolo	4	0	29	0	118, 123, 139
Odoyo	5	0	27	1	151
A Suji	5	0	26	1	
Asif Karim	4	0	31	3	
Odumbe	3	0	18	2	

WORLD CUP FINALS

Details of previous World Cup Finals can be found on the following pages. This includes a review of the competition, the Final Scorecard and details of how each team reached the final. A quick summary of each Final is produced below for ease of reference.

1975   Tournament held in England
      West Indies beat Australia by 17 runs

1979   Tournament held in England
      West Indies beat England by 92 runs

1983   Tournament held in England
      India beat West Indies by 43 runs

1987   Tournament held in Pakistan
      Australia beat England by 7 runs

1992   Tournament held in New Zealand and Australia
      Pakistan beat England by 22 runs

1996   Tournament held in India, Pakistan and Sri Lanka
      Sri Lanka beat Australia by 7 wickets

Winners

West Indies	(twice)	1975, 1979
India	(one)	1983
Australia	(one)	1987
Pakistan	(one)	1992
Sri Lanka	(one)	1996

1975

West Indies beat Australia by 17 runs

England vs India was the opener and Dennis Amiss used a fast outfield to make 137 in what was then a record one day score in 60 overs of 334 for four. India made no attempt to win the game in a bizarre start to the World Cup. There was an upset when Pakistan's Sarfraz shocked West Indies' famous batsmen with four quick wickets. A last wicket stand of 64 between Andy Roberts and Deryck Murray got West Indies home with two balls to spare. Lillee and Thomson (who had devastated England a few months before) bowled too short against the minnows Sri Lanka and won no admirers. In the clash of the Titans, the West Indies' stroke-players made easy work of the Aussie pacemen as 'little man' Kallicharan ripped into Dennis Lillee, with four fours from four bouncers.

At Headingley in the first semi, only Denness and Arnold got into double figures in a disastrous England 93. Gary Gilmour's six for 14 suited the green wicket and the ball swung and seamed. Snow, Arnold and Old then reduced the Australians to 39 for six before Walters and Gilmour rescued them. West Indies' Julian, Holder and Roberts knocked New Zealand over for 158 and the favourites won with nearly 20 overs to spare.

In the Lord's final Fredericks hit his wicket while hitting a six for the first breakthrough. At an uncharacteristic 50 for three, captain Clive Lloyd came to the middle. Dropped by Edwards, Lloyd took huge advantage with a century off 82 balls. Gilmour fought back (5 for 48) but West Indies set a total of 259 for eight. Ian Chappell replied effectively until Richards ran out Turner, Greg Chappell and Ian Chappell in succession. Walters and Marsh counter-attacked but a steady fall of wickets brought together Lillee and Thomson with 59 to win in seven overs. They needed only 18 off nine balls when Murray stumped Thompson to make West Indies the first ever world champions.

The Final

Venue: Lord's, London   Date: 21st June, 1975

Toss: Australia   Umpires: HD Bird and TW Spencer

Man of the Match: CH Lloyd

West Indies			Runs	Balls	4/6
RC Fredricks	hit wicket	b Lillee	7	13	–
CG Greenidge	c Marsh	b Thomson	13	61	1
AI Kallicharran	c Marsh	b Gilmour	12	18	2
RB Kanhai	b Gilmour		55	105	8
CH Lloyd †	c Marsh	b Gilmour	102	85	12/2
IVA Richards	b Gilmour		5	11	1
KD Boyce	c GS Chappell	b Thomson	34	37	3
BD Julien	Not Out		26	37	1
DL Murray +	c and b Gilmour		14	10	1/1
VA Holder	Not Out		6	2	1
AME Roberts					
Extras	(lb6, nb11)		17		
Total	*(60 overs, for eight wickets)*		*291*		

Australia	O	M	R	W	Fall of wickets	
Lillee	12	1	55	1	12, 27, 50, 199, 206	
Gilmour	12	2	48	5	209, 261, 285	
Thomson	12	1	44	2		
Walker	12	1	71	0		
GS Chappell	7	0	33	0		
Walters	5	0	23	0		

Australia			Runs	Balls	4/6
A Turner	Run Out		40	24	1
RB McCosker	c Kallicharran	b Boyce	7	54	4
IM Chappell †	Run Out		62	93	6
GS Chappell	Run Out		15	23	2
KD Walters	b Lloyd		35	51	5
RW Marsh +	b Boyce		11	24	–
R Edwards	c Fredricks	b Boyce	28	37	2
GJ Gilmour	c Kanhai	b Boyce	14	11	2
MHN Walker	Run Out		7	9	1
JR Thomson	Run Out		21	21	2
DK Lillee	Not Out		16	19	1
Extras	(b2, lb9, nb7)		18		
Total	*(58.4 overs – all out)*		*274*		

188

West Indies	O	M	R	W	Fall of wickets
Julien	12	0	58	0	25, 81, 115, 162
Roberts	11	1	45	0	170, 195, 221
Boyce	12	0	50	4	231, 233, 274
Holder	11.4	1	65	0	
Lloyd	12	1	38	1	

Final Route

West Indies

Group B: Beat Sri Lanka by 9 wickets at Old Trafford on 7 June
Sri Lanka: 86-10 (37.2); de Silva 21 and 1-33
West Indies: 87-1 (20.4); Fredericks 30, Julien 4-20

Group B: Beat Pakistan by 1 wicket at Edgbaston on 11 June
Pakistan: 266-7 (60); Khan 60, Nawaz 4-44
West Indies: 267-9 (59.4); Murray 61*, Richards 1-21

Group B: Beat Australia by 7 wickets at The Oval on 14 June
Australia: 192-10 (53.4); Edwards 58, Mallett 1-35
West Indies: 195-3 (46); Kallicharran 78, Roberts 3-39

Semi-Final: Beat New Zealand by 5 wickets at The Oval on 18 June
New Zealand: 158-10 (52.2); Howarth 51, Collinge 3-28
West Indies: 159-5 (40.1); Kallicharran 72, Julien 4-21

Australia

Group B: Beat Pakistan by 73 runs at Headingley on 7 June
Australia: 278-7 (60); Edwards 80*, Lillee 5-34
Pakistan: 205 all out (53); Khan 65, Malik 2-37

Group B: Beat Sri Lanka by 52 runs at The Oval on 11 June
Australia: 328-5 (60); Turner 101, Chappell 2-14
Sri Lanka: 276-4 (60); Wettimuny 53r, de Silva 2-60

Group B: Lost to West Indies by 7 wickets at The Oval on 14 June
Australia: 192-10 (53.4); Edwards 58, Mallett 1-35
West Indies: 195-3 (46); Kallicharran 78, Roberts 3-39

Semi-Final: Beat England by 4 wickets at Headingley on 18 June
England: 93 all out (36.2) – Denness 27, Old 3-29
Australia: 94-6 (28.4) – Gilmour 28* and 6-14

1979

West Indies beat England by 92 runs

The Kerry Packer circus changed the way cricket was played just prior to the second World Cup and the Australian team consisted of only those players who had stayed loyal to the traditional authorities. For the first time, two of the teams – Canada and Sri Lanka – had qualified from the new ICC Trophy. Geoff Boycott bowled a partnership-breaking over or two in the first match at Lord's against Australia. The fast bowling quintet of Roberts, Holding, Garner, Croft and King looked to make West Indies invincible but it was Greenidge who brought the crowd onto the pitch with an opening century. After two games, England and Pakistan were through. Against the odds Sri Lanka beat India but didn't progress as West Indies, with Greenidge and Lloyd in form, beat New Zealand to secure their place alongside their defeated opponents. England beat Pakistan to avoid West Indies in the semi-final. Mike Hendrick grabbed four for 15 and Boycott continued his surprising bowling career.

In the first semi, Pakistan had 280 to chase and began well but the West Indies' fast bowlers had strength in depth and West Indies went on to win by 43 runs. At a packed Old Trafford New Zealand got off to a good start chasing England's 221, until Randall ran out Wright. Boycott got another wicket and Hendrick got danger man Cairns as New Zealand ran out of overs.

Willis was lost to a knee injury for the final. Derek Randall struck again by running out Greenidge but the lesser bowlers had to bowl to Viv Richards and Collis King. Richards casually moved to a century and off the last ball, on 132, he hit a full toss from Hendrick (attempting the yorker) for six. The run rate was 4.75 an over and Garner yorked out the middle order batsmen (three in an over), as they tried to play strokes. Man of the match Lloyd was soon holding up the Prudential Cup.

The Final

Venue: Lord's, London   Date: 23rd June, 1979
Toss: England   Umpires: HD Bird and BJ Meyer
Man of the Match: IVA Richards

West Indies

			Runs	Balls	4/6
CG Greenidge	Run Out		9	31	–
DL Haynes	c Hendrick	b Old	20	27	3
IVA Richards	Not Out		138	157	11/3
AI Kallicharran		b Hendrick	4	17	–
CH Lloyd †	c and b Old		13	33	2
CL King	c Randall	b Edmonds	86	66	10/3
DL Murray +	c Gower	b Edmonds	5	9	1
AME Roberts	c Brearley	b Hendrick	0	7	–
J Garner	c Taylor	b Botham	0	5	–
MA Holding		b Botham	0	6	–
CEH Croft	Not Out		0	2	–
Extras	(b1, lb 10)		11		
Total	*(60 overs – for nine wickets)*		286		

England

	O	M	R	W		Fall of wickets
Botham	12	2	44	2		22, 36, 55, 99, 238
Hendrick	12	2	50	2		252, 258, 260, 272
Old	12	0	55	2		
Boycott	6	0	38	0		
Edmonds	12	2	40	2		
Gooch	4	0	27	0		
Larkins	2	0	21	0		

England

			Runs	Balls	4/6
JM Brearley †	c King	b Holding	64	130	7
G Boycott	c Kallicharran	b Holding	57	105	3
DW Randall	b Croft		15	22	–
GA Gooch	b Garner		32	28	4
DI Gower	b Garner		0	4	–
IT Botham	c Richards	b Croft	4	3	–
W Larkins	b Garner		0	1	–
PH Edmonds	Not Out		5	8	–
CM Old		b Garner	0	2	–
RW Taylor +	c Murray	b Garner	0	1	–
M Hendrick	b Croft		0	5	–

| Extras | (lb12, w2, nb3) | | | | 17 |
| Total | (51 overs – all out) | | | | 194 |

West Indies	O	M	R	W	Fall of wickets
Roberts	9	2	33	0	129, 135, 183
Holding	8	1	16	2	183, 186, 186
Croft	10	1	42	3	192, 192, 194
Garner	11	0	38	5	194
Richards	10	0	35	0	
King	3	0	13	0	

Final Route

West Indies

Group B: Beat India by 9 wickets at Edgbaston on 9 June
India: 190-10 (53.1); Viswanath 75, Kapil Dev 1-46
West Indies: 194-1 (51.3); Greenidge 106*, Holding 4-33

Group B: West Indies beat New Zealand by 32 runs on 16 June
West Indies: 244-7 (60); Lloyd 73*, Roberts 3-43
New Zealand: 212-9 (60); Hadlee 42, Coney 2-40

Semi-Final: Beat Pakistan by 43 runs at The Oval on 20 June
West Indies: 293-6 (60); Greenidge 73, Richards 3-52
Pakistan: 250-10 (56.2); Zaheer Abbas 93, Iqbal 4056

England

Group A: Beat Australia by 6 wickets at Lord's on 9 June
Australia: 159-9 (60); Hilditch 47, Laughlin 2-36
England: 160-4 (47.1); Gooch 53, Boycott 2-15

Group A: Beat Canada by 8 wickets at Old Trafford on 14 June
Canada: 45-10 (40.3); Dennis 21, Callender 1-14
England: 46-2 (13.5); Gooch 21*, Old 4-8

Group A: Beat Pakistan by 14 runs at Headingley on 16 June
England: 165-9 (60); Gooch 33, Hendrick 4-14
Pakistan: 151-10 (56); Asif Iqbal 51, Sikander Bahkt 3-32

Semi-Final: Beat New Zealand by 9 runs at Old Trafford on 20 June
England: 221-8 (60); Gooch 71, Hendrick 3-55
New Zealand: 212-9 (60); Wright 69, McKechnie 2-46

1983

India beat West Indies by 43 runs

With Sri Lanka now elevated to Test ranks, only one country was able to progress from the ICC trophy. Zimbabwe won through and inflicted an embarrassing 13-run defeat on Australia in their first match. As previously the teams played each other twice to determine the semi-finalists, with no quarter-finals. Australia's mishap against Zimbabwe, and another setback at India's hand, cost them a place in the semi-finals. England sailed through their group with emphatic victories, losing only once, narrowly to New Zealand at Edgbaston.

The semi-finals, at The Oval and Old Trafford, were also a bit one-sided, but from England's point of view, the wrong side. West Indies completed a straightforward victory over Pakistan and India had an equally comfortable victory over England, whose disappointing total of 213 never looked enough to test a talented batting side.

In the final at Lord's, West Indies seemed set for a comfortable victory when they dismissed India for 183, Srikkanth top scoring with 38. At 111 for six it looked all over but India batted into the 54th over to keep the winner's door slightly ajar. Andy Roberts, one of the four survivors from the 1975 final, returned the best bowling figures, three for 32, his analysis including the vital wicket of the prolific Sunil Gavaskar for two. All-rounder Larry Gomes chipped in with a couple of wickets.

West Indies seemed to be cruising to victory at 50 for one, but then a fine running catch by Kapil Dev to dispose of Richards, and an untimely injury which restricted Lloyd, slowed the champions down. India's eager medium pacers chipped away at the middle order, and suddenly West Indies were facing defeat. The gentle floaters of Amarnath, the eventual man of the match (he also scored 33), accounted for three late wickets, and India had won a famous victory.

The Final

Venue: Lord's, London   Date: 25th June, 1983
Toss: West Indies   Umpires: HD Bird and BJ Meyer
Man of the Match: M Amarnath

India			*Runs*	*Balls*	*4/6*
SM Gavaskar	c Dujon	b Roberts	2	12	–
K Srikkanth	lbw	b Marshall	38	57	7/1
M Amarnath		b Holding	26	80	3
Yashpal Sharma	c sub (Logie)	b Gomes	11	32	1
SM Patil	c Gomes	b Garner	27	29	-/1
N Kapil Dev †	c Holding	b Gomes	15	8	3
K Azad	c Garner	b Roberts	0	3	–
RMH Binny	c Garner	b Roberts	2	8	–
Madan Lal		b Marshall	17	27	-/1
SMH Kirmani		b Holding	14	43	–
BS Sandhu	Not Out		11	30	1
Extras	(b5, lb5, w9, nb1)		20		
Total	*(54.4 overs)*		*183*		

West Indies	*O*	*M*	*R*	*W*	*Fall of wickets*
Roberts	10	3	32	3	2, 59, 90, 92, 110
Garner	12	4	24	1	111, 130, 153, 161
Marshall	11	1	24	2	183
Holding	9.4	2	26	2	
Gomes	11	1	49	2	
Richards	1	0	8	0	
Larkins	2	0	21	0	

West Indies			*Runs*	*Balls*	*4/6*
CG Greenidge		b Sandhu	1	12	–
DL Haynes	c Binny	b Madan Lal	13	33	2
IVA Richards	c Kapil Dev	b Madan Lal	33	28	7
CH Lloyd †	c Kapil Dev	b Binny	8	17	1
HA Gomes	c Gavaskar	b Madan Lal	5	16	–
SFAF Bacchus	c Kirmani	b Sandhu	8	25	–
PJL Dujon +		b Amarnath	25	73	-/1
MD Marshall	c Gavaskar	b Amarnath	18	51	–
AME Roberts	lbw	b Kapil Dev	4	14	–
J Garner	Not Out		5	19	–
MA Holding	lbw	b Amarnath	6	24	–

Extras	(lb4, w10)			14	
Total	*(52 overs – all out)*			*140*	

India	*O*	*M*	*R*	*W*	*Fall of wickets*
Kapil Dev	11	4	21	1	5, 50, 57, 66, 66
Sandhu	9	1	32	2	76, 119, 124, 126
Madan Lal	12	2	31	3	140
Binny	10	1	23	1	
Amarnath	7	0	12	3	
Azad	3	0	7	0	

Final Route

West Indies

Group B: Lost to India by 34 runs at Old Trafford on 9/10 June
India: 262-8 (60); Sharma 89, Shastri 3-26
West Indies: Roberts 37*, Holding 2-32

Group B: Beat Australia by 101 runs at Headingley on 11/12 June
West Indies: 252-9 (60); Gomes 78, Davis 7-10.3
Australia: 151-10 (30.3); Hookes 45, Lawson 3-29

Group B: West Indies beat Zimbabwe by 8 wickets
at Worcester on 13 June
Zimbabwe: 217-7 (60); Fletcher 71*, Rawson 2-39
West Indies: 218-2 (48.3); Greenidge 105*, Roberts 3-36

Group B: Beat India by 66 runs at The Oval on 15 June
West Indies: 282-9 (60); Richards 119, Holding 3-40
India: 216-10 (53.1); Amarnath 80, Binny 3-71

Group B: Beat Australia by 7 wickets at Lord's on 18 June
Australia: 273-10 (60); Hughes 69, Hogg 1-25
West Indies: 276-3 (57.5); Greenidge 90, Marshall 2-36

Group B: Beat Zimbabwe by 10 wickets at Edgbaston on 20 June
Zimbabwe: 171-10 (60); Curran 62, Traicos 0-24 (12)
West Indies: 172-0 (45.1); Haynes 88*, Danie 3-28

Semi-Final: Beat Pakistan by 8 wickets at The Oval on 22 June
Pakistan: 184-8 (60); Mohsin Khan 70, Rashid Khan 1-32
West Indies: 188-2 (48.4); Richards 80*, Marshall 3-28

India

Group B: Lost West Indies by 34 runs at Old Trafford on 9/10 June
India: 262-8 (60); Sharma 89, Shastri 3-26
West Indies: Roberts 37*, Holding 2-32

Group B: Beat Zimbabwe by 5 wickets at Leicester on 11 June
Zimbabwe: 155-10 (51.4); Butchart 22*, Rawson 2-11
India:157-5 (37.3); Patil 50, Madan Lal 3-27

Group B: Lost to Australia by 162 runs at Trent Bridge on 13 June
Australia: 320-9 (60); Chappell 110, Macleay 6-39
India: 158-10 (37.5); Kapil Dev 40 and 5-43

Group B: Lost to West Indies by 66 runs at The Oval on 15 June
West Indies: 282-9 (60); Richards 119, Holding 3-40
India: 216-10 (53.1); Amarnath 80, Binny 3-71

Group B: India beat Zimbabwe by 31 runs at Tunbridge Wells
on 18 June
India: 266-8 (60); Kapil Dev 175*, Madan Lal 3-42
Zimbabwe: 235-10 (57); Curran 73, Rawson 3-47

Group B: Beat Australia by 118 runs at Chelmsford on 20 June
India: 247-10 (55.5); Sharma 40, Madan Lal 4-20
Australia: 129-10 (38.2); Border 36, Hogg 3-40

Semi-Final: Beat England by 6 wickets at Old Trafford on 22 June
England: 213-10 (60); Fowler 33, Allott 1-40
India: 217-4 (54.4); Sharma 61, Kapil Dev 3-35

1987

Australia beat England by seven runs

The fourth World Cup moved away from England, with India and Pakistan co-hosting the event. The same cast of teams as in 1983, Zimbabwe having emerged victorious from the ICC trophy, played in two groups of four, playing each other twice.

The surprise of the qualifying stages was West Indies' failure to reach the semi-finals. First England, then Pakistan conjured unlikely last-over victories against the former champions, and not even a record score of 360 for four (Richards 181) against Sri Lanka could save them. Australia made it through courtesy of two close wins over New Zealand.

The co-hosts were playing for a 'dream final' between India and Pakistan at the vast Eden Gardens ground at Calcutta, but Australia defeated Pakistan in the Lahore semi-final. With Miandad and Imran going well, Pakistan seemed set to overhaul Australia's 267 for eight, but their hopes were dashed by four quick wickets from paceman McDermott (5 for 44). At Bombay, Gooch's 115, which featured many adventurous sweep shots against India's spin-oriented attack, was the mainstay of a total of 254 for six for England. Despite 64 from the graceful Azharuddin, India fell 35 runs short, with veteran offspinner Hemmings taking four for 52.

In the final, Boon's 75, aided and abetted by useful contributions from Jones, Border, and Mike Veletta, took Australia to 253 for five in 50 overs. Despite the early loss of Robinson for a duck, England seemed set fair for victory after Athey's careful 58. Gatting and Lamb both reached 40, but Gatting tried a reverse sweep at the first ball bowled by his rival captain Border, and the ball ballooned up to be caught by the wicketkeeper. Australia's eventual winning margin of seven runs was the narrowest in any of the four World Cup finals so far.

The Final
Venue: Eden Gardens, Calcutta   Date: 8th November, 1987
Toss: Australia
Umpires: RB Gupta (I) and Mahboob Shah (P)
Man of the Match: DC Boon

Australia			*Runs*	*Balls*	*4/6*
DC Boon	c Downton	b Hemmings	75	125	7
GR Marsh		b Foster	24	49	3
DM Jones	c Athey	b Hemmings	33	57	1/1
CJ McDermott		b Gooch	14	8	2
AR Border †	Run Out		31	31	3
MRJ Veletta	Not Out		45	31	6
SR Waugh	Not Out		5	4	–
SP O'Donnell					
GC Dyer +					
TBA May					
BA Reid					
Extras	(b1, lb13, w5, nb7)		26		
Total	*(50 overs – for five wickets)*		253		

England	*O*	*M*	*R*	*W*	*Fall of wickets*	
DeFreitas	6	1	34	0	75, 151, 166, 168	
Small	6	0	33	0		241
Foster	10	0	38	1		
Hemmings	10	1	48	2		
Emburey	10	0	44	0		
Gooch	8	1	42	1		

England			*Runs*	*Balls*	*4/6*
GA Gooch	lbw	b O'Donnell	35	57	4
RT Robinson	lbw	b McDermott	0	1	–
CWJ Athey	Run Out		58	103	2
MW Gatting †	c Dyer	b Border	41	45	3/1
AJ Lamb		b Waugh	45	45	4
PR Downton +	c O'Donnell	b Border	9	8	1
JE Emburey	Run Out		10	16	–
PAJ DeFreitas	c Reid	b Waugh	17	10	2/1
NA Foster	Not Out		7	6	–
GC Small	Not Out		3	3	–

EE Hemmings

Extras	(b1, lb14, w2, nb4)			21
Total	*(50 overs – for eight wickets)*			*246*

Australia	O	M	R	W	Fall of wickets
McDermott	10	1	51	1	1, 66, 135, 170
Reid	10	0	43	0	188, 218, 220
Waugh	9	0	37	2	235
O'Donnell	10	1	35	1	
May	4	0	27	0	
Border	7	0	38	2	

Final Route

Australia

Group A: Beat India by 1 run at Madras on 9 October
Australia: 270-6 (50); Marsh 110, McDermott 4-56
India: 269-10 (49.5) Sidhu 73, Prabhaka 2-47

Group A: Beat Zimbabwe by 96 runs at Madras on 13 October
Australia: 235-9 (50); Border 67, O'Donnell 4-39
Zimbabwe: 139-10 (42.4); Curran 30 and 2-29

Group A: Beat New Zealand by 3 runs at Indore on 19 October
Australia: 199-4 (30); Boon 87, Waugh 2-36
New Zealand: 196-9 (30); Crowe 58, Snedden 2-36

Group A: Lost to India by 56 runs at Delhi on 22 October
India: 289-6 (50); Vengsarkar 63, Maninder 3-34
Australia: 233-10 (49); Boon 62, McDermott 3-61

Group A: Beat New Zealand by 17 runs at Chandigarh on 27 Oct
Australia: 251-8 (50); Marsh 126*, Border 2-27
New Zealand: 234-10 (48.4); Wright 62, Watson 2-46

Group A: Beat Zimbabwe by 70 runs at Cuttack on 30 October
Australia: 266-5 (50); Boon 93, May 2-30
Zimbabwe: 196-6 (50); Waller and Pycroft 38,
Traicos 2-45

Semi-Final: Beat Pakistan by 18 runs at Lahore on 4 November
Australia: 267-8 (50); Boon 65, McDermott 5-44
Pakistan: 249-10 (49); Miandad 70, Imran Khan 3-36

England

Group B:	Beat West Indies by 2 wickets at Gujranwala on 9 Oct
	West Indies: 243-7 (50); Richardson 53, Hooper 3-42
	England: 246-8 (49.3); Lamb 67*, Foster 3-52
Group B:	Lost to Pakistan by 18 runs at Rawalpindi on 13 Oct
	Pakistan: 239-7 (50); Salim Malik 65, Abdul Qadir 4-31
	England: 221-10 (48.4); Gatting 43, DeFreitas 3-42
Group B:	Beat Sri Lanka on faster scoring rate
	at Peshawar on 17 October
	England: 296-4 (50); Gooch 84, Emburey 2-26
	Pakistan: 158-8 (45); Ranatunga 40, Ratnayeke 2-62
Group B:	Lost to Pakistan by 7 wickets at Karachi on 20 Oct
	England: 244-9 (50); Athey 86, Emburey 1-34
	Pakistan: 247-3 (49); Ramiz Raja 113, Imran Khan 4-37
Group B:	Beat West Indies by 34 runs at Jaipur on 26 October
	England: 269-5 (50); Gooch 92, DeFreitas 3-28
	West Indies: 235-10 (48.1); Richardson 93, Patterson 3-56
Group B:	Beat Sri Lanka by 8 wickets at Pune on 30 October
	Sri Lanka: 218-7 (50); Dias 80, Jeganathan 2-45
	England: 219-2 (41.2); Gooch 61, Hemmings 3-57
Semi-Final:	Beat India by 35 runs at Bombay on 5 November
	England: 254-6 (50); Gooch 115, Hemmings 4-52
	India: 219-10 (45.3); Azharuddin 64, Maninder 3-54

1992

Pakistan beat England by 22 runs

This World Cup was the scene of some tremendous batting performances: from New Zealand's Martin Crowe, whose century not out helped propel his average in nine innings over the 100 mark; from veteran Pakistani Miandad with five 50s, highest score 89 and an average in the 60s; averaging in the late 60s was South Africa's Kirsten and in the 50s Australia's ebullient David Boon.

Why did Pakistan win the World Cup? Well also in the top ten performing batsmen were Raja with 349 runs, a 119 not out and average of over 58, and Sohail with 326 runs, including a 114. Fairbrother and Stewart (familiar names still) were England's best performers with the bat. The other reason Pakistan won the competition was Wasim Akram who took 18 wickets at an average of 18.78. Mushtaq Ahmed supported with 16 wickets. A certain Ian Botham was England's bowling spearhead with 16 wickets at 19 apiece. England's bowlers, including one day specialists like DeFreitas, Reeve, Small and Pringle, were very parsimonious in helping their side to another final. They lost only to New Zealand in the round-robin round and beat South Africa for the second time in their semi-final.

Pakistan meanwhile (their preliminary match with England had been abandoned) progressed to the final by beating New Zealand, the surprise team of the tournament. New Zealand set Pakistan 262 after Martin Crowe was run out on 91. Javed Miandad, not out 57 and Inzamam-ul-Haq guided Pakistan home. In the Melbourne final Pakistan's prolific openers went cheaply but captain Imran Khan rallied the troops and the middle order delivered a 249 target. Botham went in as an opener but fell for a duck. Only Gooch and Fairbrother delivered from the top order and, although the lower order batsmen hung around, Pakistan's Akram and Ahmed kept England short by 22 runs.

The Final

Venue: MCG, Melbourne   Date: 25th March, 1992
Toss: Pakistan
Umpires: BL Aldridge (NZ), SA Bucknor (WI)
Man of the Match: Wasim Akram

Pakistan			Runs	Balls	4/6
Aamir Sohail	c Stewart	b Pringle	4	19	–
Rameez Raja	lbw	b Pringle	8	26	1
Imran Khan †	c Illingworth	b Botham	72	110	5/1
Javed Miandad	c Botham	b Illingworth	58	98	4
Inzamam-ul-Haq		b Pringle	42	34	4
Wasim Akram	Run Out		33	19	4
Salim Malik	Not Out		0	1	–
Ijaz Ahmed					
Moin Khan +					
Mushtaq Ahmed					
Aaqib Javed					
Extras	(lb19, w6, nb7)		32		
Total	*(50 overs – for six wickets)*		*249*		

England	O	M	R	W	Fall of wickets
Pringle	10	2	22	3	20, 24, 163, 197
Lewis	10	2	52	0	249, 249
Botham	7	0	42	1	
DeFreitas	10	1	42	0	
Illingworth	10	0	50	1	
Reeve	3	0	22	0	

England			Runs	Balls	4/6
GA Gooch	c Aaqib	b Mushtaq	29	66	1
IT Botham	c Moin	b Akram	0	6	–
AJ Stewart	c Moin	b Aaqib	7	16	1
GA Hick	lbw	b Mushtaq	17	36	1
NH Fairbrother	c Moin	b Aaqib	62	70	3
AJ Lamb		b Akram	31	41	2
CC Lewis		b Akram	0	1	–
DA Reeve	c Rameez	b Mushtaq	15	32	–
DR Pringle	Not Out		18	16	1
PAJ DeFreitas	Run Out		10	8	–
RK Illingworth	c Rameez	b Imran	14	11	2

| Extras | (lb5, w13, nb6) | | | | 24 |
| Total | (50 overs – all out) | | | | 227 |

Pakistan	O	M	R	W	Fall of wickets
Akram	10	0	49	3	6, 21, 59, 69, 141
Aaqib	10	2	27	2	141, 180, 183
Mushtaq	10	1	41	3	208, 227
Ijaz	3	0	13	0	
Imran	6.2	0	43	1	
Aamir	10	0	49	0	

Final Route

England

Group: Beat India by 9 runs at WACA on 22 February
England: 236-9 (50); Smith 91, Reeve 3-38
India: 227-10 (49.2); Shastri 57, Prabhaka 2-34

Group: Beat West Indies by 6 wickets at MCG on 27 February
West Indies: 157-10 (49.2); Arthurton 54, Benjamin 2-22
England: 160-4 (39.5); Gooch 65, Lewis 3-30

Group: No Result verses Pakistan at Adelaide on 1 March
Pakistan: 74-10 (40.2); Salim Malik 17, Wasim Akram 1-7
England: 24-1 (8); Botham 6*, Pringle 3-8

Group: Beat Australia by 8 wickets at SCG on 5 March
Australia: 171-10 (49); Moody 51, Whitney 1-28
England: 173-2 (40.5); Gooch 58, Botham 4-31

Group: Beat Sri Lanka by 106 runs at Ballarat on 9 March
England: 280-6 (50); Fairbrother 63, Lewis 4-30
Sri Lanka 174-10 (44); Ranatunga 36, Gurusinha 2-67

Group: Beat South Africa by 3 wickets at MCG on 12 March
(revised target to 226 from 41 overs)
South Africa: 236-4 (50); Wessels 85, Snell 3-42
England: 226-7 (40.5); Stewart 77*, Hick 2-44

Group: Lost to New Zealand by 7 wickets at Wellington on 15 March
England: 200-8 (50); Hick 56, Botham 1-19
New Zealand: 201-3 (40.5); Jones 78, Patel 2-26

Group: Lost to Zimbabwe by 9 runs at Albury on 18 March
Zimbabwe: 134-10 (46.1); Houghton 29, Brandes 4-21
England: 125-10 (49.1); Stewart 29, Botham 3-23

Semi-Final:

       Beat South Africa by 19 runs at SCG on 22 March
       (revised target to 252 runs from 43 overs)
       England: 252-6 (45); Hick 83, Illingworth 2-46
       South Africa: 232-6 (43); Hudson 46, Pringle 2-36

Pakistan

Group: Lost to West Indies by 10 wickets at MCG on 23 February
       Pakistan: 220-2 (50); Ramiz Raja 102
       West Indies: Haynes 93*, Harper 1-33

Group: Beat Zimbabwe by 53 runs at Hobart on 27 February
       Pakistan: 254-4 (50); Sohail 114, Wasim Akram 3-21
       Zimbabwe: 2-1-7 (50); Houghton/Waller 44, Butchart 3-57

Group: No Result verses England at Adelaide on 1 March
       Pakistan: 74-10 (40.2); Salim Malik 17, Wasim Akram 1-7
       England: 24-1 (8); Botham 6*, Pringle 3-8

Group: Lost to India by 43 runs at SGC on 4 March
       India: 216-7 (49); Tendulkar 54*, Prabhakar 2-22
       Pakistan: 173-10 (48.1); Sohail 62, Mushtaq Ahmed 3-59

Group: Lost to South Africa by 20 runs at Brisbane on 8 March
       (revised target to 194 from 36 overs)
       South Africa: 211-7 (50); Hudson 54, Kuiper 3-40
       Pakistan: 173-8 (36); Inzamam-ul-Haq 48, Imran Khan 2-34

Group: Beat Australia by 48 runs at WACA on 11 March
       Pakistan: 220-9 (50); Sohail 76, Aaqib Javed 3-21
       Australia: 172-10 (45.2); Jones 47, Waugh 3-36

Group: Beat Sri Lanka by 4 wickets at WACA on 15 March
       Sri Lanka: 212-6 (50); de Silva 43, Ramanayake 2-37
       Pakistan: 216-6 (49.1);Miandad 57, Mushtaq Ahmed 2-43

Group: Beat New Zealand by 7 wickets at Christchurch on 18 March
       New Zealand: 166-10 (48.2); Greatbatch 42, Morrison 3-42
       Pakistan: 167-3 (44.4); Ramiz Raja 119*, Wasim Akram 4-32

Semi-Final:

       Beat New Zealand by 4 wickets at Auckland on 21 March
       New Zealand: 262-7 (50); Crowe 91, Watson 2-39
       Pakistan: 264-6 (49); Inzaman-ul-Haq 91,
       Wasim Akram and Mushtaq Ahmed 2-40

1996

Sri Lanka beat Australia by seven wickets

This was the second time India and Pakistan had hosted the World Cup and on this occasion Sri Lanka were also involved as co-hosts. Tamil Tiger terrorism in that country meant that the Australian and West Indies team refused to play there and conceded their games. Bookmakers Ladbrokes rated Sri Lanka 125-20 outsiders but they won their other group games and scored an all-time highest total in one-dayers against Kenya. Kenya in turn completed a shock win over West Indies. The controversy continued as Pakistan lost to India in the quarter-finals by 39 runs. Javed Miandad was appearing in his sixth consecutive World Cup. England and South Africa also fell in the quarters so all the semi finalists came from group A.

The subcontinent semi was a classic. The Sri Lankans, despite Aravinda de Silva's class innings (66 runs, 47 balls, 12 fours), were in danger of not making enough runs. In India's reply Tendulkar (65) and Sanjay Manjrekar (25) handled the Sri Lanka spinners with aplomb but the game was turned by the opportunism of Kaluwitharana who stumped Tendulkar. The Calcuttans started throwing water bottles and the generally riotous atmosphere led to the match being awarded to Sri Lanka.

West Indies took on Australia in a day/night match in Mohali in Punjab. It was Ambrose and Walsh against Taylor and Mark Waugh, Lara and Richardson against Warne and Reiffel. Five runs was the difference in Australia's favour.

In the final Taylor hit eight fours and a six and Ponting and Bevan supported in an OK total of 241. Gurusinha (65 in 99 balls), de Silva (not out 107 in 124 balls) and Ranatunga (not out 47 in 37 balls) wrapped it up in the 47th over. Sri Lanka, still rated 4-1 outsiders, therefore scored a seven-wicket win, a record sixth win in a row, eight if you count the conceded games.

The Final

Venue: Gaddafi Stadium, Lahore   Date: 17th March, 1996

Toss: Sri Lanka

Umpires: SA Bucknor (WI), DR Shepherd (E)

Man of the Match: PA de Silva

Australia			Runs	Balls	4/6
MA Taylor †	c Jayasuriya	b de Silva	74	83	8
ME Waugh	c Jayasuriya	b Vaas	12	15	1
RT Ponting		b de Silva	45	73	2
SR Waugh	c de Silva	b Dharmasena	13	25	–
SK Warne	s Kaluwitharana	b Muralitharan	2	5	–
SG Law	c de Silva	b Jayasuriya	22	30	–/1
MG Bevan	Not Out		36	49	2
IA Healy +		b de Silva	2	3	–
PR Reiffel	Not Out		13	18	–
DW Fleming					
GD McGrath					
Extras	(lb10, w11, nb1)		22		
Totals	*(50 overs – for seven wickets)*		*241*		

Sri Lanka	O	M	R	W	Fall of wickets
Wickremasinghe	7	0	38	0	36, 137, 152, 156
Vaas	6	1	30	1	170, 202, 205
Muralitharan	10	0	31	1	
Dharmasena	10	0	47	1	
Jayasuriya	8	0	43	1	
de Silva	9	0	42	3	

Sri Lanka			Runs	Balls	4/6
AST Jayasuriya	Run Out		9	7	–
RS Kaluwitharana +	c Bevan	b Fleming	6	13	–
AP Gurusinha		b Reiffel	65	99	6/1
PA de Silva	Not Out		107	124	13
A Ranatunga †	Not Out		47	37	4/1
HP Tillekeratne					
RS Mahanama					
HDPK Dharmasena					
WPUJC Vaas					
M Muralitharan					
GP Wickremasinghe					

Extras	(b1, lb4, w5, nb1)			11	
Total	*(46.2 overs – for three wickets)*			*245*	

Australia	*O*	*M*	*R*	*W*	*Fall of wickets*
McGrath	8.2	1	28	0	12, 23, 148
Fleming	6	0	43	1	
Warne	10	0	58	0	
Reiffel	10	0	49	1	
ME Waugh	6	0	35	0	
S R Waugh	3	0	15	0	
Bevan	3	0	12	0	

Final Route

Sri Lanka

Group A: Beat Australia by default – team refused to travel.

Group A: Beat Zimbabwe by 6 wickets at Colombo on 21 February
Zimbabwe: 228-6 (50); Campbell 75, Streak 3-60
Sri Lanka: 229-4 (37); de Silva 91, Vaas 2-30

Group A: Beat West Indies by default – team refused to travel.

Group A: Beat India by 6 wickets at Delhi on 2 March
India: 271-3 (50); Tendulkar 137, Kumble 2-39
Sri Lanka: 272-4 (48.4); Jayasuriya 79,
Pushpakumara and Dharmasena 1-53

Group A: Beat Kenya by 144 runs at Kandy on 6 March
Sri Lanka: 398-5 (50); de Silva 145, Muralitharan 2-40
Kenya: 254-7 (50); S.Tikolo 96, Odumbe 2-34

Quarter-Final:
Beat England by 5 wickets at Faisalabad on 9 March
England: 235-8 (50); DeFreitas 67, Reeve 1-14
Sri Lanka: 236-5 (40.4); Jayasuriya 82, Dharmasena 2-30

Semi-Final: Beat India by default after crowd trouble
Sri Lanka: 251-8 (50); de Silva 66 and 1-3
India: 120-8 (34.1); Tendulkar 65, Srinath 3-34

Australia

Group A: Lost to Sri Lanka by default – team refused to travel.

Group A: Beat Kenya by 97 runs at Vishakhapatnam on 23 Feb
             Australia: 304-7 (50); M.Waugh 130, Reiffel 2-18
             Kenya: 207-7 (50); Otieno 85, Ali 3-45

Group A: Beat India by 16 runs at Bombay on 27 February
             Australia: 258-10 (50); M.Waugh 126, Fleming 5-36
             India: 242-10 (48); Tendulkar 90, Raju 2-48

Group A: Beat Zimbabwe by 8 wickets at Nagpur on 1 March
             Zimbabwe: 154-10 (45.3); Waller 67, Strang 2-33
             Australia: 158-2 (36); M.Waugh 76*, R.Waugh 2-22

Group A: Lost to West Indies by 4 wickets at Jaipur on 4 March
             Australia: 229-6 (50); Ponting 102, M.Waugh 3-38
             West Indies: 232-6 (48.5); Richardson 93*, Walsh 2-35

Quarter-Final:
             Beat New Zealand by 6 wickets at Madras on 11 March
             New Zealand: 286-9 (50); Harris 130, Astle 1-21
             Australia: 289-4 (47.5); M.Waugh 110, McGrath 2-50

Semi-Final: Beat West Indies by 5 runs at Mohali on 14 March
             Australia: 207-8 (50); Law 72, Warne 4-36
             West Indies: 202-10 (49.3);
             Chanderpaul 80, Ambrose 2-26

WORLD CUP RECORDS

The following pages contain all-time statistics and take into account the six World Cup tournaments prior to 1999.

Highest Innings Totals

Scr	Ovs	R/O	Match	Venue	Yr
398-5	(50)	7.96	Sri Lanka vs Kenya	Kandy	95-96
360-4	(50)	7.20	West Indies vs Sri Lanka	Karachi	87-88
338-5	(60)	5.63	Pakistan vs Sri Lanka	Swansea	83
334-4	(60)	5.56	England vs India	Lord's	75
333-9	(60)	5.55	England vs Sri Lanka	Taunton	83
330-6	(60)	5.50	Pakistan vs Sri Lanka	Nottingham	75
328-3	(50)	6.56	South Africa vs Holland	Rawalpindi/2	95-96
328-5	(60)	5.46	Australia vs Sri Lanka	The Oval	75
322-6	(60)	5.36	England vs N.Zealand	The Oval	83
321-2	(50)	6.42	South Africa vs UAE	Rawalpindi/2	95-96
320-9	(60)	6.40	Australia vs India	Nottingham	83
313-7	(49.2)	6.34	Sri Lanka vs Zimbabwe	New Plymouth	91-92
312-4	(50)	6.24	Zimbabwe vs Sri Lanka	New Plymouth	91-92
309-5	(60)	5.15	N.Zealand vs East Africa	Birmingham	75
307-8	(50)	6.14	N.Zealand vs Holland	Baroda	95-96
304-7	(50)	6.08	Australia vs Kenya	Vishakhapatnam	95-96

Highest Total Batting Second – To Win

Scr	Ovs	R/O	Match	Venue	Yr
313-7	(49.2)	6.34	Sri Lanka vs Zimbabwe	New Plymouth	91-92
289-4	(47.5)	6.04	Australia vs N.Zealand	Madras	95-96
276-3	(57.5)	4.77	West Indies vs Australia	Lord's	83
272-4	(48.4)	5.58	Sri Lanka vs India	Delhi	95-96
267-9	(59.4)	4.47	West Indies vs Pakistan	Birmingham	75
264-6	(49)	5.38	Pakistan vs N.Zealand	Auckland	91-92
250-3	(47.4)	5.24	Pakistan vs England	Karachi	95-96

Highest Total Batting Second – To Lose

Scr	Ovs	R/O	Match	Venue	Yr
288-9	(60)	4.80	Sri Lanka vs Pakistan	Swansea	83
286	(58)	4.93	Sri Lanka vs England	Taunton	83
276-4	(60)	4.60	Sri Lanka vs Australia	The Oval	75
274	(58.4)	4.67	Australia vs West Indies	Lord's	75
269	(49.5)	5.39	India vs Australia	Madras	87-88
254-7	(50)	5.08	Kenya vs Sri Lanka	Kandy	95-96
252	(49.2)	5.10	Sri Lanka vs Pakistan	Hyderabad-P	87-88
250	(56.2)	4.43	Pakistan vs West Indies	The Oval	79
250	(59.1)	4.22	New Zealand vs Pakistan	Nottingham	83

Highest Match Aggregate

Scr	Ovs	R/O	Match	Venue	Yr
652-12	(100)	6.52	Sri Lanka vs Kenya	Kandy	95-96
626-14	(120)	5.21	Pakistan vs Sri Lanka	Swansea	83
625-11	(99.2)	6.29	Zimbabwe vs Sri Lanka	New Plymouth	91-92
619-19	(118)	5.24	England vs Sri Lanka	Taunton	83
604-9	(120)	5.03	Australia vs Sri Lanka	The Oval	75
575-13	(97.5)	5.87	N.Zealand vs Australia	Madras	95-96
565-18	(118.4)	4.76	West Indies vs Australia	Lord's	75

Lowest Innings Total

Scr	Ovs	R/O	Match	Venue	Yr
45	(40.3)	1.11	Canada vs England	Manchester	79
74	(40.2)	1.83	Pakistan vs England	Adelaide	91-92
86	(37.2)	2.30	N.Zealand vs West Indies	Manchester	75
93	(36.2)	2.55	England vs Australia	Leeds	75
93	(35.2)	2.63	West Indies vs Kenya	Pune	95-96
94	(52.3)	1.79	East Africa vs England	Birmingham	75

Lowest Match Aggregate

Scr	Ovs	R/O	Match	Venue	Yr
91-12	(54.2)	1.67	Canada vs England	Manchester	79
173-11	(58)	2.98	Sri Lanka vs West Indies	Manchester	75

187-16 (65)   2.87   England vs Australia   Leeds   75
Details for finished matches only.

Largest Margin of Victory – By Runs

Runs	Match	Venue	Yr
202	England (334-4) beat India (132-3)	Lord's	75
196	England (290-5) beat East Africa (94)	Birmingham	75
192	Pakistan (330-6) beat Sri Lanka (138)	Nottingham	75
191	West Indies (360-4) beat Sri Lanka (169-4)		
		Karachi	87-88
181	N.Zealand (309-5) beat East Africa (128-8)		
		Birmingham	75
169	South Africa (321-2) beat UAE (152-8)	Rawalpindi/2	95-96
162	Australia (320-9) beat India (158)	Nottingham	83
160	South Africa (328-3) beat Holland (168-8)		
		Rawalpindi/2	95-96
144	Sri Lanka (398-5) beat Kenya (254-7)	Kandy	95-96
128	Australia (265-6) beat Zimbabwe (137)	Hobart	91-92
119	New Zealand (307-8) beat Holland (188-7)		
		Baroda	95-96
118	India (247) beat Australia (129)	Chelmsford	83
113	Pakistan (297-7) beat Sri Lanka (184-8)	Faisalabad	87-88
109	N.Zealand (276-8) beat UAE (167-9)	Faisalabad	95-96
106	England (322-6) beat N.Zealand (216)	The Oval	83
106	England (280-6) beat Sri Lanka (174)	Ballarat	91-92
101	West Indies (252-9) beat Australia (151)	Leeds	83

Largest Margin of Victory – By Wickets

Wkts	Match	Venue	Yr
10	India (123-0) beat East Africa (120)	Leeds	75
10	West Indies (172-0) beat Zimbabwe (171)		
		Birmingham	83
10	West Indies (221-0) beat Pakistan (220-2)		
		Melbourne	91-92
9	West Indies (87-1) beat Sri Lanka (86)	Manchester	75
9	West Indies (194-1) beat India (190)	Birmingham	79
9	New Zealand (190-1) beat Sri Lanka	Nottingham	79
9	England (137-1) beat Sri Lanka (136)	Leeds	83

9	India (224-1) beat N.Zealand (221-9)	Nagpur	87-88
9	South Africa (171-1) beat Australia (170)	Sydney	91-92
9	Pakistan (112-1) beat UAE (109-9)	Gujranwala	95-96

Smallest Margin of Victory – By Runs

Runs	Match	Venue	Yr
1	Australia (270-6) beat India (269) *	Madras	87-88
	Australia (237-9) beat India (234) *	Brisbane	91-92
3	N.Zealand (242-7) beat Zimbabwe (239)	Hyderabad	87-88
	Australia (199-4) beat N.Zealand (196-9)	Indore	87-88
5	Australia (207-8) beat West Indies (202)	Mohali	95-96
7	Australia (253-5) beat England (246-8)	Calcutta	87-88
9	England (221-8) beat N.Zealand (212-9)	Manchester	79
	England (236-9) beat India (227)	Perth	91-92
	Zimbabwe (134) beat England 127	Albury	91-92

* revised target

Smallest Margin of Victory – By Wickets

Wkts	Match	Venue	Yr
1	West Indies (267-9) beat Pakistan (266-7)	Birmingham	75
	Pakistan (217-9) beat West Indies (216)	Lahore	87-88
2	N.Zealand (238-8) beat England (234)	Birmingham	83
	England (246-8) beat West Indies (243-7)	Gujranwala	87-88

Smallest Margin of Victory – By Wickets

Runs	bp	Player	Match	Venue	Yr
188no	2	G Kirsten	S.Africa vs UAE	Rawalpindi	95-96
181	4	IVA Richards	W.Indies vs Sri Lanka	Karachi	87-88
175no	6	N Kapil Dev	India vs Zimbabwe	Tun. Wells	83
171no	1	GM Turner	N.Zealand vs E.Africa	Birmingham	75
161	2	AC Hudson	S.Africa vs Holland	Rawalpindi	95-96
145	4	PA de Silva	Sri Lanka vs Kenya	Kandy	95-96
142	3	DL Houghton	Zimbabwe vs N.Zealand	Hyderabad	87-88
138no	3	IVA Richards	W.Indies vs England	Lord's	79
137	2	DL Amiss	England vs India	Lord's	75
137	2	SR Tendulkar	India vs Sri Lanka	Delhi	95-96
131	3	KWR Fletcher	England vs N.Zealand	Nottingham	75

130	3	DI Gower	England vs Sri Lanka	Taunton	83
130	2	ME Waugh	Australia vs Kenya	Vis'patnam	95-96
130	5	CZ Harris	N.Zealand vs Australia	Madras	95-96
127no	2	SR Tendulkar	India vs Kenya	Cuttack	95-96
126no	1	GR Marsh	Australia vs N.Zealand	Chandigarh	87-88
126	1	ME Waugh	Australia vs India	Bombay	95-96

Records including all innings of 120 plus runs. bp=Batting Position.

Partnership Records

Man	Total	Players (Runs) / Match and Venue		Yr
1st	186	G Kirsten (83), AC Hudson (161)		
		South Africa vs UAE	Rawalpindi/2	95-96
2nd	176	DL Amiss (137), KWR Fletcher (68)		
		England vs India	Lord's	75
3rd	207	ME Waugh (130), SR Waugh (82)		
		Australia vs Kenya	Vishakhapatnam	95-96
4th	168	LK Germon (89), CZ Harris (130)		
		N.Zealand vs Australia	Madras	95-96
5th	*145	A Flower (115no), AC Waller (83no)		
		Zimbabwe vs SL (New Plymouth)		91-92
6th	144	Imran Khan (102no), Shahid Mahboob (77)		
		Pakistan vs Sri Lanka	Leeds	83
7th	*75	DAG Fletcher (69no), IP Butchart (34no)		
		Zimbabwe vs Australia	Nottingham	83
8th	117	DL Houghton (142), IP Butchart (54)		
		Zimbabwe vs N.Zealand	Hyderabad-I	87-88
9th	*126	N Kapil Dev (175no) SMH Kirmani (24no)		
		India vs Zimbabwe	Tunbridge Wells	83
10th	71	AME Roberts (37no), J Garner (37)		
		West Indies vs India	Manchester	83

* Player or players not out. Players from team listed first.

Five Wickets Taken in an Innings

Rec	Type	Bowler	Match	Venue	Yr
7-51	rfm	WW Davis	West Indies vs Australia	Leeds	83
6-14	lfm	GJ Gilmour	Australia vs England	Leeds	75
6-39	rfm	KH Macleay	Australia vs India	Nottingham	83
5-21	rfm	AG Hurst	Australia vs Canada	Birmingham	79

5-21	lbg	P A Strang	Zimbabwe vs Kenya	Patna	95-96
5-25	rf	RJ Hadlee	N.Zealand vs Sri Lanka	Bristol	83
5-29		S Dukanwala	UAE vs Holland	Lahore	95-96
5-32	rfm	ALF DeMel	Sri Lanka vs N.Zealand	Derby	83
5-34	rf	DK Lillee	Australia vs Pakistan	Leeds	75
5-36	rfm	DW Fleming	Australia vs India	Bombay	95-96
5-38	rfm	J Garner	West Indies vs England	Lord's	79
5-39	ob	VJ Marks	England vs Sri Lanka	Taunton	83
5-39	rfm	ALF DeMel	Sri Lanka vs Pakistan	Leeds	83
5-43	rfm	N Kapil Dev	India vs Australia	Nottingham	83
5-44	lbg	Abdul Qadir	Pakistan vs Sri Lanka	Leeds	83
5-44	rfm	CJ McDermott	Australia vs Pakistan	Lahore	87-88
5-48	lfm	GJ Gilmour	Australia vs West Indies	Lord's	75

Player from team listed first.

Most Economical Bowling

o-m-r-w	R/O	Arm	Bowler	Match/Venue	Yr
12-8-6-1	0.50	sla	BS Bedi	India vs East Africa Leeds	75
10-5-8-4	0.80	rfm	CM Old	England vs Canada Manchester	79
12-6-10-1	0.83	rf	RJ Hadlee	N.Zealand vs East Africa Birmingham	75
12-6-11-4	0.91	rf	JA Snow	England vs East Africa Birmingham	75
11-4-11-1	1.00	ob	Majid Khan	Pakistan vs Canada Leeds	79
10-3-11-4	1.04	rf	RGD Willis	England vs Canada Manchester	79
10-5-11-0	1.10	sla	DL Underwood	England vs East Africa Birmingham	75
12-6-14-6	1.16	rfm	GJ Gilmour	Australia vs England Leeds	75
10-4-12-2	1.20	rm	IT Botham	England vs Pakistan Adelaide	91-92
12-6-15-4	1.25	rfm	M Hendrick	England vs Pakistan Leeds	79
12-5-16-2	1.33	rf	AME Roberts	West Indies vs Sri Lanka Manchester	75

| 12-3-16-1 | 1.33 | rf | RJ Hadlee | New Zealand vs Sri Lanka | |
| | | | | Derby | 83 |

Requirement is a minimum of ten overs.

Most Expensive Bowling

o-m-r-w	R/O	Arm	Bowler	Match/Venue	Yr
10-0-97-1	9.70	rfm	ALF de Mel	Sri Lanka vs West Indies	
				Karachi	87-88
12-1-105-2	8.75	rfm	MC Snedden	New Zealand vs England	
				The Oval	83
10-0-83-0	8.30	rm	DR Pringle	England vs West Indies	
				Gujranwala	87-88
11-1-83-0	7.54	lfm	KD Ghavri	India vs England	
				Lord's	75
10-0-72-2	7.20	rm	AP Gurusinha	Sri Lanka vs Zimbabwe	
				New Plymouth	91-92
10-0-72-0	7.20	rm	KG Duers	Zimbabwe vs Sri Lanka	
				New Plymouth	91-92
10-0-72-1	7.20	rm	CZ Harris	New Zealand vs Pakistan	
				Auckland	91-92
10-1-71-1	7.10	rm	MP Jarvis	Zimbabwe vs West Indies	
				Brisbane	91-92
10-0-70-3	7.00	rfm	EA Brandes	Zimbabwe vs Sri Lanka	
				New Plymouth	91-92

Requirement is a minimum of ten overs.

Most Dismissals by Wicket-Keeper

Wkt	How	Keeper	Match/Venue	Yr
5	(5 ct)	SMH Kirmani	India vs Zimbabwe	
			Leicester	83
5	(4ct/1st)	JC Adams	West Indies vs Kenya	
			Pune	95-96
5	(4ct/1st)	Rashid Latif	Pakistan vs N.Zealand	
			Lahore	95-96
4	(4 ct)	DL Murray	West Indies vs N.Zealand	
			Manchester	75
4	(3ct/1st)	Wasim Bari	Pakistan vs N.Zealand	
			Birmingham	83

4	(4 ct)	DL Houghton	Zimbabwe vs India	
			Tunbridge Wells	83
4	(2ct/2st)	S More	India vs Zimbabwe	
			Bombay	87-88
4	(4 ct)	GC Dyer	Australia vs Pakistan	
			Lahore	87-88
4	(4 ct)	D Williams	West Indies vs N.Zealand	
			Auckland	91-92

Most Catches by a Fielder

Cts	Fielder	Match	Venue	Yr
4	CL Cairns	N.Zealand vs UAE	Faisalabad	95-96
3	CH Lloyd	West Indies vs N.Zealand	Manchester	75
3	DA Reeve	England vs Pakistan	Adelaide	91-92
3	Ijaz Ahmed	Pakistan vs Australia	Perth	91-92
3	AR Border	Australia vs Zimbabwe	Hobart	91-92

WORLD CUP '99
PLAYER A-Z

The following pages contain an A-Z of players profiled in this book. There are 200 players in all and the list arranges them alphabetically with details of country and their batting and bowling style. To locate a player locate him in this index and then refer to the country referred to in the team section for a detailed profile.

Player	Country	Bat/Bowl
BOJE, Nico	South Africa	LHB/LS
BOUCHER, Mark Verdon	South Africa	RHB/WK
BRANDES, Eddo Andre	Zimbabwe	RHB/RFM
BRINKLEY, James Edward	Scotland	RHB/RFM
BROWN, Alistair Duncan	England	RHB/RLB
BUTT, Asim	Scotland	RHB/MF
CAIRNS, Christopher Lance	New Zealand	RHB/RFM
CAMPBELL, Alistair Douglas Ross	Zimbabwe	LHB/ROB
CAMPBELL, Sherwin	West Indies	RHB/ROB
CHANDANA, Umagiliya Durage Upul		
	Sri Lanka	RHB/LB
CHANDERPAUL, Shivnarine	West Indies	LHB/LBG
CHUDASAMA, Dipak	Kenya	RHB
COWAN, David	Scotland	LHB/RFM
CRAWLEY, Stephen Thomas	Scotland	RHB/RFM
CROFT, Robert Damien Bale	England	RHB/ROB
CRONJE, Wessel Johannes	South Africa	RHB/RM
CULLINAN, Daryll John	South Africa	RHB/ROB
DALE, Adam Craig	Australia	LHB/RFM
DAVIES, Alec	Scotland	RHB/WK
DE SILVA, Pinnaduwage Aravinda	Sri Lanka	RHB/ROB
DHARMASENA, Handunettige Deepthi Priyantha Kumara		
	Sri Lanka	RHB/OF
DILLON, Mervyn	West Indies	RHB/RFM
DONALD, Allan Anthony	South Africa	RHB/RF
DOULL, Simon Blair	New Zealand	RHB/RM
DRAVID, Rahul	India	RHB
DYER, Nick	Scotland	
EALHAM, Mark Alan	England	RHB/RFM
ELWORTHY, Steven	South Africa	RHB/RFM
EVANS, Craig Neil	Zimbabwe	RHB/RM
FAIRBROTHER, Neil Harvey	England	LHB/LM
FLEMING, Damien William	Australia	RHB/RFM
FLEMING, Stephen Paul	New Zealand	LHB
FLINTOFF, Andrew	England	RHB/RM

Player	Country	Bat/Bowl
FLOWER, Andrew	Zimbabwe	LHB/ROB
FLOWER, Grant William	Zimbabwe	RHB/SLO
FRASER, Angus Robert Charles	England	RHB/RF
GANGA, Daren	West Indies	RHB
GANGULY, Saurav Chandidas	India	LHB/RM
GIBBS, Herschelle Herman	South Africa	RHB/RMF
GILCHRIST, Adam Craig	Australia	LHB/WK
GILLESPIE, Jason Neil	Australia	RHB/RF
GOODWIN, Murray William	Zimbabwe	RHB/RM,LB
GOUGH, Darren	England	RHB/RF
GOURLAY, Scott	Scotland	RHB/RM
HALL, Andrew James	South Africa	RHB/RFM
HARRIS, Chris Zinzan	New Zealand	LHB/RM
HEADLEY, Dean Warren	England	RHB/RMF
HEALY, Ian Andrew	Australia	RHB/WK
HEGG, Warren Kevin	England	RHB/WK
HICK, Graeme Ashley	England	LHB/LOB
HOLLIOAKE, Adam John	England	RHB/RMF
HOOPER, Carl Llewellyn	West Indies	RHB/ROB
HORNE, Matthew Jeffery	New Zealand	RHB/RM
HOSSAIN, Mehrab Opee	Bangladesh	RHB/RM
HOSSAIN, Mohammad Shahriar Bidyut	Bangladesh	RHB
HUCKLE, Adam George	Zimbabwe	RHB/LBG
HUSSAIN, Mohammad Hasibul Shanto	Bangladesh	RHB/RFM
HUSSAIN, Nasser	England	RHB/RLS
INZAMAM-UL-HAQ	Pakistan	RHB/SLA
ISLAM, Mohammad Aminul Bulbul	Bangladesh	RHB/ROB
JADEJA, Ajaysingh	India	RHB/RM
JAYASURIYA, Sanath Teran	Sri Lanka	LHB/SL
JAYAWARDENE, Denagamage Proboth Mahela de Silva	Sri Lanka	RHB/RM
JOHNSON, Neil Clarkson	Zimbabwe	LHB/RFM
JULIAN, Brendon Paul	Australia	RHB/LFM

219

Player	Country	Bat/Bowl
KALLIS, Jacques Henry	South Africa	RHB/RM
KALPAGE, Ruwan Senani	Sri Lanka	LHB/ROB
KALUWITHARANA, Romesh Shantha		
	Sri Lanka	RHB/WK
KAMBLI, Vinod Ganpat	India	LHB/ROB
KANITKAR, Hrishikesh Hemant	India	LHB/ROB
KARIM, Aasif	Kenya	RHB/SO
KASPROWICZ, Michael Scott	Australia	RHB/RF
KHAN, Mohammad Akram Hussain	Bangladesh	RHB/RM
KHAN, Moin	Pakistan	RHB/WK
KIRSTEN, Gary	South Africa	RHB/ROB
KLUSENER, Lance	South Africa	LHB/RFM
KNIGHT, Nicholas Verity	England	LHB/RM
KUMBLE, Anil	India	RHB/LBG
LAMBERT, Clayton Benjamin Lambert		
	West Indies	LHB/ROB
LANGER, Justin Lee	Australia	LHB/RM/WK
LARA, Brian	West Indies	LHB/LB
LARSEN, Gavin Rolf	New Zealand	RHB/RM
LAXMAN, Vangipurappu Venkata Sai	India	RHB/ROB
LEHMANN, Darren Scott	Australia	LHB/SLO
LOCKHART, Douglas	Scotland	RHB
LOCKIE, Bryn	Scotland	RHB
MACGILL, Stuart Charles Glyndwr	Australia	RHB/LBG
MAHANAMA, Roshan Siriwardene	Sri Lanka	RHB
MAHMOOD, Azhar	Pakistan	RHB/RFM
MALIK, Salim	Pakistan	RHB, LB
MARTYN, Damien Richard	Australia	RHB/ROB
MASHUD, Mohammad Khaled Pilot	Bangladesh	RHB/WK
MBANGWA, Mpumelelo	Zimbabwe	RHB/RFM
MCGRATH, Glenn Donald	Australia	RHB/RF
MCLEAN, Nixon Alexei McNamara	West Indies	LHB/RF
MCMILLAN, Craig Douglas	New Zealand	RHB/RM
MILLER, Colin Reid	Australia	RHB/ROB
MODI, Hitesh	Kenya	LHB/ROB
MONGIA, Nayan Ramlal	India	RHB/WK

Player	Country	Bat/Bowl
MPITSANG, Victor	South Africa	RHB/RFM
MULLALLY, Alan David	England	RHB/FM
MURALITHARAN, Mutiah	Sri Lanka	RHB/LOB
MURRAY, Junior Randalph	West Indies	RHB/WK
MUSHTAQ, Saqlain	Pakistan	RHB/OB
NASH, Dion Joseph	New Zealand	RHB/RM
NGOCHE, Lameck Onyango	Kenya	RHB/RFM
OBUYA, Kennedy Otieno	Kenya	RHB/WK
ODOYO, Thomas	Kenya	RHB/RMF
ODUMBE, Maurice Omondi	Kenya	RHB/ROB
ODUOL, Angara Joseph	Kenya	RM
OLONGA, Henry Khaaba	Zimbabwe	RHB/RF
OMAR, Mohammad Javed Belim Golla		
	Bangladesh	RHB
ONDIK, Anthony Suji	Kenya	RHB/RM
PARORE, Adam Craig	New Zealand	RHB/WK
PARSONS, Robert Andrew	Scotland	LHB/M
PATTERSON, Brian Matthew Winston		
	Scotland	RHB
PERERA, Anhettige Suresh Asanka	Sri Lanka	RHB/RM
PHILIP, Ian	Scotland	RHB/SL/WK
POLLOCK, Shaun Maclean	South Africa	RHB/RFM
PONTING, Ricky Thomas	Australia	RHB/RM/WK
PRASAD, Bapu Krishnarao Venkatesh		
	India	RHB/RM
PUSHPAKUMARA, Karuppiahyage Ravindra		
	Sri Lanka	RHB/RFM
RAFIQUE, Mohammad	Bangladesh	LHB/SLO
RAHMAN, Mafizur Munna	Bangladesh	RHB/RM
RAHMAN, Naimur Durjoy	Bangladesh	RHB/ROB
RAMESH, Sadagoppan	India	LHB/ROB
RAMPRAKASH, Mark Ravin	England	RHB/ROB
RANATUNGA, Arjuna	Sri Lanka	LHB/RM
RAZA, Hasan	Pakistan	RHB/LB
RENNIE, Gavin James	Zimbabwe	LHB/SLO

Player	Country	Bat/Bowl
RHODES, Jonathan Neil	South Africa	RHB/RM
RINDEL, Michael John Raymond	South Africa	LHB/RMF
ROSE, Franklyn Albert	West Indies	RHB/RF
SALMOND, George	Scotland	RHB/RM
SHAH, Ravindu	Kenya	RHB
SHERIDAN, Keith	Scotland	LHB/SLO
SIDHU, Navjot Singh	India	RHB
SIMMONS, Philip Verant	West Indies	RHB/RM
SINGH, Rabindra Ramanarayan	India	LHB/RMF
SLATER, Michael Jonathon	Australia	RHB/LB
SMITH, Mike	Scotland	RHB/RM
SOHAIL, Aamir	Pakistan	LHB/SLA
SRINATH, Javagal	India	RHB/RFM
STANGER, Ian Michael	Scotland	RHB/RFM
STEINDL, Peter David	Scotland	RHB/RM
STEWART, Alec James	England	RHB/WK
STRANG, Paul Andrew	Zimbabwe	RHB/LBG
STREAK, Heath Hilton	Zimbabwe	RHB/RFM
SUJI, Martin	Kenya	RHB/RFM
SYMCOX, Patrick Leonard	South Africa	RHB/RO
TENDULKAR, Sachin Rumesh	India	RHB, RM/LB
TENNANT, Andy M	Scotland	LHB/SLO
TERBRUGGE, David John	South Africa	RHB/RFM
THOMSON, Kevin	Scotland	RHB/RMF
THORPE, Graham	England	LHB/RM
TIKOLO, Stephen Ogomji	Kenya	RHB/ROB
TILLAKARATNE, Hashan Prasantha	Sri Lanka	LHB/RM
TWOSE, Roger Graham	New Zealand	LHB/RM
VAAS, Warnakulasuriya Patabendige Ushantha Joseph Chaminda		
	Sri Lanka	LHB/LFM
VADER, Alpesh	Kenya	RHB
VETTORI, Daniel Luca	New Zealand	LHB/SO
WALLACE, Philo Alphonso	West Indies	RHB/RM
WARNE, Shane Keith	Australia	RHB/LBG
WAUGH, Mark Edward	Australia	RHB/ROB

Player	Country	Bat/Bowl
WAUGH, Stephen Rodger	Australia	RHB/RM
WELLS, Vincent John	England	RHB/RM/WK
WHITTALL, Andrew Richard	Zimbabwe	RHB/ROB
WICKREMASINGHE, Gallage Pramodya	Sri Lanka	RHB/RFM
WILLIAMS, Stuart Clayton	West Indies	RHB
WILLIAMSON, J Greig	Scotland	RHB/RM
WISEMAN, Paul John	New Zealand	RHB/ROB
WISHART, Craig Brian	Zimbabwe	RHB/RM
WRIGHT, Craig McIntyre	Scotland	RHB/RM
YOUHANNA, Yousuf	Pakistan	RHB
YOUNIS, Waqar	Pakistan	RHB/RF

Notes